Mastering Clojure Data Analysis

Leverage the power and flexibility of Clojure through
this practical guide to data analysis

Eric Rochester

[PACKT] PUBLISHING

open source*
community experience distilled

BIRMINGHAM - MUMBAI

Mastering Clojure Data Analysis

First published: May 2014

Production Reference: 1200514

Published by Packt Publishing Ltd.
Livery Place
35 Livery Street
Birmingham B3 2PB, UK.

ISBN 978-1-78328-413-9

www.packtpub.com

Cover Image by Jarosław Blaminsky (milak6@wp.pl)

Credits

Author
Eric Rochester

Reviewers
Masato Hagiwara
Bart Kastermans
Nicholas Quirk
Andrew Stine

Commissioning Editor
Edward Gordon

Acquisition Editor
Greg Wild

Content Development Editor
Athira Laji

Technical Editors
Arwa Manasawala
Mrunmayee Patil
Nachiket Vartak

Copy Editors
Aditya Nair
Stuti Srivastava

Project Coordinator
Neha Thakur

Proofreaders
Simran Bhogal
Ameesha Green
Clyde Jenkins

Indexers
Tejal Soni
Priya Subramani

Graphics
Ronak Dhruv
Yuvraj Mannari

Production Coordinator
Komal Ramchandani

Cover Work
Komal Ramchandani

About the Author

Eric Rochester enjoys reading, writing, and spending time with his wife and kids. When he's not doing these things, he likes to work on programs in a variety of languages and platforms. Currently, he is exploring functional programming languages, including Clojure and Haskell. He has also written *Clojure Data Analysis Cookbook, Packt Publishing*. He works at the Scholars' Lab library at the University of Virginia, helping the professors and graduate students of humanities realize their digitally informed research agendas.

I'd like to thank almost everyone. My technical reviewers proved invaluable. Also, thank you to the editorial staff at Packt Publishing. This book is much stronger for all of their feedback, and any remaining deficiencies are mine alone.

Thank you to Bethany Nowviskie and Wayne Graham. They've made the Scholars' Lab a great place to work at; they have interesting projects and give us space to explore our own interests as well.

A special thank you to Jackie, Melina, and Micah. They've been exceptionally patient and supportive while I worked on this project. Without them, it wouldn't be worth it.

About the Reviewers

Masato Hagiwara works as a lead scientist at the Rakuten Institute of Technology, New York. He received his PhD in Information Science from Nagoya University in 2009. Before joining Rakuten, he worked at Google and Microsoft Research as an intern, and at Baidu, Japan as a full-time R&D engineer, focusing on Japanese language processing related to search engines. His research interests include Japanese and Chinese word segmentation, knowledge acquisition, transliteration, and language education. He received several awards from Japanese domestic conferences for his work on knowledge acquisition and transliteration. He extensively uses Clojure for his research projects.

> To Lynn and Daphne, thank you for filling my life with smiles and happiness.

Bart Kastermans is an academician turned software developer. He has worked in set and computability theory, before giving in to his long-standing interest in information technology. Currently, he is working as a data scientist at AdGoji, a mobile marketing start-up in Amsterdam.

Nicholas Quirk has been a lifelong resident of Massachusetts. He currently works as one of the few in-house programmers for a billion-dollar manufacturing company. Working there for only three years, he was the sole designer and programmer responsible for the rewriting of some legacy applications, most notably, the production scheduling and order entry software. He has a continuous drive for self improvement. His interests tend to sit in two realms; arts and technology, which he likes to meld when the opportunity presents itself. His art interests include watercolors, drawing (traditional and digital), digital photography, learning languages, and playing the piano. His technical interests include learning about functional programming (Clojure, Haskell, or just about any LISP), language design, compilers, virtual machines, and game design. He also has an unending curiosity in typography, sequential art, text editor color schemes, and knowing how to trick the brain into learning.

You can find more information about him at www.nicholas-quirk.com.

I'd like to thank my partner Caitlin. She has a great set of ears and did a fantastic job editing my biography.

Andrew Stine is a software developer from Northern Virginia. He loves coding and has used a wider variety of technologies than he would care to recall. His favorite language is Clojure.

www.PacktPub.com

Support files, eBooks, discount offers, and more

You might want to visit `www.PacktPub.com` for support files and downloads related to your book.

Did you know that Packt offers eBook versions of every book published, with PDF and ePub files available? You can upgrade to the eBook version at `www.PacktPub.com` and as a print book customer, you are entitled to a discount on the eBook copy. Get in touch with us at `service@packtpub.com` for more details.

At `www.PacktPub.com`, you can also read a collection of free technical articles, sign up for a range of free newsletters and receive exclusive discounts and offers on Packt books and eBooks.

PACKTLIB

`http://PacktLib.PacktPub.com`

Do you need instant solutions to your IT questions? PacktLib is Packt's online digital book library. Here, you can access, read and search across Packt's entire library of books.

Why subscribe?

- Fully searchable across every book published by Packt
- Copy and paste, print and bookmark content
- On demand and accessible via web browser

Free access for Packt account holders

If you have an account with Packt at `www.PacktPub.com`, you can use this to access PacktLib today and view nine entirely free books. Simply use your login credentials for immediate access.

Table of Contents

Preface

Data has become increasingly important almost everywhere. It's been said that *software is eating the world*, but that seems even truer of data. Sometimes, it seems that the focus has shifted: companies no long seem to want more users in order to show them advertisements. Now they want more users to gather data on them. Having more data is seen as a tremendous business advantage.

However, data by itself isn't really useful. It has to be analyzed, interrogated, and interpreted. Data scientists are settling on a number of great tools to do this, from R and Python to Hadoop and the web browser.

This book looks at 10 data analysis tasks. Unlike *Clojure Data Analysis Cookbook*, *Packt Publishing*, this book examines fewer problems and tries to go into more depth. It's more of a case study approach.

Why use Clojure? Clojure was first released in 2007 by Rich Hickey. It's a member of the lisp family of languages, and it has the strengths and flexibility that they provide. It's also functional, so Clojure programs are easy for reasoning. Also, it has amazing features to work concurrently and in parallel. All of these can help us as we analyze data, while keeping things simple and fast.

Moreover, Clojure runs on Java Virtual Machine (JVM), so any libraries written for Java are available as well. Throughout this book, we'll see many examples of leveraging Java libraries for machine learning and other tasks. This gives Clojure an incredible amount of breadth and power.

I hope that this book will help you analyze your data further and in a better manner and also make the process more fun and enjoyable.

What this book covers

Chapter 1, Network Analysis – The Six Degrees of Kevin Bacon, will discuss how people are socially organized into networks. These networks are reified in interesting ways in online social networks. We'll take the opportunity to get a small dataset from an online social network and analyze and look at how people are related in it.

Chapter 2, GIS Analysis – Mapping Climate Change, will explore how we can work with geographical data. It also walks us through getting the weather data and tying it to a geographical location. It then involves analyzing nearby points together to generate a graphic of a simplified and somewhat naive notion of how climate has changed over the period the weather has been tracked.

Chapter 3, Topic Modeling – Changing Concerns in the State of the Union Addresses, will address how we can scrape free text information off the Internet. It then uses topic modeling to look at the problems that presidents have faced and the themes that they've addressed over the years.

Chapter 4, Classifying UFO Sightings, will take a look at UFO sightings and talk about different ways to explore and get a grasp of what's in the dataset. It will then classify the UFO sightings based on various attributes related to the sightings as well as their descriptions.

Chapter 5, Benford's Law – Detecting Natural Progressions of Numbers, will take a look at the world population data from the World Bank data site. It will discuss **Benford's Law** and how it can be used to determine whether a set of numbers is naturally generated or artificially or randomly constructed.

Chapter 6, Sentiment Analysis – Categorizing Hotel Reviews, will take a look at the problems and possibilities related to sentiment analysis tasks. These are typically difficult and fraught categorizations of documents based on a notion of positive or negative. In this chapter, we'll also take a look at categorizing, both manually and automatically, a dataset of hotel reviews.

Chapter 7, Null Hypothesis Tests – Analyzing Crime Data, will take a look at planning, constructing, and performing null-hypothesis tests for statistical significance. It will use international crime data to look at the relationship between economic indicators and some types of crime.

Chapter 8, A/B Testing – Statistical Experiments for the Web, will take a look at how to determine which version of a website engages with the users in a better way. Although conceptually simple, this task does have a few pitfalls and danger points to be aware of.

Chapter 9, Analyzing Social Data Participation, will take a look at how people participate in online social networks. We will discuss and demonstrate some ways to analyze this data with an eye toward encouraging more interaction, contributions, and participation.

Chapter 10, Modeling Stock Data, will take a look at how to work with time-series data, stock data, natural language, and neural networks in order to find relationships between news articles and fluctuations in stock prices.

What you need for this book

One piece of software required for this book is JDK, which you can get from `http://www.oracle.com/technetwork/java/javase/downloads/index.html`. JDK is necessary to run and develop on the Java platform.

The other major piece of software that you'll need is Leiningen 2, which you can download and install from `https://github.com/technomancy/leiningen`. Leiningen 2 is a tool that is used to manage Clojure projects and their dependencies. It's quickly becoming the de facto standard project tool in the Clojure community.

Throughout this book, we'll use a number of other Clojure and Java libraries, including Clojure itself. Leiningen will take care of downloading these for us as and when we need them.

You'll also need a text editor or **Integrated Development Environment** (IDE). If you already have a text editor that you like, you can probably use it. Refer to `http://dev.clojure.org/display/doc/Getting+Started` for tips and plugins to use your particular favorite environment. If you don't have a preference, I'd suggest that you look at using **Eclipse** with **Counterclockwise**. There are instructions to get this setup at `http://dev.clojure.org/display/doc/Getting+Started+with+Eclipse+and+Counterclockwise`.

Who this book is for

If you are a programmer or data scientist who is familiar with Clojure and wants to use it in your data analysis processes, this book is for you. This isn't a tutorial on Clojure—there are already a number of excellent introductory books out there—so you'll need to be familiar with the language; however, you don't need to be an expert at it.

Likewise, you don't need to be an expert on data analysis, although you should probably be familiar with its tasks, processes, and techniques. While you might be able to gain enough from these case studies to get started, you'll want to get a more thorough introduction to this field to be truly effective.

Conventions

In this book, you will find a number of styles of text that distinguish between different kinds of information. Here are some examples of these styles, and an explanation of their meaning.

Code words in text, database table names, folder names, filenames, file extensions, pathnames, dummy URLs, user input, and Twitter handles are shown as follows: "However, before we start looking at the code, let's check out the Leiningen 2 `project.clj` file."

A block of code is set as follows:

```
(ns network-six.graph
  (:require [clojure.set :as set]
            [clojure.core.reducers :as r]
            [clojure.data.json :as json]
            [clojure.java.io :as io]
            [clojure.set :as set]
            [network-six.util :as u]))
```

When we wish to draw your attention to a particular part of a code block, the relevant lines or items are set in bold:

```
clojure.lang.PersistentStructMap
(extract-text [x]
    (concat
      (extract-text (:content x))
      (when (contains? #{:span :p} (:tag x))
        ["\n\n"]))))
```

Any command-line input or output is written as follows:

```
$ cd www
$ python -m SimpleHTTPServer
Serving HTTP on 0.0.0.0 port 8000 …
```

New terms and **important** words are shown in bold. Words that you see on the screen, in menus or dialog boxes for example, appear in the text like this: "Right-click on the new layer and select **Properties**."

> Warnings or important notes appear in a box like this.

> Tips and tricks appear like this.

Reader feedback

Feedback from our readers is always welcome. Let us know what you think about this book—what you liked or may have disliked. Reader feedback is important for us to develop titles that you really get the most out of.

To send us general feedback, simply send an e-mail to feedback@packtpub.com, and mention the book title via the subject of your message.

If there is a topic that you have expertise in and you are interested in either writing or contributing to a book, see our author guide on www.packtpub.com/authors.

Customer support

Now that you are the proud owner of a Packt book, we have a number of things to help you to get the most from your purchase.

Downloading the example code

You can download the example code files for all Packt books you have purchased from your account at http://www.packtpub.com. If you purchased this book elsewhere, you can visit http://www.packtpub.com/support and register to have the files e-mailed directly to you.

Downloading the color images of this book

We also provide you a PDF file that has color images of the screenshots/diagrams used in this book. The color images will help you better understand the changes in the output. You can download this file from `https://www.packtpub.com/sites/default/files/downloads/4139OS_ColoredImages.pdf`.

Errata

Although we have taken every care to ensure the accuracy of our content, mistakes do happen. If you find a mistake in one of our books—maybe a mistake in the text or the code—we would be grateful if you would report this to us. By doing so, you can save other readers from frustration and help us improve subsequent versions of this book. If you find any errata, please report them by visiting `http://www.packtpub.com/submit-errata`, selecting your book, clicking on the **errata submission form** link, and entering the details of your errata. Once your errata are verified, your submission will be accepted and the errata will be uploaded on our website, or added to any list of existing errata, under the Errata section of that title. Any existing errata can be viewed by selecting your title from `http://www.packtpub.com/support`.

Piracy

Piracy of copyright material on the Internet is an ongoing problem across all media. At Packt, we take the protection of our copyright and licenses very seriously. If you come across any illegal copies of our works, in any form, on the Internet, please provide us with the location address or website name immediately so that we can pursue a remedy.

Please contact us at `copyright@packtpub.com` with a link to the suspected pirated material.

We appreciate your help in protecting our authors, and our ability to bring you valuable content.

Questions

You can contact us at `questions@packtpub.com` if you are having a problem with any aspect of the book, and we will do our best to address it.

1
Network Analysis – The Six Degrees of Kevin Bacon

With the popularity of **Facebook, Twitter, LinkedIn,** and other social networks, we're increasingly defined by who we know and who's in our **network**. These websites help us manage who we know — whether personally, professionally, or in some other way — and our interactions with those groups and individuals. In exchange, we tell these sites who we are in the network.

These companies, and many others, spend a lot of time on and pay attention to our social networks. What do they say about us, and how can we sell things to these groups?

In this chapter, we'll walk through learning about and analyzing social networks:

- Analyzing social networks
- Getting the data
- Understanding graphs
- Implementing the graphs
- Measuring social network graphs
- Visualizing social network graphs

Analyzing social networks

Although the Internet and popular games such as *Six Degrees of Kevin Bacon* have popularized the concept, social network analysis has been around for a long time. It has deep roots in sociology. Although the sociologist John A. Barnes may have been the first person to use the term in 1954 in the article *Class and communities in a Norwegian island parish* (`http://garfield.library.upenn.edu/classics1987/A1987H444300001.pdf`), he was building on a tradition from the 1930s, and before that, he was looking at social groups and interactions relationally. Researchers contended that the phenomenon arose from social interactions and not individuals.

Slightly more recently, starting in the 1960s, Stanley Milgram has been working on a small world experiment. He would mail a letter to a volunteer somewhere in the mid-western United States and ask him or her to get it to a target individual in Boston. If the volunteer knew the target on a first-name basis, he or she could mail it to him. Otherwise, they would need to pass it to someone they knew who might know the target. At each step, the participants were to mail a postcard to Milgram so that he could track the progress of the letter.

This experiment (and other experiments based on it) has been criticized. For one thing, the participants may decide to just throw the letter away and miss huge swathes of the network. However, the results are evocative. Milgram found that the few letters that made it to the target, did so with an average of six steps. Similar results have been born out by later, similar experiments.

Milgram himself did not use the popular phrase *six degrees of separation*. This was probably taken from John Guare's play and film *Six Degrees of Separation* (1990 and 1993). He said he got the concept from Guglielmo Marconi, who discussed it in his 1909 Nobel Prize address.

The phrase "six degrees" is synonymous with social networks in the popular imagination, and a large part of this is due to the pop culture game *Six Degrees of Kevin Bacon*. In this game, people would try to find a link between Kevin Bacon and some other actor by tracing the films in which they've worked together.

In this chapter, we'll take a look at this game more critically. We'll use it to explore a network of Facebook (`https://www.facebook.com/`) users. We'll visualize this network and look at some of its characteristics.

Specifically, we're going to look at a network that has been gathered from Facebook. We'll find data for Facebook users and their friends, and we'll use that data to construct a social network graph. We'll analyze that information to see whether the observation about the six degrees of separation applies to this network. More broadly, we'll see what we can learn about the relationships represented in the network and consider some possible directions for future research.

Getting the data

A couple of small datasets of the Facebook network data are available on the Internet. None of them are particularly large or complete, but they do give us a reasonable snapshot of part of Facebook's network. As the Facebook graph is a private data source, this partial view is probably the best that we can hope for.

We'll get the data from the **Stanford Large Network Dataset Collection** (http://snap.stanford.edu/data/). This contains a number of network datasets, from Facebook and Twitter, to road networks and citation networks. To do this, we'll download the facebook.tar.gz file from http://snap.stanford.edu/data/ egonets-Facebook.html. Once it's on your computer, you can extract it. When I put it into the folder with my source code, it created a directory named facebook.

The directory contains 10 sets of files. Each group is based on one primary vertex (user), and each contains five files. For vertex 0, these files would be as follows:

- 0.edges: This contains the vertices that the primary one links to.
- 0.circles: This contains the groupings that the user has created for his or her friends.
- 0.feat: This contains the features of the vertices that the user is adjacent to and ones that are listed in 0.edges.
- 0.egofeat: This contains the primary user's features.
- 0.featnames: This contains the names of the features described in 0.feat and 0.egofeat. For Facebook, these values have been anonymized.

For these purposes, we'll just use the *.edges files.

Now let's turn our attention to the data in the files and what they represent.

Understanding graphs

Graphs are the Swiss army knife of computer science data structures. Theoretically, any other data structure can be represented as a graph, although usually, it won't perform as well.

For example, binary trees can be seen as a graph in which each node has two outgoing edges at most. These edges link it to the node's children. Or, an array can be seen as a graph in which each item in the array has edges that link it to the items adjacent to it.

However, in this case, the data that we're working with is naturally represented by a graph. The people in the network are the nodes, and their relationships are the edges.

Graphs come in several flavors, but they all have some things in common. First, they are a series of nodes that are connected by edges. Edges can be unidirectional, in which case, the relationship they represent goes only one way (for example, followers on Twitter), or it goes bidirectional, in which the relationship is two-way (for example, friends on Facebook).

Graphs generally don't have any hierarchy or structure like trees or lists do. However, the data they represent may have a structure. For example, Twitter has a number of users (vertices) who have a lot of followers (inbound edges). However, most users only have a few followers. This dichotomy creates a structure to the graph, where a lot of data flows through a few vertices.

Graphs' data structures typically support a number of operations, including adding edges, removing edges, and traversing the graph. We'll implement a graph data structure later. At that point, we'll also look at these operations. This may not be the best performing graph, especially for very large datasets, but it should help make clear what graphs are all about.

Implementing the graphs

As the graph data structure is so central to this chapter, we'll take a look at it in more detail before we move on.

There are a number of ways to implement graphs. In this case, we'll use a variation of an **adjacency list**, which maps each node to a list of its neighbors. We'll store the nodes in a hash map and keep separate hash maps for each node's data. This representation is especially good for sparse graphs, because we only need to store existing links. If the graph is very dense, then representing the set of neighboring nodes as a matrix instead of a hash table will take less memory.

However, before we start looking at the code, let's check out the **Leiningen 2** project.clj file. Apart from the **Clojure** library, this makes use of the Clojure JSON library, the me.raynes file utility library (https://github.com/Raynes/fs), and the **Simple Logging Facade for Java** library (http://www.slf4j.org/):

```
(defproject network-six "0.1.0-SNAPSHOT"
  :description "FIXME: write description"
  :url "http://example.com/FIXME"
  :license {:name "Eclipse Public License"
    :url "http://www.eclipse.org/legal/epl-v10.html"}
```

```
:plugins [[lein-cljsbuild "0.3.2"]]
:dependencies [[org.slf4j/slf4j-simple "1.7.5"]
  [org.clojure/clojure "1.5.1"]
  [org.clojure/data.json "0.2.2"]
  [me.raynes/fs "1.4.4"]
  [org.clojure/clojurescript "0.0-2202"]]
:cljsbuild {:builds [{:source-paths ["src-cljs"],
  :compiler {:pretty-printer true,
    :output-to "www/js/main.js",
    :optimizations :whitespace}}]})
```

If you're keeping track, there are several sections related to **ClojureScript** (`https://github.com/clojure/clojurescript`) as well. We'll talk about them later in the chapter.

For the first file that we'll work in, open up `src/network_six/graph.clj`. Use this for the namespace declaration:

```
(ns network-six.graph
  (:require [clojure.set :as set]
            [clojure.core.reducers :as r]
            [clojure.data.json :as json]
            [clojure.java.io :as io]
            [clojure.set :as set]
            [network-six.util :as u]))
```

In this namespace, we'll create a `Graph` record that contains two slots. One is for the map between vertex numbers and sets of neighbors. The second is for the data maps. We'll define an empty graph that we can use anywhere, as follows:

```
(defrecord Graph
  [neighbors data])
(def empty-graph (Graph. {} {}))
```

The primary operations that we'll use for this chapter are functions that modify the graph by adding or removing edges or by merging two graphs. The `add` and `delete` operations both take an optional flag to treat the edge as bidirectional. In that case, both functions just call themselves with the ends of the edges swapped so that they operate on the edge that goes in the other direction:

```
(defn update-conj [s x]
  (conj (if (nil? s) #{} s) x))
(defn add
  ([g x y] (add g x y false))
  ([g x y bidirectional?]
```

```
        ((if bidirectional? #(add % y x false) identity)
           (update-in g [:neighbors x] #(update-conj % y))))))
   (defn delete
     ([g x y] (delete g x y false))
     ([g x y bidirectional?]
      ((if bidirectional? #(delete % y x false) identity)
           (update-in g [:neighbors x] #(disj % y)))))
   (defn merge-graphs [a b]
     (Graph. (merge-with set/union (:neighbors a) (:neighbors b))
             (merge (:data a) (:data b))))
```

The final low-level functions to work with graphs are two functions that are used to set or retrieve data associated with the vertices. Sometimes, it's also useful to be able to store data of the edges, but we won't use that for this implementation. However, we will associate some information with the vertices themselves later on, and when we do that, we'll use these functions.

All of these functions are overloaded. Passed in a graph, a vertex number, and a key, they set or retrieve a value on a hash map that is that vertex's value. Passed in just a graph and a vertex number, they set or retrieve the vertex's value — either the hash map or another value that is there in its place:

```
   (defn get-value
     ([g x] ((:data g) x))
     ([g x k] ((get-value g x) k)))
   (defn set-value
     ([g x v] (assoc-in g [:data x] v))
     ([g x k v] (set-value g x (assoc (get-value g x) k v))))
   (defn update-value
     ([g x f] (set-value g x (f (get-value g x))))
     ([g x k f] (set-value g x k (f (get-value g x k)))))
```

We will also want to get the vertices and the edges for the graph. The vertices are the union of the set of all the nodes with outbound edges and the set of nodes with inbound edges. There should be some, or even a lot, of overlap between these two groups. If the graph is bidirectional, then get-edges will return each edge twice — one going from a to b and the other going from b to a:

```
   (defn get-vertices [graph]
     (reduce set/union (set (keys (:neighbors graph)))
             (vals (:neighbors graph))))
   (defn get-edges [graph]
     (let [pair-edges (fn [[v neighbors]]
                         (map #(vector v %) neighbors))]
       (mapcat pair-edges (:neighbors graph))))
```

We'll write some more basic utilities later, but right now, let's take a look at a function that is a slightly higher-level function, but still a fundamental operation on graphs: a **breadth-first walk** over the graph and a search based on that.

A breadth-first walk traverses the graph by first looking at all the neighbors of the current node. It then looks at the neighbors of those nodes. It continues broadening the search one layer at a time.

This is in opposition to a **depth-first walk**, which goes deep down one path until there are no outgoing edges to be tried. Then, it backs out to look down other paths.

Which walk is more efficient really depends on the nature of the individual graph and what is being searched for. However, in our case, we're using a breadth-first walk because it ensures that the shortest path between the two nodes will be found first. A depth-first search can't guarantee that.

The backbone of the `breadth-first` function is a **First In, First Out** (FIFO) queue. To keep track of the vertices in the paths that we're trying, we use a vector with the index of those vertices. The queue holds all of the active paths. We also keep a set of vertices that we've reached before. This prevents us from getting caught in loops.

We wrap everything in a lazy sequence so that the caller can control how much work is done and what happens to it.

At each step in the loop, the algorithm is pretty standard:

1. If the queue is empty, then we've exhausted the part of the graph that's accessible from the start node. We're done, and we return null to indicate that we didn't find the node.
2. Otherwise, we pop a path vector off the queue. The current vertex is the last one.
3. We get the current vertex's neighbors.
4. We remove any vertices that we've already considered.
5. For each neighbor, we append it to the current path vector, creating that many new path vectors. For example, if the current path vector is [0, 171, 4] and the new neighbors are 7, 42 and 532, then we'll create three new vectors: [0, 171, 4, 7], [0, 171, 4, 42], and [0, 171, 4, 532].
6. We push each of the new path vectors onto the queue.
7. We add each of the neighbors onto the list of vertices that we've seen.
8. We output the current path to the lazy sequence.
9. Finally, we loop back to step one for the rest of the output sequence.

The following code is the implementation of this. Most of it takes place in bf-seq, which sets up the processing in the first clause (two parameters) and constructs the sequence in the second clause (three parameters). The other function, breadth-first, is the public interface to the function:

```
(defn bf-seq
  ([get-neighbors a]
   (bf-seq
     get-neighbors
     (conj clojure.lang.PersistentQueue/EMPTY [a])
     #{a}))
  ([get-neighbors q seen]
   (lazy-seq
     (when-not (empty? q)
       (let [current (first q)
             nbors (remove seen (get-neighbors (last current)))]
         (cons current
               (bf-seq get-neighbors
                       (into (pop q)
                             (map #(conj current %) nbors))
                       (into seen nbors))))))))
(defn breadth-first [graph a]
  (bf-seq (:neighbors graph) a))
```

Notice that what makes this a breadth-first search is that we use a FIFO queue. If we used a **LIFO (Last In, First Out)** queue (a Clojure list works well for this), then this would be a depth-first search. Instead of going broadly and simultaneously trying a number of paths, it would dive deep into the graph along one path and not backtrack to try a new one until it had exhausted the first path.

This is a flexible base on which one can build a number of functionalities. For example, a breadth-first search is now a two-line function:

```
(defn bfs [graph a b]
  (first (filter #(= (last %) b) (breadth-first graph a))))
```

These are just filters that find all paths that start from a and end at b and then return the first of those.

Loading the data

Now that we have the fundamental data structure that we're going to use, we can read the data files that we downloaded into a graph.

For the purposes of analyzing the network itself, we're only interested in the *.edges files. This lists the edges in the graph, one edge per line. Each edge is defined by the node numbers that it connects. As Facebook relationships are two-way, the edges represented here are bidirectional. For example, the first few lines of 0.edges are shown as follows:

```
236 186
122 285
24 346
271 304
176 9
```

We'll first define a function that reads one edge file into a Graph, and then we'll define another function that walks a directory, reads each edge file, and merges the graphs into one. I'm keeping these in a new namespace, network-six.ego. This is defined in the src/network_six/ego.clj file. It uses the following namespace declaration:

```
(ns network-six.ego
  (:require [clojure.java.io :as io]
            [clojure.set :as set]
            [clojure.string :as string]
            [clojure.data.json :as json]
            [clojure.core.reducers :as r]
            [network-six.graph :as g]
            [network-six.util :as u]
            [me.raynes.fs :as fs])
  (:import [java.io File]))
```

Now we'll define the function that reads the *.edges files from a data directory:

```
(defn read-edge-file [filename]
  (with-open [f (io/reader filename)]
    (->>
      f
      line-seq
      (r/map #(string/split % #"\s+"))
      (r/map #(mapv (fn [x] (Long/parseLong x)) %))
      (r/reduce #(g/add %1 (first %2) (second %2))
```

```
                 g/empty-graph))))
(defn read-edge-files [ego-dir]
  (r/reduce g/merge-graphs {}
            (r/map read-edge-file
                   (fs/find-files ego-dir #".*\.edges$"))))
```

We can use these from **read-eval-print loop** (**REPL**) to load the data into a graph that we can work with. We can get some basic information about the data at this point, and the following how we'll go about doing that:

```
User=> (require '[network-six.graph :as g]
                '[network-six.ego :as ego])
user=> (def graph (ego/read-edge-files "facebook/"))
#'user/graph
user=> (count (g/get-vertices graph))
3959
user=> (count (g/get-edges graph))
168486
```

Now let's dive deeper into the graph and get some other metrics.

Measuring social network graphs

There are a variety of metrics that we can use to describe graph data structures in particular and social network graphs in general. We'll look at a few of them and think about both, what they can teach us, and how we can implement them.

Density

Recall that a network's density is the number of actual edges versus the number of possible edges. A completely dense network is one that has an edge between each vertex and every other vertex. For example, in the following figure, the graph on the upper-right section is completely dense. The graph in the lower-left section has a density factor of 0.5333.

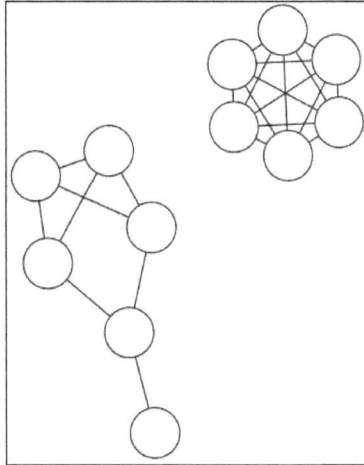

The number of possible edges is given as `N(N-1)`. We'll define the density formula as follows:

```
(defn density [graph]
  (let [n (count (get-vertices graph))
        e (count (get-edges graph))]
    (/ (* 2.0 e) (* n (dec n)))))
```

We can use this to get some information about the number of edges in the graph:

```
user=> (g/density graph)
0.021504657198130255
```

Looking at this, it appears that this graph is not very dense. Maybe some other metrics will help explain why.

Degrees

A vertex's degree is the number of other vertexes connected to it, and another summary statistic for social networks is the average degree. This is computed by the formula $2E/N$. The Clojure to implement this is straightforward:

```
(defn avg-degree [graph]
  (/ (* 2.0 (count (get-edges graph)))
     (count (get-vertices graph))))
```

Similarly, it is easy to use it:

```
user=> (g/avg-degree graph)
85.11543319019954
```

So, the typical number of edges is around 85. Given that there are almost 4,000 vertices, it is understandable why the density is so low (0.022).

Paths

We can get a number of interesting metrics based on all of the paths between two elements. For example, we'll need those paths to get the centrality of nodes later in this chapter. The average path length is also an important metric. To calculate any of these, we'll need to compute all of the paths between any two vertices.

For weighted graphs that have a weight or cost assigned to each edge, there are a number of algorithms to find the shortest path. **Dijkstra's algorithm** and **Johnson's algorithm** are two common ones that perform well in a range of circumstances.

However, for non-weighted graphs, any of these search algorithms evolve into a breadth-first search. We just implemented this.

We can find the paths that use the `breadth-first` function that we walked through earlier. We simply take each vertex as a starting point and get all the paths from there. To make access easier later, we convert each path returned into a hash map as follows:

```
(defn find-all-paths [graph]
  (->> graph
    get-vertices
    (mapcat #(breadth-first graph %))
    (map #(hash-map :start (first %) :dest (last %) :path %))))
```

Unfortunately, there's an added complication; the output will probably take more memory than available. Because of this, we'll also define a couple of functions to write the paths out to a file and iterate over them again. We'll name them `network-six.graph/write-paths` and `network-six.graph/iter-paths`, and you can find them in the code download provided for this chapter on the Packt Publishing website. I saved it to the file `path.json`, as each line of the file is a separate JSON document.

Average path length

The first metric that we can get from the paths is the average path length. We can find this easily by walking over the paths. We'll use a slightly different definition of mean that doesn't require all the data to be kept in the memory. You can find this in the `network-six.util` namespace:

```
user=> (double
         (u/mean
           (map count (map :path (g/iter-paths "path.json")))))
6.525055748717483
```

This is interesting! Strictly speaking, the concept of six degrees of separation says that all paths in the network should be six or smaller However, experiments often look at the paths in terms of the average path length. In this case, the average distance between any two connected nodes in this graph is just over six. So, the six degrees of separation do appear to hold in this graph.

We can see the distribution of path lengths more clearly by looking at a histogram of them:

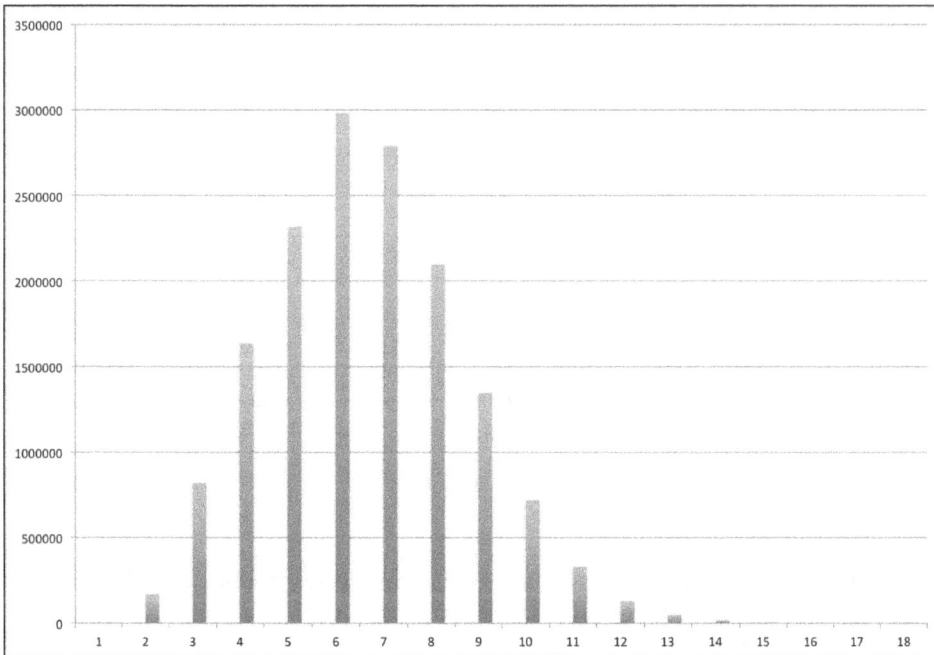

So, the distribution of path lengths appears to be more or less normal, centered on 6.

Network diameter

The network diameter is the longest of the shortest paths between any two nodes in the graph. This is simple to get:

```
user=> (reduce
          max Integer/MIN_VALUE
          (map count (map :path (g/iter-paths "path.json"))))
18
```

So the network diameter is approximately three times larger than the average.

Clustering coefficient

Clustering coefficient is a measure of how many densely linked clusters there are in the graph. This is one measure of the small world effect, and it's sometimes referred to as the "all my friends know each other" property. To find the clustering coefficient for one vertex, this basically cuts all of its neighbors out of the network and tries to find the density of the subgraph. In looking at the whole graph, a high clustering coefficient indicates a small world effect in the graph.

The following is how to find the clustering coefficient for a single vertex:

```
(defn clustering-coeff [graph n]
  (let [cluster ((:neighbors graph) n)
        edges (filter cluster (mapcat (:neighbors graph) cluster))
        e (count edges)
        k (count cluster)]
    (if (= k 1)
      0
      (/ (* 2.0 e) (* k (dec k))))))
```

The function to find the average clustering coefficient for the graph is straightforward, and you can find it in the code download. The following is how it looks when applied to this graph:

```
user=> (g/avg-cluster-coeff graph)
1.0874536731229358
```

So it's not overly large. Chances are, there are a few nodes that are highly connected throughout the graph and most others are less connected.

Centrality

There are several ways to measure how central a vertex is to the graph. One is **closeness centrality**. This is the distance of any particular vertex from all other vertices. We can easily get this information with the `breadth-first` function that we created earlier. Unfortunately, this only applies to complete networks, that is, to networks in which every vertex is reachable from every other vertex. This is not the case in the graph we're working with right now. There are some small pockets that are completely isolated from the rest of the network.

However, there are other measures of centrality that we can use instead. **Betweenness centrality** counts the number of shortest paths that a vertex is found in. Betweenness finds the vertices that act as a bridge. The original intent of this metric was to identify people who control the communication in the network.

To get this done efficiently, we can rely on the paths returned by the `breadth-first` function again. We'll get the paths from each vertex and call `reduce` over each. At every step, we'll calculate the total number of paths plus the number of times each vertex appears in a path:

```
(defn accum-betweenness
  [{:keys [paths betweenness reachable]} [v v-paths]]
  (let [v-paths (filter #(> (count %) 1) v-paths)]
    {:paths (+ paths (count v-paths)),
     :betweenness (merge-with +
                              betweenness
                              (frequencies (flatten v-paths))),
     :reachable (assoc reachable v (count v-paths))}))
```

Next, once we reach the end, we'll take the total number of paths and convert the betweenness and reachable totals for each vertex to a ratio, as follows:

```
(defn ->ratio [total [k c]]
  [k (double (/ c total))])
(defn finish-betweenness
  [{:keys [paths betweenness reachable] :as metrics}]
  (assoc metrics
         :betweenness (->> betweenness
                           (map #(->ratio paths %))
                           (into {}))
         :reachable (->> reachable
                         (map #(->ratio paths %))
                         (into {}))))
```

While these two functions do all the work, they aren't the public interface. The function metrics tie these two together in something we'd want to actually call:

```
(defn metrics [graph]
  (let [mzero {:paths 0, :betweenness {}, :reachable {}}]
    (->> graph
      get-vertices
      (pmap #(vector % (breadth-first graph %)))
      (reduce accum-betweenness mzero)
      finish-betweenness)))
```

We can now use this to find the betweenness centrality of any vertex as follows:

```
user=> (def m (g/metrics graph))
user=> ((:betweenness m) 0)
5.092923145895773E-4
```

Or, we can sort the vertices on the centrality measure to get those vertices that have the highest values. The first number in each pair of values that are returned is the node, and the second number is the betweenness centrality of that node. So, the first result says that the betweenness centrality for node `1085` is `0.254`:

```
user=> (take 5 (reverse (sort-by second (seq (:betweenness m)))))
([1085 0.2541568423150047] [1718 0.1508391907570839] [1577
  0.1228894724115601] [698 0.09236806137867479]
  [1505 0.08172539570689669])
```

This has all been interesting, but what about Kevin Bacon?

Degrees of separation

We started this chapter talking about the *Six Degrees of Kevin Bacon*, a pop culture phenomenon and how this captures a fundamental nature of many social networks. Let's analyze our Facebook network for this.

First, we'll create a function called `degrees-between`. This will take an origin vertex and a degree of separation to go out, and it will return a list of each level of separation and the vertices at that distance from the origin vertex. The `degrees -between` function will do this by accumulating a list of vertices at each level and a set of vertices that we've seen. At each step, it will take the last level and find all of those vertices' neighbors, without the ones we've already visited. The following is what this will look like:

```
(defn degrees-between [graph n from]
  (let [neighbors (:neighbors graph)]
    (loop [d [{:degree 0, :neighbors #{from}}],
```

```
            seen #{from}]
    (let [{:keys [degree neighbors]} (last d)]
      (if (= degree n)
        d
        (let [next-neighbors (->> neighbors
                                  (mapcat (:neighbors graph))
                                  (remove seen)
                                  set)]
          (recur (conj d {:degree (inc degree)
                          :neighbors next-neighbors})
                 (into seen next-neighbors)))))))))
```

Earlier, we included a way to associate data with a vertex, but we haven't used this yet. Let's exercise that feature to store the degrees of separation from the origin vertex in the graph. We can either call this function with the output of degrees-between or with the parameters to degrees-between:

```
(defn store-degrees-between
  ([graph degrees]
   (let [store (fn [g {:keys [degree neighbors]}]
                 (reduce #(set-value %1 %2 degree) g neighbors))]
     (reduce store graph degrees)))
  ([graph n from]
   (store-degrees-between graph (degrees-between graph n from))))
```

Finally, the full graph is a little large, especially for many visualizations. So, let's include a function that will let us zoom in on the graph identified by the degrees-between function. It will return both the original graph, with the vertex data fields populated and the subgraph of vertices within the n levels of separation from the origin vertex:

```
(defn degrees-between-subgraph [graph n from]
  (let [marked (store-degrees-between graph n from)
        v-set (set (map first (filter second (:data marked))))
        sub (subgraph marked v-set)]
    {:graph marked, :subgraph sub}))
```

With these defined, we can learn some more interesting things about the network that we're studying. Let's see how much of the network with different vertices can reach within six hops. Let's look at how we'd do this with vertex 0, and then we can see a table that presents these values for several vertices:

```
user=> (def v-count (count (g/get-vertices g)))
#'user/v-count
user=> (double
```

```
(/ (count
      (g/get-vertices
        (:subgraph (g/degrees-between-subgraph g 6 0)))))
      v-count))
0.8949229603435211
```

Now, it's interesting to see how the betweenness values for these track the amount of the graph that they can access quickly:

Vertex	Betweenness	Percent accessible
0	0.0005093	89.5000
256	0.0000001	0.0005
1354	0.0005182	75.9500
1085	0.2541568	96.1859

These are some interesting data points. What does this look like for the network as a whole?

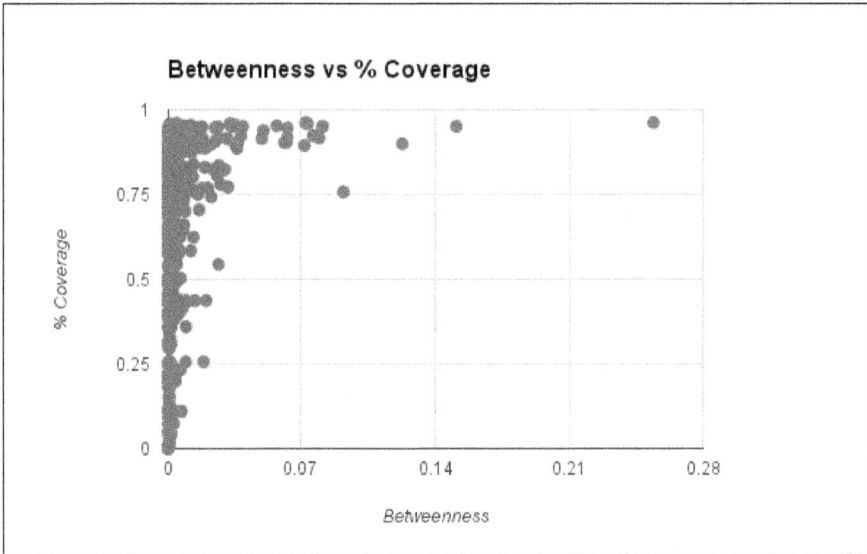

This makes it clear that there's probably little correlation between these two variables. Most vertices have a very low betweenness, although they range between 0 and 100 in the percent of the network that they can access.

At this point, we have some interesting facts about the network, but it would be helpful to get a more intuitive overview of it, like we just did for the betweenness centrality. Visualizations can help here.

Visualizing the graph

At this point, it would be really useful to visualize this graph. There are a number of different ways to visualize graphs. We'll use the JavaScript library D3 (data-driven documents, http://d3js.org/) to generate several graph visualizations on subgraphs of the Facebook network data, and we'll look at the pros and cons of each. Finally, we'll use a simple pie chart to visualize how much of the graph is affected as we move outward from a node through its degrees of separation.

Setting up ClojureScript

As I just mentioned, D3 is a JavaScript library. JavaScripts are not bad, but this is a book about Clojure. There's an implementation of the Clojure compiler that takes Clojure and generates JavaScript. So, we'll use that to keep our focus on Clojure while we call JavaScript libraries and deploy them on a browser.

Before we can do that, however, we need to set up our system to use ClojureScript. The first thing we'll need to do is to add the configuration to our project.clj file for this project. This is fairly simple. We just need to declare lein-cljsbuild as a plugin for this project and then configure the ClojureScript compiler. Our project.clj file from earlier is shown as follows, with the relevant lines highlighted as follows:

```
(defproject network-six "0.1.0-SNAPSHOT"
  :description "FIXME: write description"
  :url "http://example.com/FIXME"
  :license {:name "Eclipse Public License"
            :url "http://www.eclipse.org/legal/epl-v10.html"}
  :plugins [[lein-cljsbuild "0.3.2"]]
  :dependencies [[org.slf4j/slf4j-simple "1.7.5"]
                 [org.clojure/clojure "1.5.1"]
                 [org.clojure/data.json "0.2.2"]
                 [me.raynes/fs "1.4.4"]
                 [org.clojure/clojurescript "0.0-2202"]]
  :cljsbuild {:builds
              [{:source-paths ["src-cljs"],
                :compiler {:pretty-printer true,
                :output-to "www/js/main.js",
                :optimizations :whitespace}}]})
```

The first line adds the lein-cljsbuild plugin to the project. The second block of lines tell Leiningen to watch the src-cljs directory for ClojureScript files. All of these files are then compiled into the www/js/main.js file.

We'll need an HTML file to frame the compiled JavaScript. In the code download, I've included a basic page that's modified from an HTML5 Boilerplate template (`http://html5boilerplate.com/`). The biggest change is that I've taken out everything that's in the `div` content.

Also, I added some `script` tags to load D3 and a D3 plugin for one of the types of graphs that we'll use later. After the tag that loads `bootstrap.min.js`, I added these:

```
<script src="http://d3js.org/d3.v3.min.js"></script>
<script src="http://d3js.org/d3.hive.v0.min.js"></script>
```

Finally, to load the data files asynchronously with AJAX, the www directory will need to be accessible from a web server. There are a number of different options, but if you have Python installed, the easiest option is to probably navigate to the www directory and execute the following command:

```
$ cd www
$ python -m SimpleHTTPServer
Serving HTTP on 0.0.0.0 port 8000 ...
```

Now we're ready to proceed. Let's make some charts!

A force-directed layout

One of the standard chart types to visualize graphs is a **force-directed layout**. These charts use a dynamic-layout algorithm to generate charts that are more clear and look nice. They're modeled on springs. Each vertex repels all the other vertices, but the edges draw the vertices closer.

To have this graph compiled to JavaScript, we start by creating a file named `src-cljs/network-six/force.cljs`. We'll have a standard namespace declaration at the top of the file:

```
(ns network-six.force)
```

Generally, when we use D3, we first set up part of the graph. Then, we get the data. When the data is returned, we continue setting up the graph. In D3, this generally means selecting one or more elements currently in the tree and then selecting some of their children using `selectAll`. The elements in this new selection may or may not exist at this point. We join the `selectAll` elements with the data. From this point, we use the `enter` method most of the time to enter the data items and the nonexistent elements that we selected earlier. If we're updating the data, assuming that the elements already exist, then the process is slightly different. However, the process that uses the `enter` method, which I described, is the normal workflow that uses D3.

So, we'll start with a little setup for the graph by creating the color palette. In the graph that we're creating, colors will represent the node's distance from a central node. We'll take some time to understand this, because it illustrates some of the differences between Clojure and ClojureScript, and it shows us how to call JavaScript:

```
(defn make-color []
  (.. js/d3
    -scale
    category10
    (domain (array 0 1 2 3 4 5 6))))
```

Let's take this bit by bit so that we can understand it all. I'll list a line and then point out what's interesting about it:

```
(.. js/d3
```

There are a couple of things that we need to notice about this line. First, . . is the standard member access macro that we use for Java's interoperability with the main Clojure implementation. In this case, we're using it to construct a series of access calls against a JavaScript object. In this case, the ClojureScript that the macro expands to would be (.domain (.category10 (.-scale js/d3)) (array 0 1 2 3 4 5 6)).

In this case, that object is the main D3 object. The js/ namespace is available by default. It's just an escape hatch to the main JavaScript scope. In this case, it would be the same as accessing a property on the JavaScript window object. You can use this to access anything from JavaScript without having to declare it. I regularly use it with js/console for debugging, for example:

```
-scale
```

This resolves into the JavaScript d3.scale call. The minus sign before scale just means that the call is a property and not a function that takes no arguments. As Clojure doesn't have properties and everything here would look like a function call, ClojureScript needs some way to know that this should not generate a function call. The dash does that as follows:

```
category10
```

This line, combined with the preceding lines, generates JavaScript that looks like d3.scale.category10(). In this case, the call doesn't have a minus sign before it, so the ClojureScript compiler knows that it should generate a function call in this case:

```
(domain (array 0 1 2 3 4 5 6))))
```

Finally, this makes a call to the scale's `domain` method with an array that sets the domain to the integers between 0 and 6, inclusive of both. These are the values for the distances that we'll look at. The JavaScript for this would be `d3.scale.category10().domain([0, 1, 2, 3, 4, 5, 6])`.

This function creates and returns a color object. This object is callable, and when it acts as a function that takes a value and returns a color, this will consistently return the same color whenever it's called with a given value from the domain. For example, this way, the distance 1 will also be associated with the same color in the visualization.

This gives us an introduction to the rules for interoperability in ClojureScript. Before we make the call to get the data file, we'll also create the object that takes care of managing the force-directed layout and the D3 object for the `svg` element. However, you can check the code download provided on the Packt Publishing website for the functions that create these objects.

Next, we need to access the data. We'll see that in a minute, though. First, we need to define some more functions to work with the data once we have it.For the first function, we need to take the force-layout object and associate the data with it.

The data for all of the visualizations has the same format. Each visualization is a JSON object with three keys. The first one, `nodes`, is an array of JSON objects, each representing one vertex in the graph. The main property of these objects that we're interested in is the `data` property. This contains the distance of the current vertex from the origin vertex. Next, the `links` property is a list of JSON objects that represent the edges of the graph. Each link contains the index of a source vertex and a target vertex. Third, the `graph` property contains the entire graph using the same data structures as we did in Clojure.

The force-directed layout object expects to work with the data from the `nodes` and the `links` properties. We set this up and start the animation with the `setup-force-layout` function:

```
(defn setup-force-layout [force-layout graph]
  (.. force-layout
    (nodes (.-nodes graph))
    (links (.-links graph))
    start))
```

As the animation continues, the force-layout object will assign each node and link the object with one or more coordinates. We'll need to update the circles and paths with those values.

We'll do this with a handler for a `tick` event that the layout object will emit:

```
(defn on-tick [link node]
  (fn []
    (.. link
      (attr "x1" #(.. % -source -x))
      (attr "y1" #(.. % -source -y))
      (attr "x2" #(.. % -target -x))
      (attr "y2" #(.. % -target -y)))
    (.. node
      (attr "cx" #(.-x %))
      (attr "cy" #(.-y %)))))
```

Also, at this stage, we create the `circle` and `path` elements that represent the vertices and edges. We won't list these functions here.

Finally, we tie everything together. First, we set up the initial objects, then we ask the server for the data, and finally, we create the HTML/SVG elements that represent the data. This is all tied together with the `main` function:

```
(defn ^:export main [json-file]
  (let [width 960, height 600
        color (make-color)
        force-layout (make-force-layout width height)
        svg (make-svg width height)]
    (.json js/d3 json-file
      (fn [err graph]
        (.. graph
          -links
          (forEach #(do (aset %1 "weight" 1.0)
                        (aset %1 "index" %2))))
        (setup-force-layout force-layout graph)
        (let [link (make-links svg graph color)
              node (make-nodes svg graph color force-layout)]
          (.on force-layout "tick"
            (on-tick link node)))))))
```

There are a couple of things that we need to notice about this function, and they're both highlighted in the preceding snippet. The first is that the function name has an `:export` metadata flag attached to it. This just signals that the ClojureScript compiler should make this function accessible from JavaScript outside this namespace. The second is the call to `d3.json`. This function takes a URL for a JSON data file and a function to handle the results. We'll see more of this function later.

Before we can use this, we need to call it from the HTML page. After the `script` tag that loads `js/main.js`, I added this `script` tag:

```
<script>
network_six.force.main('facebook-49.json');
</script>
```

This loads the data file for vertex number `49`. This vertex had a betweenness factor of 0.0015, and it could reach four percent of the larger network within six hops. This is small enough to create a meaningful, comprehensible graphic, as seen in the following figure:

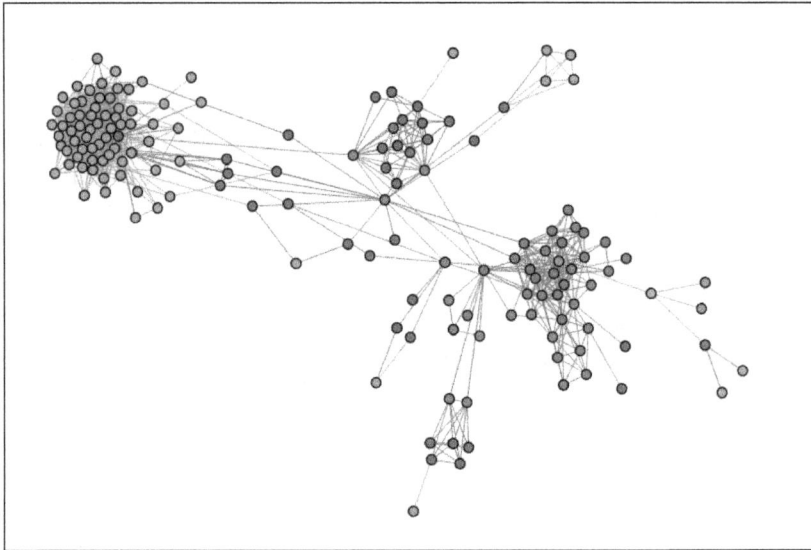

The origin vertex (`49`) is the blue vertex on the lower-right section, almost the farthest-right node of the graph. All the nodes at each hop away from that node will be of a different color. The origin vertex branches to three orange vertices, which link to some green ones. One of the green vertices is in the middle of the larger cluster on the right.

Some aspects of this graph are very helpful. It makes it relatively easy to trace the nodes as they get farther from the origin. This is even easier when interacting with the node in the browser, because it's easy to grab a node and pull it away from its neighbors.

However, it distorts some other information. The graph that we're working with today is not weighted. Theoretically, the links in the graph should be the same length because all the edges have the same weight. In practice, however, it's impossible to display a graph in two dimensions. Force-directed layouts help you display the graph, but the cost is that it's hard to tell exactly what the line lengths and the several clear clusters of various sizes mean on this graph.

Also, the graphs themselves cannot be compared. If we then pulled out a subgraph around a different vertex and charted it, we wouldn't be able to tell much by comparing the two.

So what other options do we have?

A hive plot

The first option is a **hive plot**. This is a chart type developed by Martin Krzywinski (`http://egweb.bcgsc.ca/`). These charts are a little different, and reading them can take some time to get used to, but they pack in more meaningful information than force-directed layout or other similar chart types do.

In hive plots, the nodes are positioned along a number of radial axes, often three. Their positions on the axis and which axis they fall on are often meaningful, although the meanings may change between different charts in different domains.

For this, we'll have vertices with a higher degree (with more edges attached to them) be positioned farther out from the center. Vertices closer in will have fewer edges and fewer neighbors. Again, the color of the lines represent the distance of that node from the central node. In this case, we won't make the selection of the axis meaningful.

To create this plot, we'll open a new file, `src-cljs/network-six/hive.cljs`. At the top, we'll use this namespace declaration:

```
(ns network-six.hive)
```

The axis on which a node falls on is an example of a D3 *scale*; its color from the force layout plot is another scale. Scales are functions that also have properties attached and are accessible via getter or setter functions. However, primarily, when they are passed a data object and a key function, they know how to assign that data object a position on the scale.

In this case, the `make-angle` function will be used to assign nodes to an axis:

```
(defn make-angle []
  (.. js/d3
    -scale
    ordinal
    (domain (.range js/d3 4))
    (rangePoints (array 0 (* 2.0 pi))))))
```

We'll position the nodes along each axis with the `get-radius` function. This is another scale that takes a vertex and positions it in a range between `40` and `400` according to the number of edges that are connected to it:

```
(defn get-radius [nodes]
  (.. js/d3
    -scale
    linear
    (range (array 40 400))
    (domain (array (.min js/d3 nodes #(.-count %))
                   (.max js/d3 nodes #(.-count %))))))))
```

We use these scales, along with a scale for color, to position and style the nodes:

```
(defn make-circles [svg nodes color angle radius]
  (.. svg
    (selectAll ".node")
    (data nodes)
    (enter)
    (append "circle")
    (attr "stroke" #(color (.-data %)))
    (attr "transform"
          #(str "rotate(" (degrees (angle (mod (.-n %) 3))) \)))
    (attr "cx" #(radius (.-count %)))
    (attr "r" 5)
    (attr "class" #(get-classes %))))
```

I've highlighted the scales that we use in the preceding code snippet. The circle's `stroke` property comes from the color, which represents the distance of the vertex from the origin for this graph.

The `angle` is used to assign the circle to an axis using the circle's `transform` attribute. This is done more or less at random, based on the vertex's index in the data collection.

Finally, the `radius` scale positions the circle along the axis. This sets the circle's position on the *x* axis, which is then rotated using the `transform` attribute and the `angle` scale.

Again, everything is brought together in the `main` function. This sets up the scales, requests the data, and then creates and positions the nodes and edges:

```
(defn ^:export main [json-file]
  (let [width 750, height 750
        angle (make-angle), color (make-color)
        svg (make-svg width height)]
    (.json js/d3 json-file
        (fn [err data]
          (let [nodes (.-nodes data)
                radius (get-radius nodes)]
          (make-axes svg angle radius)
          (let [df (get-degreed nodes data)]
            (make-arcs svg nodes df color angle radius)
            (make-circles svg nodes color angle radius)))))))
```

Let's see what this graph looks like:

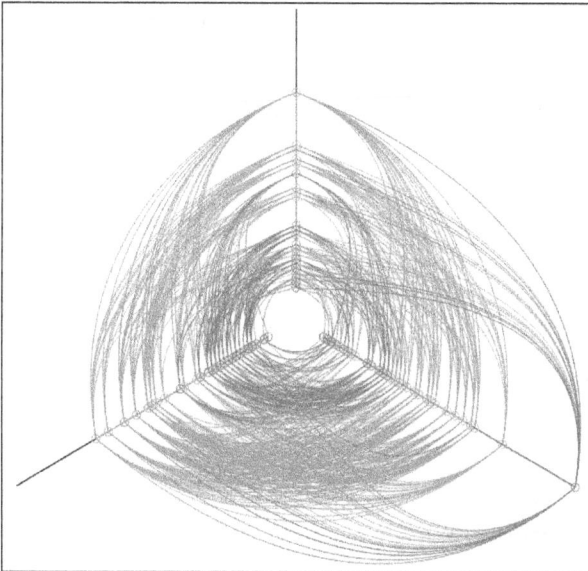

Again, the color represents the distance of the node from the central node. The distance from the center on each axis is the degree of the node.

It's clear from the predominance of the purple-pink color and the bands that the majority of the vertices are six hops from the origin vertex. From the vertices' position on the axes, we can also see that most nodes have a moderate number of edges attached to them. One has quite a few, but most are much closer to the center.

This graph is denser. Although the force-layout graph may have been problematic, it seemed more intuitive and easier to understand, whether it was meaningful or not. Hive plots are more meaningful, but they also take a bit more work to learn to read and to decipher.

A pie chart

Our needs today are simpler than the complex graph we just created; however, we're primarily interested in how much of the network is covered within six hops from a vertex. Neither of the two graphs that we've looked at so far conveyed that well, although they have presented other information and they're commonly used with graphs. We want to know proportions, and the go-to chart for proportions is the pie chart. Maybe it's a little boring, and it's does not strictly speak of a graph visualization per se, but it's clear, and we know what we're dealing with in it.

Generating a pie chart will look very similar to creating a force-directed layout graph or a hive plot. We'll go through the same steps, overall, even though some of the details will be different.

One of the first differences is the function to create an arc. This is similar to a scale, but its output is used to create the d (path description) attribute of the pie chart's wedges:

```
(defn make-arc [radius]
  (.. js/d3 -svg arc
    (outerRadius (- radius 10))
    (innerRadius 0)))
```

The pie layout controls the overall process and design of the chart. In this case, we say that we want no sorting, and we need to use the amount property of the data objects:

```
(defn make-pie []
  (.. js/d3 -layout pie
    (sort nil)
    (value #(.-amount %))))
```

The other difference in this chart is that we'll need to preprocess the data before it's ready to be fed to the pie layout. Instead of a list of nodes and links, we'll need to give it categories and counts. To make this easier, we'll create a record type for these frequencies:

```
(defrecord Freq [degree amount])
```

Also, we'll need a function that takes the same data as the other charts, counts it by distance from the origin vertex, and creates `Freq` instances to contain that data:

```
(defn get-freqs [data]
  (->> data
    .-nodes
    (map #(.-data %))
    frequencies
    (map #(Freq. (first %) (second %)))
    into-array))
```

Again, we pull all these together in the `main` function, and we do things in the usual way. First, we set up the graph, then we retrieve the data, and finally, we put the two together to create the graph.

In this case, this should give us an idea of how much of the graph this vertex can easily touch. The graph for vertex `49` is shown as follows. We can see that it really doesn't touch much of the network at all. 3799 vertices, more than 95 percent of the network, aren't within six hops of vertex `49`.

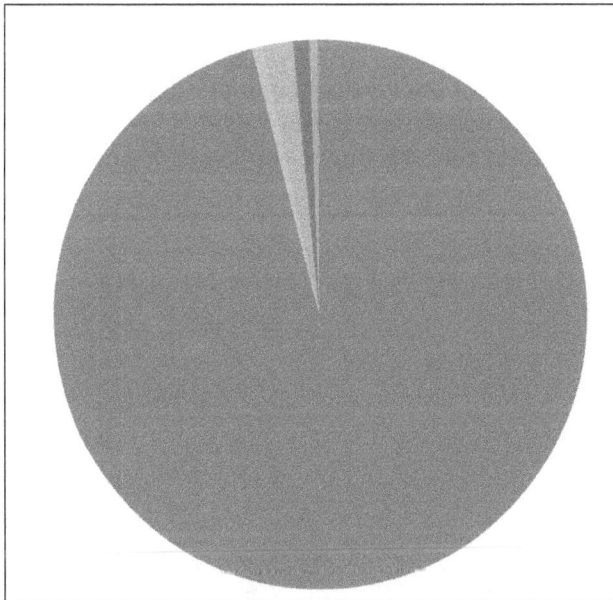

However, if we compare this with the pie chart for vertex 1085, which was the vertex with the highest betweenness factor, we see a very different picture. For that vertex, more than 95 percent of the network is reachable within 6 hops.

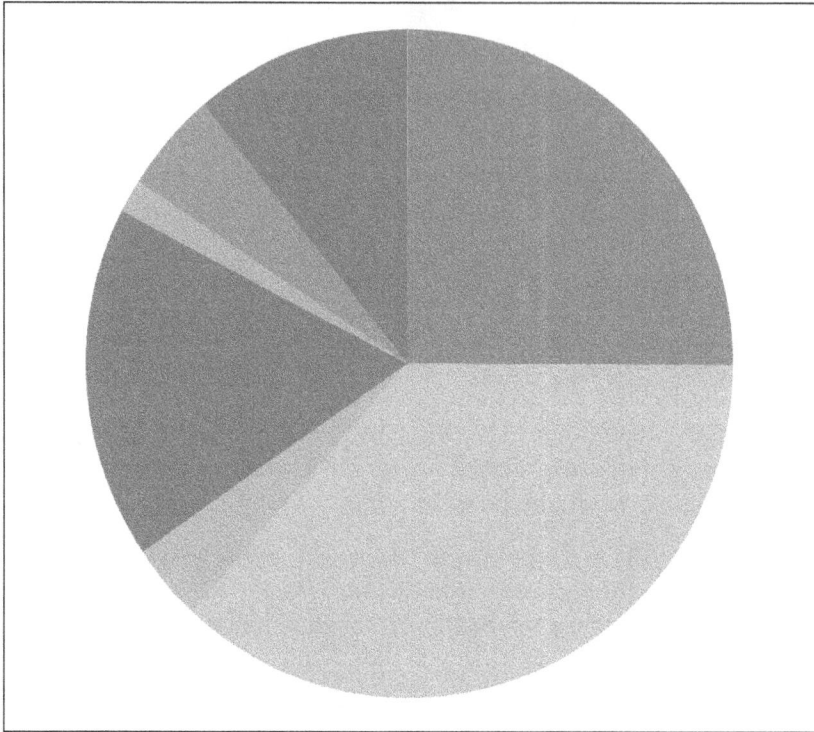

It's also interesting that most of the vertices are four edges away from the origin. For smaller networks, most vertices are further away. However, in this case, it's almost as if it had started running out of vertices in the network.

Summary

So, we discovered that this dataset does conform to a loose definition of the small world or a six-degree hypothesis. The average distance between any two nodes is about six. Also, as we're working with a sample, it's possible that working with a complete graph may fill in some links and bring the nodes closer together.

We also had an interesting time looking at some visualizations. One of the important lessons that we learned was that more complicated isn't always better. Simple, perhaps even a little boring, graphs can sometimes answer the questions we have in a better manner.

However, we've barely scratched the surface of what we can do with social graphs. We've primarily been looking at the network as a very basic, featureless graph, looking at the existence of people and their relationships without digging into the details. However, there are several directions we could go in to make our analysis more social. For one, we could look at the different types of relationships. Facebook and other social platforms allow you to specify spouses, for example, it might be interesting to look at an overlap between spouses' networks. Facebook also tracks interests and affiliations using their well-known **Like** feature. We could also look at how well people with similar interests find each other and form cliques.

In the end, we've managed to learn a lot about networks and how they work. Many real-world social networks share very similar characteristics, and there's a lot to be learned from sociology as well. These structures have always defined us but never more so than now. Being able to effectively analyze social networks, and the insights we can get from them, can be a useful and effective part of our toolkit.

In the next chapter, we'll look at using geographical analysis and applying that to weather data.

2
GIS Analysis – Mapping Climate Change

One area of data analysis that's gotten a lot of attention is **Geographic Information Systems (GIS)**. GIS is a system that is designed to store, manage, manipulate, and analyze geographic data. As such, GIS sits at the intersection of cartography, computers, statistics, and information science.

GIS is applied to fields as diverse as military planning, epidemiology, architecture, urban planning, archaeology, and many other fields. Basically, any domain or problem that involves location or topology can use GIS techniques or methods.

As you can imagine from this very brief description, we won't even scratch the surface of GIS in this chapter. However, we'll apply it to a small problem to see how it can help us understand the way climate change affects the continental **United States** in a better manner.

Understanding GIS

While the preceding description is accurate, it doesn't really help us much. As befits a field concerned with the lay of the land, GIS really begins in the field. Data is gathered using aerial and satellite photography, and it is also gathered from people on the ground using GPS, laser range finders, and surveying tools. GIS can also make use of existing maps, especially for historical research and to compare time periods. For example, this may involve studying how a city has evolved over time or national boundaries have changed. A lot of time and energy in GIS goes into gathering this data and entering it into the computer.

Once the data is in the computer, GIS can perform a wide range and variety of analyses on the data, depending on the questions being asked and the task at hand. For example, the following are some of the many things you can do with GIS:

- **View-shed analysis**: This attempts to answer the question, "What can someone standing right here at this elevation (and perhaps at a second story window) see?". This takes into account the elevation and slope of the terrain around the viewer.

- **Topological modeling**: This combines the GIS data with other data in the data mining and modeling to add a geospatial component to more mainstream data mining and modeling. This allows the models to account for the geographical proximity.

- **Hydrological modeling**: This models the way in which water interacts with the environment through rainfall, watershed, runoff, and catchment.

- **Geocoding**: This involves associating human-readable addresses with their geospatial coordinates. When you click on a **Google Map** or **Bing Map** and get the business or address of a location, it's because it's been geocoded for the coordinates you tapped on.

The primary tool for most GIS specialists is **ArcGIS** by **ESRI** (http://www.esri.com/). This is a powerful, full-featured GIS workbench. It interoperates with most data sources and performs most of the analyses. It also has an **API** for **Python** and APIs in **Java** and **.NET** to interact with ArcGIS servers. We'll use ArcGIS at the end of this chapter to generate the visualization.

However, there are other options as well. Most databases have some GIS capabilities, and **Quantum GIS** (http://www.qgis.org/) is an open source alternative to ArcGIS. It isn't as polished or as fully featured, but it's still powerful in its own right and is freely available. **GeoServer** (http://geoserver.org/) is an enterprise-level server and management system for the GIS data. There are also libraries in a number of programming languages; **Geospatial Data Abstraction Layer**, also known as **GDAL**, (http://www.gdal.org/) deserves special mention here, both in its own right and because it serves as the foundation for libraries in a number of other programming languages. One of the libraries for Java is **GeoTools** (http://www.geotools.org/), and part of it calls GDAL under the table.

Mapping the climate change

So, let's roll up our sleeves and perform some geospatially informed data analysis.

For our problem, we'll look at how the climate change affects the continental United States over the last century or so. Specifically, we'll look at how the average maximum temperature for July has changed. For North America, this should give us a good snapshot of the hottest temperatures.

One nice thing about working with the weather data is that there's a lot of it, and it's easily available. **US National Oceanic and Atmospheric Administration (NOAA)** collects it and maintains archives of it.

For this project, we'll use the **Global Summary of the Day** (http://www.ncdc.noaa. gov/cgi-bin/res40.pl). This includes daily summaries from each active weather station. We'll filter out any weather stations that aren't in the US, and we'll filter out any data that is not in use for the month of July.

Climate is typically defined on thirty-year periods. For example, the climate for a location would be the average temperature of thirty years, not the temperature for the year. However, there won't be that many thirty-year periods for the time span that we're covering, so instead, we'll look at the maximum temperature for July from each weather station in ten-year rolling averages.

To find out how much the maximum temperature has changed, we'll find the rolling average for these ten-year periods. Then, for each station, we'll find the difference between the first ten year period's average and the last one's.

Unfortunately, the stations aren't evenly or closely spaced; as we'll see, they also open and close over the years. So we'll do the best we can with this data, and we'll fill in the geospatial gaps in the data.

Finally, we'll graph this data over a map of the US. This will make it easy to see how temperatures have changed in different places. What will this process look like? Let's outline the steps for the rest of this chapter:

1. Download the data from NOAA's FTP servers. Extract it from the files.

2. Filter out the data that we won't need for this analysis. We'll only hang onto places and the month that we're interested in (the US for July).

3. Average the maximum temperatures for each month.

4. Calculate the ten-year rolling averages of the averages from step three.

5. Get the difference between the first and last ten-year averages for each weather station.

6. Interpolate the temperature differences for the areas between the stations.

7. Create a heat map of the differences.

8. Review the results.

Downloading and extracting the data

As mentioned above, NOAA maintains an archive of GSOD. For each weather station around the world, these daily summaries track a wide variety of weather data for all active weather stations around the globe. We'll use the data from here as the basis of our analysis.

The data is available at `ftp://ftp.ncdc.noaa.gov/pub/data/gsod/`. Let's look at how this data is stored and structured:

● ○ ○	Index of /pub/data/gsod/ ✕	
← → C	ftp://ftp.ncdc.noaa.gov/pub/data/gsod/	☆ » ≡
2001/		4/19/13 11:15:00 PM
2002/		4/19/13 10:08:00 PM
2003/		4/19/13 8:58:00 PM
2004/		4/19/13 7:33:00 PM
2005/		4/19/13 6:02:00 PM
2006/		4/19/13 12:12:00 PM
2007/		4/19/13 10:34:00 AM
2008/		4/18/13 1:24:00 PM
2009/		4/17/13 11:30:00 AM
2010/		4/16/13 5:05:00 PM
2011/		6/19/13 12:56:00 AM
2012/		3/13/13 5:57:00 AM
2013/		7/12/13 3:10:00 PM
GSOD-IMPROVEMENTS.TXT	808 B	7/11/13 2:24:00 PM
GSOD_DESC.txt	14.6 kB	10/25/11 12:00:00 AM
country-list.txt	26.2 kB	8/24/06 12:00:00 AM
ish-history.csv	3.0 MB	7/8/13 1:33:00 PM
ish-history.txt	3.1 MB	7/8/13 1:33:00 PM
readme.txt	14.4 kB	9/8/10 12:00:00 AM

So, the main directory on the FTP site (`/pub/data/gsod/`) has a directory for each year that has the weather data. There's also a file called `ish-history.csv`. This contains information about the weather stations, when they were operational, and where they were located. (Also, the text files and `README` files are always important for more specific, detailed information about what's in each file.)

Now let's check out one of the data directories; this is for 2013.

The data directories contain a large number of data files. Each of the files that ends in `.op.gz` has three components for its file name. The first two parts are identifiers for the weather station and the third is the year.

Each data directory also has a tarball that contains all of the `*.op.gz` data files. That file will be the easiest to download, and then we can extract the `*.op.gz` files from it. Afterwards, we'll need to decompress these files to get the `*.op` data files. Let's do that, and then we can look at the data that we have.

Downloading the files

Before we actually get into any of the code to do this, let's take a look at the dependencies that we'll need.

Before we get started, let's set up our project. For this chapter, our Leiningen 2 (http://leiningen.org/) project.clj file should look something like the following code:

```
(defproject clj-gis "0.1.0-SNAPSHOT"
  :dependencies [[org.clojure/clojure "1.5.1"]
                 [me.raynes/fs "1.4.4"]
                 [com.velisco/clj-ftp "0.3.0"]
                 [org.clojure/data.csv "0.1.2"]
                 [clj-time "0.5.1"]
                 [incanter/incanter-charts "1.5.1"]]
  :jvm-opts ["-Xmx4096m"])
```

Now for this section of code, let's open the src/clj_gis/download.clj file. We'll use this namespace declaration for this code as follows:

```
(ns clj-gis.download
  (:require [clojure.java.io :as io]
            [me.raynes.fs.compression :as compression]
            [me.raynes.fs :as fs]
            [miner.ftp :as ftp]
            [clj-gis.locations :as loc]
            [clj-gis.util :as u])
  (:import [org.apache.commons.net.ftp FTP]
           [java.util.zip GZIPInputStream]
           [java.io BufferedInputStream]))
```

Now, the next two functions together download the GSOD data files. The main function is download-data. It walks the directory tree on the FTP server, and whenever it identifies a file to be downloaded, it hands it off to download-file. This function figures out where to put the file and downloads it to that location. I've left out the source code for some of the utilities and secondary functions listed here, such as download-src, so that we can focus on the larger issues. You can find these functions in the file in this chapter's code download. The following code snippet is part of the code that is available for download:

```
(defn download-file
  "Download a single file from FTP into a download directory."
  [client download-dir dirname]
  (let [src (download-src dirname)
        dest (download-dest download-dir dirname)]
```

```
          (ftp/client-get client src dest)))

(defn download-data
    "Connect to an FTP server and download the GSOD data files."
    [uri download-dir data-dir]
    (let [download-dir (io/file download-dir)
          data-dir (io/file data-dir)]
      (ensure-dir download-dir)
      (ensure-dir data-dir)
      (ftp/with-ftp [client uri]
        (.setFileType client FTP/BINARY_FILE_TYPE)
        (doseq [dirname
                  (filter get-year
                          (ftp/client-directory-names client))]
          (download-file client download-dir dirname)))))
```

Extracting the files

Now, we've downloaded the files from the NOAA FTP server onto the local
hard drive. However, we still need to use the `tar` utility to extract the files we've
downloaded and then decompress them.

We'll use the **FS** library to extract the downloaded files. Currently, the individual
data files are in a common Unix file format called `tar`, which collects multiple files
into one larger file. These files are also compressed using the utility **gzip**. We'll use
Java's `GZIPOutputStream` to decompress `gz`. Let's see how this works:

```
(defn untar
    "Untar the file into the destination directory."
    [input-file dest-dir]
    (compression/untar input-file dest-dir))

(defn gunzip
    "Gunzip the input file and delete the original."
    [input-file]
    (let [input-file (fs/file input-file)
          parts (fs/split input-file)
          dest (fs/file (reduce fs/file (butlast parts))
                        (first (fs/split-ext (last parts))))]
      (with-open [f-in (BufferedInputStream.
                          (GZIPInputStream.
                            (io/input-stream input-file)))]
        (with-open [f-out (io/output-stream dest)]
          (io/copy f-in f-out)))))
```

We can put these functions together with the download functions that we just looked at. This function, download-all, will download all the data and then decompress all of the data files into a directory specified by clj-gis.locations/*data-dir*:

```
(defn download-all []
  (let [tar-dir (fs/file loc/*download-dir*)
        data-dir (fs/file loc/*data-dir*)]
    (download-data tar-dir data-dir)
    (doseq [tar-file (fs/list-dir tar-dir)]
      (untar (fs/file tar-dir tar-file) data-dir))
    (doseq [gz-file (fs/list-dir data-dir)]
      (gunzip (fs/file data-dir gz-file)))))
```

Now, what do these files look like? The header line of one of them is as follows:

```
STN--- WBAN    YEARMODA    TEMP       DEWP       SLP        STP
   VISIB     WDSP    MXSPD    GUST    MAX     MIN    PRCP   SNDP
   FRSHTT
```

The following is one of the data rows:

```
007032 99999  20130126     80.1 12     65.5 12  9999.9  0  9999.9  0
   999.9  0    2.5 12    6.0  999.9     91.4*   71.6*  0.00I
   999.9  000000
```

So, there are some identification fields, some for temperature, dew point, wind, and other weather data. Next, let's see how to winnow the data down to just the information that we plan to use.

Transforming the data – filtering

As we just noticed, there's a lot of data in the GSOD files that we don't plan to use. This includes the following:

- Too many files with data for places that we aren't interested in
- Too many rows with data for months that we aren't interested in
- Too many columns with weather data that we aren't interested in (dew points, for instance)

At this point, we'll only worry about the first problem. Just filtering out the places we're not looking at will dramatically reduce the amount of data that we're dealing with from approximately 20 GB of data to just 3 GB.

The code for this section will be in the `src/clj_gis/filter_data.clj` file. Give it the following namespace declaration:

```
(ns clj-gis.filter-data
  (:require
    [clojure.string :as str]
    [clojure.data.csv :as csv]
    [clojure.java.io :as io]
    [me.raynes.fs :as fs]
    [clj-gis.locations :as loc]
    [clj-gis.util :refer (ensure-dir)]))
```

Now it's time for the code that is to be put in the rest of the file.

To filter out the data that we won't use, we'll copy files for stations in the United States into their own directory. We can create a set of these stations from the `ish-history.csv` file that we noticed earlier, so our first task will be parsing that file. This code will read the CSV file and put the data from each line into a new data record, `IshHistory`. Having its own data type for this information isn't necessary, but it makes the rest of the code much more readable. For example, we can reference the country field using `(:country h)` instead of `(nth h 3)` later. This type can also reflect the column order from the input file, which makes reading the data easier:

```
(defrecord IshHistory
  [usaf wban station_name country fips state call
   lat lon elevation begin end])
(defn read-history
  "Read the station history file."
  [filename]
  (with-open [f (io/reader filename)]
    (doall
      (->> (csv/read-csv f)
        (drop 1)
        (map #(apply ->IshHistory %))))))
```

The stations are identified by the combination of the USAF and WBAN fields. Some stations use USAF, some use WBAN, and some use both. So we'll need to track both to uniquely identify the stations. This function will create a set of the stations in a given country:

```
(defn get-station-set
  "Create a set of all stations in a country."
  [country histories]
  (set (map #(vector (:usaf %) (:wban %))
         (filter #(= (:country %) country)
           histories))))
```

Finally, we need to tie these functions together. This function, `filter-data-files`, reads the history and creates the set of stations that we want to keep. Then, it walks through the data directory and parses the file names to get the station identifiers for each file. Files from the stations in the set are then copied to a directory with the same name as the country code, as follows:

```
(defn filter-data-files
  "Read the history file and copy data files matching the
  country code into a new directory."
  [ish-history-file data-dir country-code]
  (let [history (read-history ish-history-file)
        stations (get-station-set country-code history)]
    (ensure-dir (fs/file country-code))
    (doseq [filename (fs/glob (str data-dir "*.op"))]
      (let [base (fs/base-name filename)
            station (vec (take 2 (str/split base #"-")))]
        (when (contains? stations station)
          (fs/copy filename (fs/file country-code base)))))))
```

This set of functions will filter out most of the data and leave us with only the observations from the stations we're interested in.

Rolling averages

We aren't plotting the raw data. Instead, we want to filter it further and summarize it. This transformation can be described in the following steps:

1. Process only the observations for the month of July.

2. Find the mean temperature for the observations for the month of July for each year, so we'll have an average for July 2013, July 2012, July 2011, and so on.

3. Group these monthly averages into rolling ten-year windows. For example, one window will have the observations for 1950 to 1960, another window will have observations for 1951 to 1961, and so on.

4. Find the mean temperature for each of these windows for a climatic average temperature for July for that period.

5. Calculate the change in the maximum temperature by subtracting the climatic average for the last window for a station from the average of its first window.

This breaks down the rest of the transformation process pretty well. We can use this to help us structure and write the functions that we'll need to implement the process. However, before we can get into that, we need to read the data.

Reading the data

We'll read the data from the space-delimited data files and store the rows in a new record type. For this section, let's create the `src/clj_gis/rolling_avg.clj` file. It will begin with the following namespace declaration:

```clojure
(ns clj-gis.rolling-avg
  (:require
    [clojure.java.io :as io]
    [clojure.string :as str]
    [clojure.core.reducers :as r]
    [clj-time.core :as clj-time]
    [clj-time.format :refer (formatter parse)]
    [clojure.data.csv :as csv]
    [me.raynes.fs :as fs]
    [clj-gis.filter-data :as fd]
    [clj-gis.locations :as loc]
    [clj-gis.types :refer :all]
    [clj-gis.util :as u]))
```

Now, we can define a data type for the weather data. We'll read the data into an instance of `WeatherRow`, and then we'll need to normalize the data to make sure that the values are ones that we can use. This will involve converting strings to numbers and dates, for instance:

```clojure
(defrecord WeatherRow
  [station wban date temp temp-count dewp dewp-count slp
   slp-count stp stp-count visibility vis-count wdsp
   wdsp-count max-wind-spd max-gust max-temp min-temp
   precipitation snow-depth rfshtt])
(defn read-weather
  [filename]
  (with-open [f (io/reader filename)]
    (doall
      (->> (line-seq f)
        (r/drop 1)
        (r/map #(str/split % #"\s+"))
        (r/map #(apply ->WeatherRow %))
        (r/map normalize)
        (r/remove nil?)
        (into [])))))
```

Now that we have the weather data, we can work it through the pipeline as outlined in the preceding code snippet. This series of functions will construct a sequence of reducers.

Reducers, introduced in Clojure 1.5, are a relatively new addition to the language. They refine traditional functional-style programming. Instead of map taking a function and a sequence and constructing a new sequence, the reducers' version of map takes a function and a sequence or folder (the core reducer data type) and constructs a new folder that will apply the function to the elements of the input when required. So, instead of constructing a series of sequences, it composes the functions into a larger function that performs the same processing, but only produces the final output. This saves on allocating the memory, and if the input data types are structured correctly, the processing can also be automatically parallelized as follows:

1. For the first step, we want to return only the rows that fall in the month we're interested in. This looks almost exactly like a regular call to filter, but instead of returning a new, lazy sequence, it returns a folder that has the same effect; it produces a sequence with only the data rows we want. Or, we can compose this with other folders to further modify the output. This is what we will do in the next few steps:

    ```
    (defn only-month
      "1. Process only the observations for the month of July."
      [month coll]
      (r/filter #(= (clj-time/month (:date %)) month) coll))
    ```

2. This function takes the reducer from the first step and passes it through a few more steps. The group-by function finally reifies the sequence into a hash map. However, it's immediately fed into another reducer chain that averages the accumulated temperatures for each month:

    ```
    (defn mean [coll]
      (/ (sum coll) (double (count coll))))
    (defn get-monthly-avgs
      "2. Average the observations for each year's July, so
      we'll have an average for July 2013, one for July 2012,
      one for July 2011, and so on."
      [weather-rows]
      (->> weather-rows
        (group-by #(clj-time/year (:date %)))
        (r/map (fn [[year group]]
              [year (mean (map :max-temp group))]))))
    ```

3. For step three, we create a series of moving windows across the monthly averages. If there aren't enough averages to create a full window, or if there are only enough to create one window, then we throw those extra observations out:

```
(defn get-windows
  "3. Group these monthly averages into a rolling ten-year
  window. For example, one window will have the
  observations for 1950-1960. Another window will have
  observations for 1951-1961. And so on."
  [period month-avgs]
  (->>
    month-avgs
    (into [])
    (sort-by first)
    (partition period 1)
    (r/filter #(> (count %) 1))
    (r/map #(vector (ffirst %) (map second %))))))
```

4. This step uses a utility function, mean, to get the average temperature for each window. We saw this defined in step two. This keeps hold of the starting year for that window so they can be properly ordered:

```
(defn average-window
  "4. Average each of these windows for a climatic average
  temperature for July for that period."
  [windows]
  (r/map (fn [[start-year ws]] [start-year (mean ws)])
         windows))
```

5. After this, we do a little more filtering to only pass the averages through, and then we replace the list of averages with the difference between the initial and the final averages:

```
(defn avg-diff
  "5. Calculate the change in maximum temperature by
  subtracting the climatic average for the last window for
  a station from the average of its first window."
  [avgs]
  (- (last avgs) (first avgs)))
```

There's more to this, of course. We have to get a list of the files to be processed, and we need to do something with the output; either send it to a vector or to a file.

Now that we've made it this far, we're done transforming our data, and we're ready to start our analysis.

Interpolating sample points and generating heat maps using inverse distance weighting (IDW)

In the end, we're going to feed the data we've just created to ArcGIS in order to create the heat map, but before we do that, let's try to understand what will happen under the covers.

For this code, let's open up the `src/clj_gis/idw.clj` file. The namespace for this should be like the following code:

```
(ns clj-gis.idw
  (:require [clojure.core.reducers :as r]
            [clj-gis.types :refer :all]))
```

To generate a **heat map**, we first start with a sample of points for the space we're looking at. Often, this space is geographical, but it doesn't have to be. Values for a complex, computationally-expensive, two-dimensional function are another example where a heat map would be useful. It would take too long to completely cover the input domain, and inverse distance weighting could be used to fill in the gaps.

The sample data points each have a value, often labeled z to imply a third dimension. We want a way to interpolate the z value from the sample points onto the spaces between them. The heat map visualization is just the result of assigning colors to ranges of z and plotting these values.

One common technique to interpolate the value of z to points between the sample points is called **inverse distance weighting (IDW)**. To find the interpolated value of z for a point x, y, IDW sees how much the value of each sample point influences that location, given each sample's distance away and a value p that determines how far each sample point's influence carries. Low values of p don't project much beyond their immediate vicinity. High values of p can be projected too far. We'll see some examples of this in a minute.

There are a variety of ways to calculate the IDW. One general form is to sum the weighted difference between the data point in question and all others, and divide it by the non-weighted sum.

$$u(x) = \frac{\sum\limits_{i=1}^{N} w_i(x) u_i}{\sum\limits_{i=1}^{N} w_i(x)} \qquad\qquad w_i(x) = \frac{1}{d(x, x_i)^P}$$

There are several variations of IDW, but here, we'll just describe the base version, as outlined by Donald Shepard in 1968. First, we have to determine the inverse distance function. It's given here as w. Also, x_i is the sample point, and x is the point to estimate the interpolation for, just as given in the preceding formula:

```
(defn w
  "Finds the weighted inverse distance between the points x and
  x_i. "
  ([p dist-fn x] (partial w p dist-fn x))
  ([p dist-fn x x_i]
   (/ 1.0 (Math/pow (dist-fn x x_i) p))))
```

With this in place, IDW is the sum of w for each point in the sample, multiplied by that sample point's value and divided by the sum of w for all the samples. It's probably easier to parse the code than it is to describe it verbosely:

```
(defn sum-over [f coll] (reduce + (map f coll)))
(defn idw
  ([sample-points data-key p dist-fn]
   (partial idw sample-points data-key p dist-fn))
  ([sample-points data-key p dist-fn point]
   (float
     (/ (sum-over #(* (w p dist-fn point %) (data-key %))
                  sample-points)
        (sum-over (w p dist-fn point) sample-points))))
  ([sample-points data-key p dist-fn lat lon]
   (idw sample-points data-key p dist-fn
        (->DataPoint lat lon nil))))
```

The highlighted part of the function is the part to pay attention to. The rest makes it easier to call idw in different contexts. I precompute the denominator in the let form, as it won't change for each sample point that is considered. Then, the distances of each sample point and the target point are multiplied by the value of each sample point and divided by the denominator, and this is summed together.

This function is easy to call with the charting library that **Incanter** provides, which has a very nice heat map function. Incanter is a library used to perform data analysis and visualization in Clojure by interfacing with high-performance Java libraries. This function first gets the bounding box around the data and pads it a little. It then uses Incanter's heat-map function to generate the heat map. To make it more useful, however, we then make the heat map transparent and plot the points from the sample onto the chart. This is found in src/clj_gis/heatmap.clj:

```
(defn generate-hm
  [sample p border]
```

```
(let [{:keys [min-lat max-lat min-lon max-lon]}
      (min-max-lat-lon sample)]
  (->
    (c/heat-map (idw sample :value p euclidean-dist)
                (- min-lon border) (+ max-lon border)
                (- min-lat border) (+ max-lat border))
    (c/set-alpha 0.5)
    (c/add-points (map :lon sample) (map :lat sample)))))
```

Let's take a random data sample and use it to see what different values of p do.

For the first experiment, let's look at *p=1*:

```
(i/view (hm/generate-hm sample 1.0 5.0))
```

The graph it produces looks like the following figure:

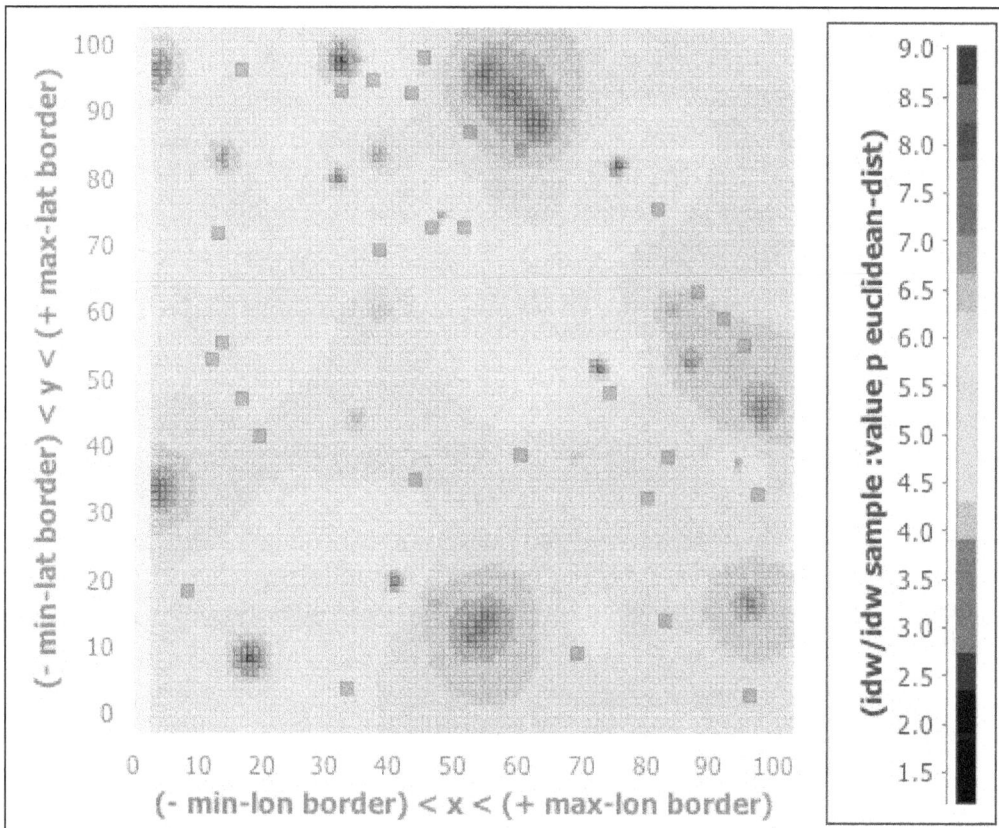

We can see that the influence for each sample point is tightly bound to its immediate neighborhood. More moderate values, around 4 and 5, dominate.

For *p=8*, the picture is a bit different, as shown in the following screenshot:

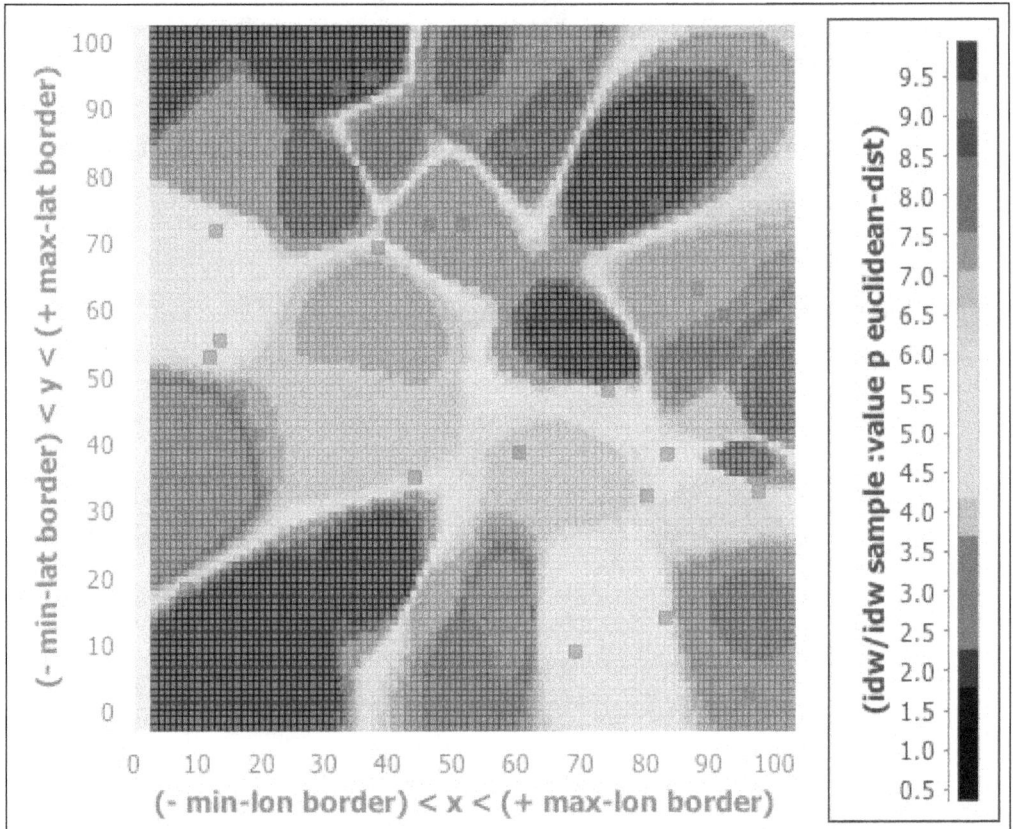

In the preceding figure, each interpolated point is more heavily influenced by the data points closest to it, and further points are less influential. More extreme regions have great influence over larger distances, except around sample points with moderate values.

Finally, we'll look at an interpolated point that's more balanced. The following is the chart for when *p=3*:

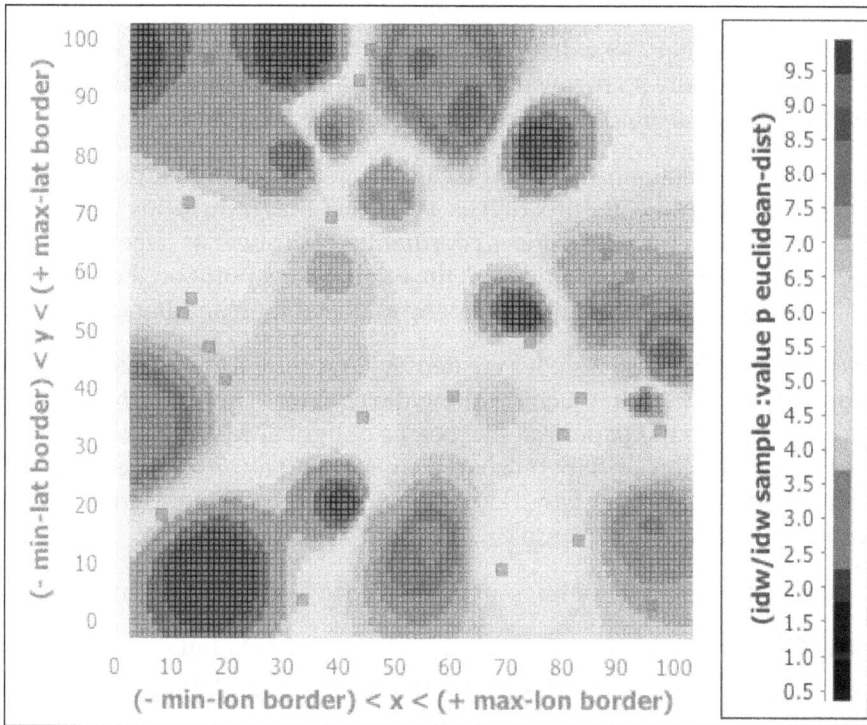

This seems much more balanced. Each sample point clearly exerts its influence across its own neighborhood. However, no point, and no range of values, appears to dominate. A more meaningful graph with real data would probably look quite good.

So far, we've been playing with the toy data. Before we can apply this to the climate data that we prepared earlier, there are several things we need to take into consideration.

Working with map projections

Have you looked at a world wall map and noticed how big Greenland is? It's huge. It's larger than China, the United States, and Australia, and is about as big as Africa. Too bad it's so cold, or we could fit a lot of people up there. Or could we?

Actually, Australia is about three and a half times as big as Greenland, China is almost four and a half times as big, and Africa is almost fourteen times as large!

What's going on? The **Mercator projection** is what's going on. It was developed by the Flemish cartographer Gerardus Mercator in 1569. Over time, it's become very popular, at least partially so because it fits nicely onto a rectangular page without wasting a lot of space around the edges, the way some projections do.

A map projection is a transformation of locations on a sphere or ellipsoid onto locations on a plane. You can think of it as a function that transforms latitudes and longitudes of the earth into the x and y coordinates on a sheet of paper. This allows us to take a point on a map and find it on the earth, take a point on the earth and find it on the map, or take a point on one map and find it on another.

Mercator is a common projection. It's created by wrapping a cylindrical sheet of paper around the globe, only touching along the equator. Then, the shapes on the globe are cast out onto the paper roll like beams of light spreading out. This was developed for navigation, and if you chart a course with a constant bearing, it plots on a Mercator map as a straight line. However, its major problem is that it distorts shapes around the edges, for example, Greenland or Antarctica.

There are a number of other common projections, such as the following:

- The **Gall-Peters** projection accurately shows the area but distorts the shape.

- The **Eckert IV** projection distorts the outer shape of the map onto an ovoid to minimize the area distortions of the Mercator projection, although it still distorts the shapes of things near the poles.

- The **Goode homolosine** projection attempts to accurately portray both the area and shape by cutting the *skin* off the globe into some awkward shapes. It's sometimes called the *orange peel map* because the outlines of the map look like you peeled an orange by hand and flattened it on the table top.

So how does this apply to our project?

On the one hand, we need some way to accurately measure the distances between points in the real world. For example, as we're working in the northern hemisphere, the points near the top of the map, to the north, will be closer together than the points near the bottom. We need to know the projection in order to measure these distances correctly and correctly calculate the interpolations.

To put it another way, the distance between two points that are a degree of longitude apart would be different, depending on their latitude. In Grand Forks, North Dakota, the distance between longitude -97 and -96 is approximately 46 miles (74.5 km). On the other hand, the distance between longitudes -97 and -96, just west of Houston, Texas, is almost 60 miles (96.52 km). Think of the way in which two lines that are parallel on the equator have to curve towards each other as they converge at the poles.

On the other hand, we also need to then be able to know which pixel a set of latitude and longitude correspond to. In order to actually plot the heat map on the screen, we have to be able to determine which pixel gets which color, depending on the interpolated points on the map.

Finding a base map

Related to the projections, we also need to have a base layer to display the heat map on top of it. Without being able to see the context of the underlying geography, a heat map is more confusing than it is illuminating.

There are maps available that have their locations encoded in their metadata. **GeoTIFF** is one such format. GIS packages can layer the data and information on top of these base maps to provide more complex, interesting, and useful visualizations and analyses.

Working with ArcGIS

Working with projections and base maps can be fiddly and prone to errors. While there are Java libraries that can help us with this, let's use the major software package in this domain, **ArcGIS**, for the purposes of this demonstration. While it's awesome to be able to program solutions in a powerful, flexible language like Clojure, sometimes, it's nicer to get pretty pictures quickly.

We're going to start this by getting the base layer. ESRI maintains a set of topological maps, and this map of the United States is perfect for this:

1. Navigate to `http://www.arcgis.com/home/item.html?id=99cd5fbd98934 028802b4f797c4b1732` to view ESRI's page on the **US Topo Maps**.

2. Click on the **Open** dropdown.

3. Select the option that allows you to get **ArcGIS Desktop** to open the layer.

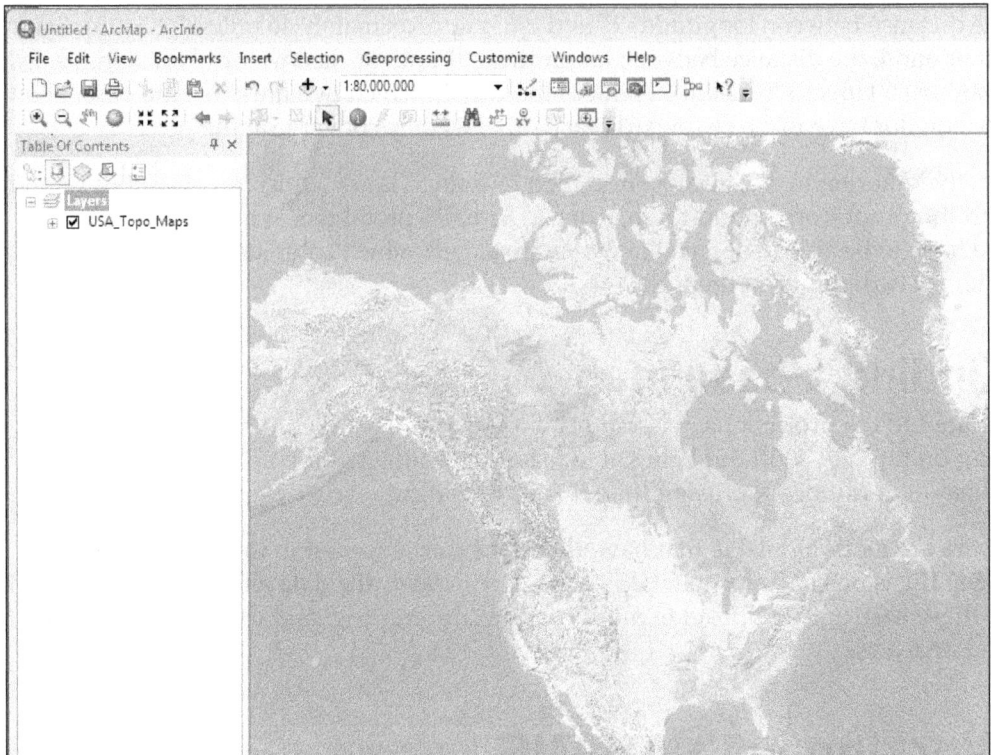

Now we'll add our data. This was created using the functions that we defined earlier as well as a few more that are available in this chapter's code download:

1. The data is available at `http://www.ericrochester.com/clj-data-master/temp-diffs.csv`. Point your web browser there and download the file. Don't forget where you put it!

2. In ArcGIS, navigate to **File | Add Data | Add XY Data**.

3. Select the `temp-diffs.csv` file, and specify `z` for the **z** field.

4. We'll also need to change the projection of the input data. To do this, click on **Edit...** to edit the projection.

5. In the new dialog box, **Select** a predefined coordinate system. Navigate to **Coordinate Systems | Geographic Coordinate Systems | North America | NAD 1983**.

6. When the file is ready to load, the dialog should look like what is shown in the following screenshot:

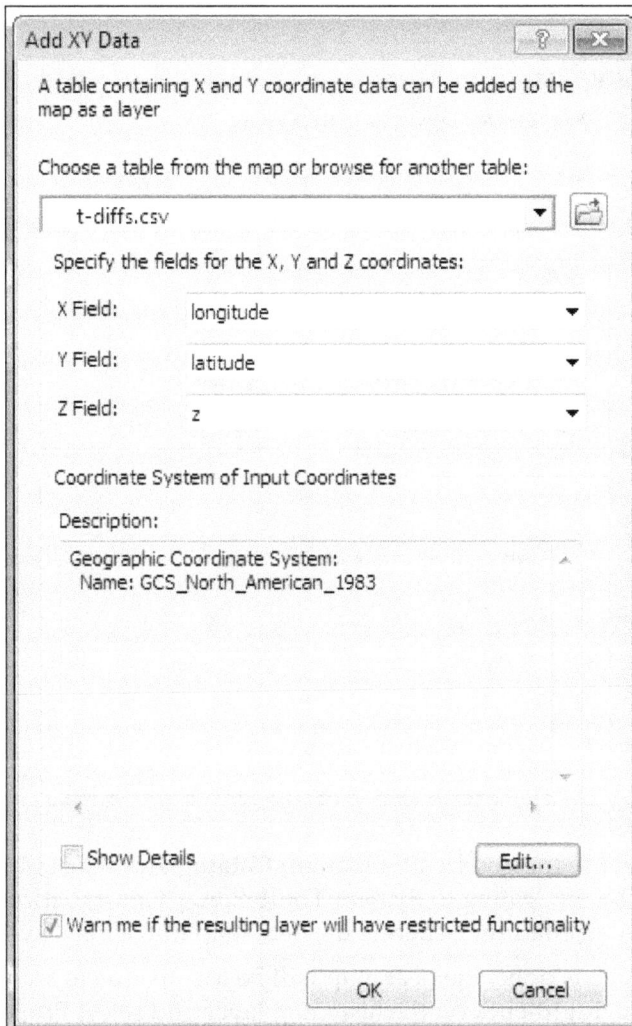

```
Add XY Data                                              [?] [X]

A table containing X and Y coordinate data can be added to the
map as a layer

Choose a table from the map or browse for another table:

  t-diffs.csv                                   [▼]  [📁]

  Specify the fields for the X, Y and Z coordinates:

  X Field:      longitude                          ▼

  Y Field:      latitude                           ▼

  Z Field:      z                                  ▼


Coordinate System of Input Coordinates

Description:

  Geographic Coordinate System:
    Name: GCS_North_American_1983








   ◄                                    ►

   [ ] Show Details                        [ Edit... ]

 [✓] Warn me if the resulting layer will have restricted functionality

                        [ OK ]          [ Cancel ]
```

7. Once the data is in place, we need to set the color scheme for the **z** field. Right-click on the new layer and select **Properties**. Select the **Symbology** tab and get the graduated colors the way you like them.

8. After I was done playing, the dialog box looked like what is shown in the following screenshot:

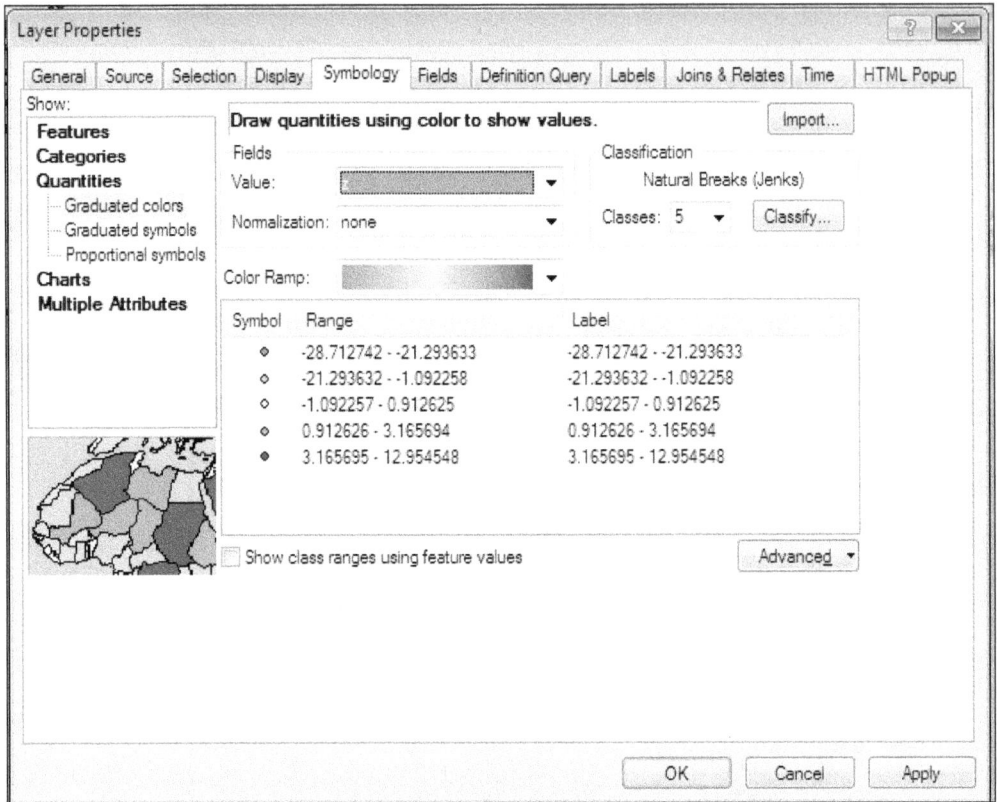

9. Now we get to the good part. Open up **Catalog** and select **IDW tool**. It is done by navigating to **System Toolboxes | Geostatistical Analyst Tools | Interpolation**. Generate the heat map into a new layer.

10. Once ArcGIS is done, the heat map will be too opaque to see the underlying geography. Right-click on the heat map layer and select **Properties**. In the **Display** tab, change the opacity to something reasonable. I used 0.40.

The final results are shown as follows:

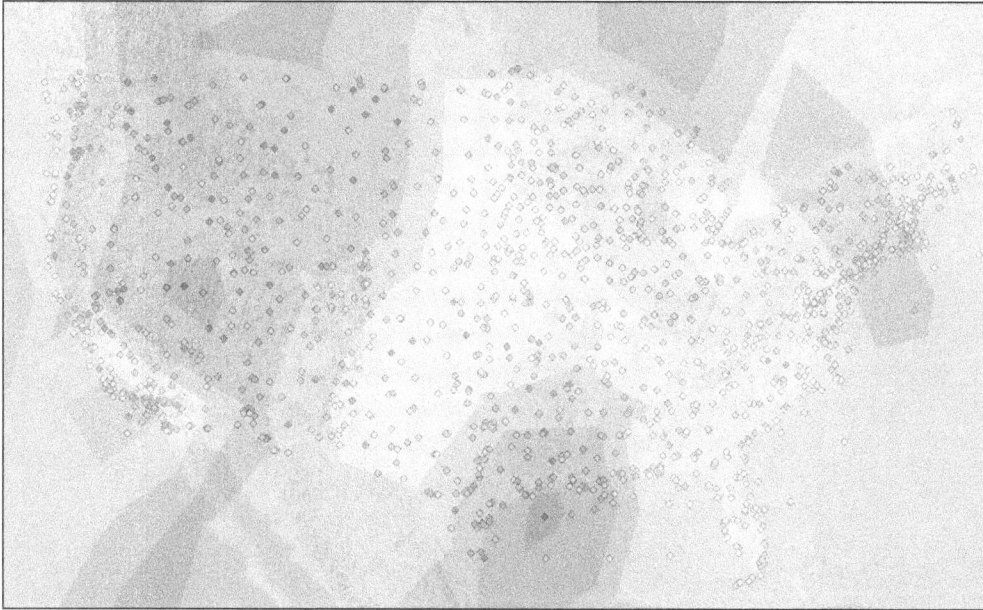

We can see that for a large part of the nation, things have heated up. The west part of the great lakes have cooled a bit, but the Rocky Mountains have especially gotten warmer.

Summary

This has been a fun little experiment. Looking at the data, however, suggests caution. Some of the stations have been in operation long enough to have only a few of the sliding windows defined. Others have been operational for much longer. This makes it difficult to compare the aggregated numbers from the different different stations, which is what we're doing by creating the heat map.

Nevertheless, this does point to some interesting areas of future enquiry, and it provides a brief glimpse of what geographical information systems can provide and how to use them. They can add a geospatially informed edge to the modeling and analysis, which isn't possible with the data, tools, and techniques they bring to the table.

In this next chapter, we'll turn our attention to sifting through free-form textual data using topic modeling.

3
Topic Modeling – Changing Concerns in the State of the Union Addresses

A huge source of data right now is the volumes of unstructured, natural-language data that's everywhere on the Internet. Think of all the news articles, blog posts, Twitter posts, and YouTube comments as well as the thousands of other ways that people can create and share textual content online. What they're saying may be important to you, and being able to track what subjects they are talking about is incredibly useful to become aware of the trends and conversations.

A tool to explore the information a group of text documents discusses is called **topic modeling**. This is a technique to identify the "topics" discussed in a collection of documents, although as we'll see, "topics" is defined a little differently here than it is in informal conversation. The strength of these models is that they don't assume that each document talks only about one thing. Instead, they model documents as collections of topics. This is incredibly powerful in that it allows more complex conceptions of what a document is as well as more complex patterns between documents.

In this chapter, we will cover the following topics:

- Understanding data in State of the Union addresses
- Understanding topic modeling
- Preparing for visualizations
- Setting up the project
- Getting the data
- Visualizing data with D3 and ClojureScript
- Exploring the topics

Understanding data in the State of Union addresses

In this chapter, we'll apply topic modeling to the (**SOTU**) **State of the Union** addresses presented by the presidents of the United States of America. Each January or February, the President addresses the US Senate and the House of Representatives either in person or in writing, and talks about how the country is doing as well as outlining his agenda for the coming year. The speeches can be fairly short, but the written reports can be much longer. George Washington's first State of the Union address from 1790 had less than 500 words. Barack Obama's latest SOTU (at the time of this writing in 2013) had over 3,000 words. Jimmy Carter had the longest SOTU address, which he delivered in writing in 1981. It is almost 14,000 words long.

The gradual increase in the length of the SOTU address, which climaxed around 1910, was because starting from Thomas Jefferson's 1801 address up until William H. Taft's 1912 address, the SOTU address was a written report delivered before Congress. The following graph represents the increase in the word counts of SOTU addresses:

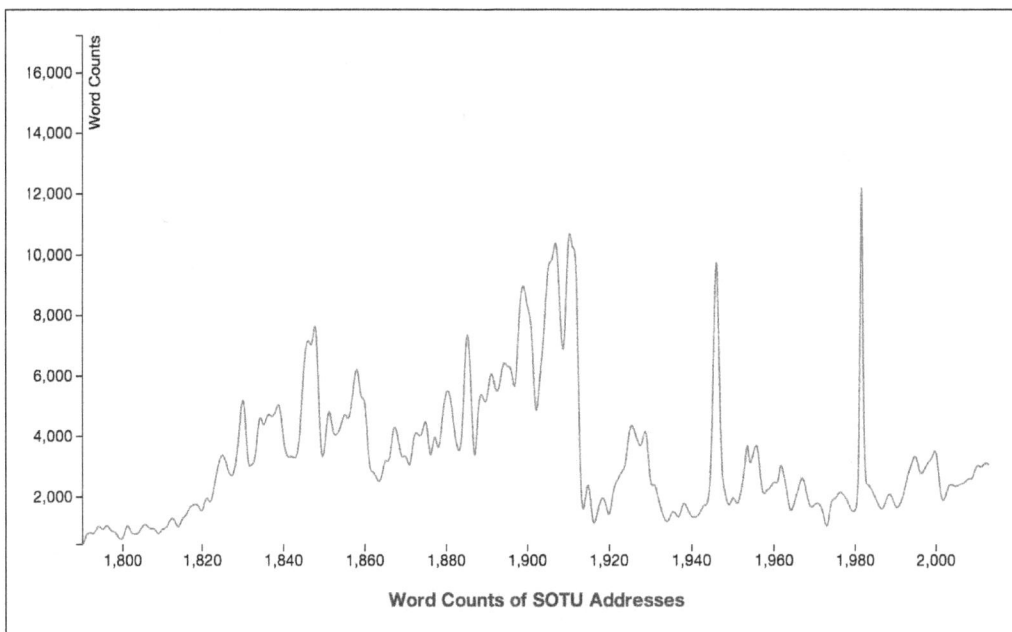

Word Counts of SOTU Addresses

Of course, as the situation has changed both domestically and internationally, so have the topics that the President discusses in the SOTU addresses. You wouldn't expect John Adams' 1800 address to talk about the same things as Bill Clinton's 2000 address. This immediately raises the question: what topics have the Presidents talked about in their SOTU addresses and how have those topics changed over time?

This isn't a new question, even for topic modeling. Xuerui Wang and Andrew McCallum covered it as one of several examples in their 2006 paper, *Topics over time: A non-Markov continuous-time model of topical trends (2006)* (http://citeseer. ist.psu.edu/viewdoc/summary?doi=10.1.1.152.2460). In this paper, they present a way of analyzing a series of time-stamped documents in order to get an improved understanding of how the topics interact over time. In fact, this is an area of considerable further research, and there are a number of other extensions to topic modeling that take time into account.

In this chapter, we're only going to cover the most widely used topic modeling algorithm today: **LDA** (**Latent Dirichlet Allocation**). With an understanding of this procedure and the underlying thought behind it, you can understand Wang's and McCallum's Topics over Time algorithm without too much difficulty.

Understanding topic modeling

A topic model is a statistical model of the topics in a document. The assumption is that if 10 percent of a document talks about the military and 40 percent of it talks about the economy (and 50 percent talks about other things), then there should be roughly four times as many words about economics as about the military.

An early form of topic modeling was described by Christos Papadimitriou and others in their 1998 paper, *Latent Semantic Indexing: A probabilistic analysis* (http://www. cs.berkeley.edu/~christos/ir.ps). This was refined by Thomas Hofmann in 1999 with *Probabilistic Latent Semantic Indexing* (http://www.cs.brown.edu/~th/papers/ Hofmann-SIGIR99.pdf).

In 2003, David Blei, Andrew Ng, and Michael I. Jordan published their paper, *Latent Dirichlet Allocation* (http://jmlr.csail.mit.edu/papers/v3/blei03a. html). Currently, this is the most common type of topic modeling. It's simple, easy to get started, and widely available. Most work in the field since then has been developing extensions to the original LDA topic modeling method. This is the procedure that we'll learn about and use in this chapter.

In LDA, each document is modeled as a bag of words, each word drawn from a number of topics. So each word in the document is the result of one of those topics. The model takes the following steps to create each document:

1. Select a distribution for the topic in the document.

2. Select a distribution for the words from the topic.

3. Select a topic and then a word from that topic from those distributions for each word in the document.

The distributions for the topics and words use a Dirichlet distribution for their prior probability, which is the assumed uncertainty about the distribution of topics and words before considering any evidence or documents. However, as they are trained on a set of input documents, these distributions more accurately reflect the data they've seen so far, and so they are able to more accurately categorize future documents.

A short example may be helpful. Initially the distributions are picked randomly. Afterwards, we'll train on one document. Say we have a document with the following words: budget, spending, army, navy, plane, soldier, and dollars. The model knows from previous training that the words *budget, spending,* and *dollars* all relate to a topic on finance, while army, navy, plane, and soldier relate to a topic on the military, and plane relates to one on travel. This may suggest that the document is 35 percent about finance, 50 percent about the military, and 10 percent about travel. Military would be the dominant topic, but other topics would be represented as well.

If the LDA is in its training phase, then the presence of those words would slightly strengthen the association between all of the words listed, between those words and the other words in the document, and between those words and the topics that represent the relationship between them.

One twist to this is that the topics aren't named. In the previous example, I said that there were topics about finance, the military, and travel. However, LDA would see those as topics 1, 2, and 3. The labels are interpretations I would give based on the terms in those topics and the documents that scored high in them. One of the tasks when using LDA is investigating and interpreting the topics. We'll see several examples of this at the end of the chapter when we explore the results of our analysis.

Preparing for visualizations

One of the basic tools of data analysis is visualization. Good, flexible visualizations make it easier to explore and understand the data, and this is useful at all stages of the data analysis process. At the beginning, visualizations make it easier to find errors and inconsistencies and to get to know your data and developing an intuition for it. It continues to drive insights throughout the process. In the end, visualizations make great supporting evidence and explanations in reports and presentations.

Visualizations will be an important part of this chapter and in understanding the results of topic modeling. To create and interact with the graphs, we're going to use some software that's recently become an important part of many data scientists' toolkits: the Web browser.

As we did in *Chapter 1, Network Analysis – The Six Degrees of Kevin Bacon*, we'll use D3 (`http://d3js.org/`) and ClojureScript (`https://github.com/clojure/clojurescript/`).

The graph of the word counts earlier in this chapter as well as the ones that will come later are examples of this system. They're part of a static website. That is, the resources that load in the browser are read from the filesystem, not generated dynamically by a server-side web application. The data is read from **CSV** (**comma-separated values**) files that we'll create from the topic model data. Finally, the ClojureScript is compiled into a JavaScript file that's loaded by the browser.

We'll see later how to set up this site with ClojureScript as well as how to create the graphs. As usual, for the full code, refer to the source code download from the Packt Publishing website.

Setting up the project

Before we dive in further, however, we'll need to set up our project for this chapter. So with all of that in mind, let's tackle the solution. The first thing we'll need is the following Leiningen 2 `project.clj` file:

```
(defproject tm-sotu "0.1.0-SNAPSHOT"
  :license {:name "Eclipse Public License"
            :url "http://www.eclipse.org/legal/epl-v10.html"}
  :plugins [[lein-cljsbuild "0.3.2"]]
```

```
:dependencies [[org.clojure/clojure "1.5.1"]
               [enlive "1.1.1"]
               [org.clojure/data.csv "0.1.2"]
               [cc.mallet/mallet "2.0.7"]]
:cljsbuild {:builds [{:source-paths ["src-cljs"],
                      :compiler {:pretty-printer true,
                                 :output-to "www/js/main.js",
                                 :optimizations :whitespace}}]})
```

We use a couple of dependencies for this: Enlive to download the text of the SOTU addresses and MALLET for topic modeling. We'll talk more about both of these in the forthcoming sections.

Getting the data

To get a copy of the SOTU addresses, we'll visit the website for the American Presidency Project at the University of California, Santa Barbara (http://www. presidency.ucsb.edu/). This site has the text for the SOTU addresses as well as an archive of many messages, letters, public papers, and other documents for various presidents. It's a great resource for looking at political rhetoric.

In this case, we'll write some code to visit the index page for the SOTU addresses. From there, we'll visit each of the pages that contain an address; remove the menus, headers, and footers; and strip out the HTML. We'll save this in a file in the data directory.

We won't see all of the code for this. To see the rest, look at the download.clj file in the src/tm_sotu/ directory in the downloaded code.

To handle downloading and parsing the files, we'll use the Enlive library (https:// github.com/cgrand/enlive/wiki). This library provides a DSL to navigate and pull data from HTML pages. The syntax and concepts are similar to CSS selectors, so if you're familiar with those, using Enlive will seem very natural.

We'll tackle this problem piece by piece. First, we need to set up the namespace and imports for this module with the following code:

```
(ns tm-sotu.download
  (:require [net.cgrand.enlive-html :as enlive]
            [clojure.java.io :as io])
  (:import [java.net URL]
           [java.io File]))
```

Now, we can define a function that downloads the index page for the SOTU addresses as shown in the following code (`http://www.presidency.ucsb.edu/sou.php`). It will take this URL as a parameter, download the resource, pull out the list of links, and remove any text that isn't a year:

```
(defn get-index-links [index-url]
  (->
    index-url
    enlive/html-resource
    (enlive/select [:.doclist :a])
    filter-year-content?))
```

Let's walk through these lines step by step:

1. First, `index-url` is just the URL of the index page that needs to be downloaded. This line just kicks off the processing pipeline.

2. The `enlive/html-resource` function downloads and parses the web page. Most processing that uses Enlive will start with this function.

3. Now, `(enlive/select [:.doclist :a])` only pulls out certain anchor tags. The vector that specifies the tags to return is similar to a CSS selector. In this case, it would be equivalent to the `.doclist :a` selector. I found which classes and tags to look for by examining the source code for the HTML file and experimenting with it for a few minutes.

4. Finally, I called `filter-year-content?` on the sequence of tags. This looks at the text within the anchor tag and throws out any text that is not a four-digit year.

The `get-index-links` function returns a sequence of anchor tags that need to be downloaded. Between the tag's `href` attribute and its content, we have the URL for the address and the year it was delivered, and we'll use both of them.

The next step of the process is the `process-speech-page` function. It takes an output directory and a tag, and it downloads the page the tag points to, gets the text of the address, strips out the HTML tags from it, and saves the plain text to a file, as shown in the following code:

```
(defn process-speech-page [outputdir a-tag]
  (->> a-tag
    :attrs
    :href
    URL.
    enlive/html-resource
```

```
       get-text-tags
       extract-text
       (save-text-seq
         (unique-filename
           (str outputdir \/ (first (:content a-tag)))))))))
```

This strings together a number of functions. We'll walk through these a little more quickly, and then dive into one of the functions this calls in more detail.

First, the sequence of keywords :attrs and :href gets the URL from the anchor tag. We pass this to enlive/html-resource to download and parse the web page. Finally, we identify the text (get-text-tags), strip out the HTML (extract-text), and save it (save-text-seq). Most of these operations are fairly straightforward, but let's dig into extract-text.

This procedure is actually the sole method from a protocol of types that we can pull text from, stripping out HTML tags in the process. The following code gives the definition of this protocol. It's also defined over all the data structures that Enlive uses to return data: Strings for text blocks, hash maps for tags, lazy sequences for lists of content, and nil to handle all the possible input values, as shown in the following code:

```
(defprotocol Textful
  (extract-text [x]
    "This pulls the text from an element.
    Returns a seq of String."))

(extend-protocol Textful
  java.lang.String
  (extract-text [x] (list x))

  clojure.lang.PersistentStructMap
  (extract-text [x]
      (concat
        (extract-text (:content x))
        (when (contains? #{:span :p} (:tag x))
          ["\n\n"])))

  clojure.lang.LazySeq
  (extract-text [x] (mapcat extract-text x))

  nil
  (extract-text [x] nil))
```

The preceding code allows us to find the parent elements for each address, pass those elements to this protocol, and get the HTML tags stripped out. Of all of these methods, the most interesting implementation is hash map's, which is highlighted in the preceding code.

First, it recursively calls the `extract-text` method to process the tag's content. Then, if the tag is p or span, the method adds a couple of new lines to format the tag as a paragraph. Having a span tag trigger a new paragraph is a bit odd, but the introduction to the address is in a span tag. Like any screen-scraping task, this is very specialized to the SOTU. Getting data from other sites will require a different set of rules and functions to get the data back out.

I've tied this process together in a function that first downloads the index page and then processes the address links one by one as shown in the following code:

```
(defn download-corpus [datadir index-url]
  (doseq [link (get-index-links (URL. index-url))]
    (println (first (:content link)))
    (process-speech-page datadir link)))
```

After this function executes, there will be a data/ directory that contains one text file for each SOTU address. Now we just need to see how to run LDA topic modeling on them.

Loading the data into MALLET

To actually perform topic modeling, we'll use the MALLET Java library (http://mallet.cs.umass.edu/). **MALLET (MAchine Learning for LanguagE Toolkit)** contains a number of algorithms for various statistical and machine learning algorithms for natural-language processing, including document classification, sequence tagging, and numerical optimization. However, it's commonly also used for topic modeling, and its support for that is very robust and flexible. We'll interact with it using Clojure's Java `interop` functions.

Each document is stored in a MALLET `cc.mallet.types.Instance` class. So to begin with, we'll need to create a processing pipeline that reads the files from disk and processes them and loads them into MALLET.

The next group of code will go into the `src/tm_sotu/topic_model.clj` file. The following code is the namespace declaration with the list of dependencies for this module. Be patient; the following list isn't short:

```
(ns tm-sotu.topic-model
  (:require [clojure.java.io :as io]
            [clojure.data.csv :as csv]
```

```
                [clojure.string :as str])
    (:import [cc.mallet.util.*]
             [cc.mallet.types InstanceList]
             [cc.mallet.pipe
              Input2CharSequence TokenSequenceLowercase
              CharSequence2TokenSequence SerialPipes
              TokenSequenceRemoveStopwords
              TokenSequence2FeatureSequence]
             [cc.mallet.pipe.iterator FileListIterator]
             [cc.mallet.topics ParallelTopicModel]
             [java.io FileFilter]
             [java.util Formatter Locale]))
```

Now we can write a function that creates the processing pipeline and the list of instances based on it, as shown in the following code:

```
(defn make-pipe-list []
  (InstanceList.
    (SerialPipes.
      [(Input2CharSequence. "UTF-8")
       (CharSequence2TokenSequence.
         #"\p{L}[\p{L}\p{P}]+\p{L}")
       (TokenSequenceLowercase.)
       (TokenSequenceRemoveStopwords. false false)
       (TokenSequence2FeatureSequence.)]))))
```

This function creates a pipeline of classes that process the input. Each stage in the process makes a small, select modification to its input, and then it passes the data down the pipeline.

The first step takes the input file's name and reads it as a sequence of characters. It tokenizes the character sequence using the regular expression given, which matches the sequence of letters with embedded punctuation.

Next, it normalizes the case of the tokens and removes stop words. Stop words are very common words. Most of these function grammatically in the sentence, but do not really add to the semantics (that is, to the content) of the sentence. Examples of stop words in English are *the*, *of*, *and*, and *are*.

Finally, it converts the token sequence to a sequence of features. A feature is a word, a token, or some metadata from a document that you want to include in the training. For example, the presence or absence of the word *president* might be a feature in this corpus. Features are often assembled into vectors; one vector for each document. The position of each feature in the vectors must be consistent. For example, the feature *president* must always be found at the seventh position in all documents' feature vectors.

Feature sequences are sequences of numbers along with mappings from words to indices, so the rest of the algorithm will deal with numbers instead of words.

For instance, the first SOTU address by George Washington (1790) begins with, "I embrace with great satisfaction the opportunity which now presents itself." The following are some of the steps that the processing pipeline would take for this input:

1. `CharSequence2TokenSequence`: After tokenization, it would be a sequence of individual strings such as *I, embrace, with, great,* and *satisfaction.*

2. `TokenSequenceLowercase`: Normalizing the case would convert the first word to *i.*

3. `TokenSequenceRemoveStopwords`: Removing stop words would leave just content words: *embrace, great, satisfaction, opportunity, now, presents,* and *itself.*

4. `TokenSequence2FeatureSequence`: This changes input into a sequence of numbers. Internally, it also maintains a mapping between the indexes and the words, so 0 would be associated with *embrace*. The next time it finds a word that it has encountered before, it will reuse the feature index, so from here on, *now* will always be replaced by 4.

We can also visually represent this process as shown in the following chart:

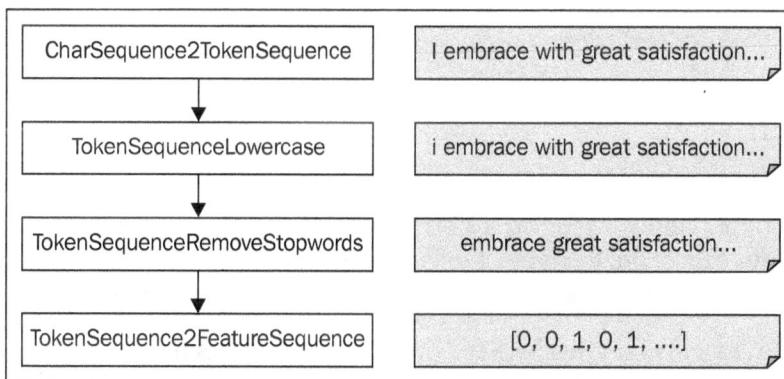

We still haven't specified which files to process or connected them to the processing pipeline. We do that using the instance list's `addThruPipe` method. To make this step easier, we'll define a function that takes a list of files and plugs them into the pipeline as shown in the following code:

```
(defn add-directory-files
  "Adds the files from a directory to the instance list."
  [instance-list data-dir]
  (.addThruPipe
```

```
instance-list
(FileListIterator.
  (.listFiles (io/file data-dir))
  (reify FileFilter
    (accept [this pathname] true))
  #"/([^/]*).txt$"
  true)))
```

The `FileListIterator` function wraps the array of files. It can also filter the array, which is more than we need. The regular expression, `#"/([^/]*).txt$"`, is used to separate the filename from the directory. This will be used to identify the instance for the rest of the processing.

That's it. Now we're ready to write a function to train the model. This process has a number of options, including how many threads to use, how many iterations to perform, how many topics to find, and a couple of hyper parameters to the algorithm itself: the a sum and β. The a parameter is the sum over the topics and β is the parameter for one dimension of the Dirichlet prior distributions that are behind topic modeling. In the following code, I've hardcoded them to `1.0` and `0.01`, and I've provided defaults for the number of topics (`100`), threads (`4`), and iterations (`50`):

```
(defn train-model
  ([instances] (train-model 100 4 50 instances))
  ([num-topics num-threads num-iterations instances]
  (doto (ParallelTopicModel. num-topics 1.0 0.01)
    (.addInstances instances)
    (.setNumThreads num-threads)
    (.setNumIterations num-iterations)
    (.estimate))))
```

Finding the right number of topics is a bit of an art. The value is an interaction between the size of your collection, the type of documents it contains, and how finely grained you wish the topics to be. The number could range from the tens to the hundreds.

One way to get a grasp on this is to see how many instances have a given topic with the top weighting. In other words, if there are a lot of topics with only one or two documents strongly associated with them, then maybe those topics are too specific, and we can run the training again with fewer documents. If none do, or only a few do, then maybe we need to use fewer topics.

However, ultimately, the number of topics depends on how fine-grained and precise you want the topic categories to be, and that will depend upon exactly what questions you're attempting to answer. If you need to find topics that are only important for a year or two, then you'll want more topics; however, if you're looking for broader, more general trends and movements, then fewer topics will be more helpful.

For example, the following graph shows the weightings for each topic in each SOTU address when ten topics are used:

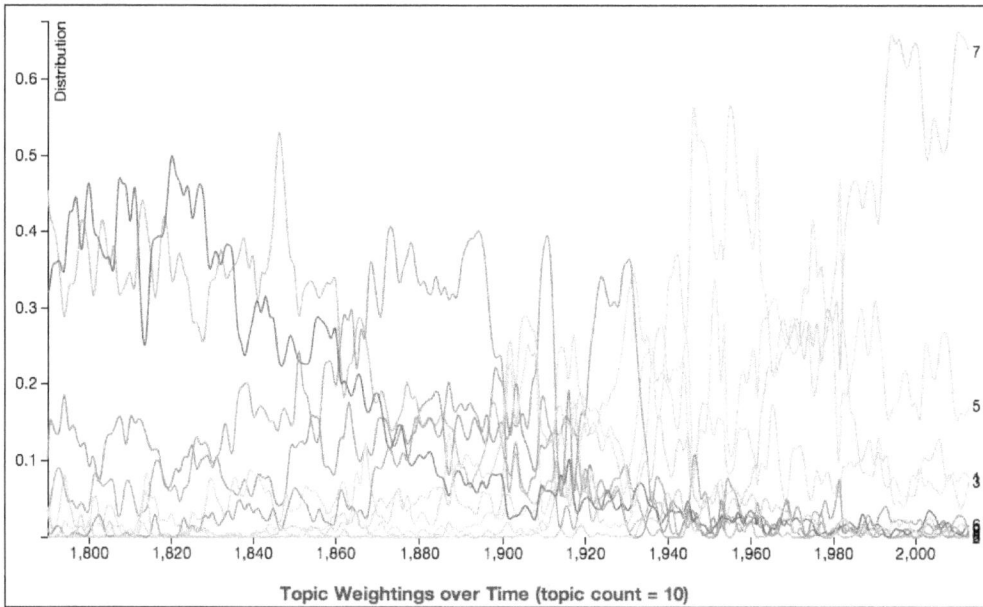

Topic Weightings over Time (topic count = 10)

We can see that the lines describe large arcs. Some lines begin strong and then taper off. Others have a hump in the middle and fall away to both sides. Others aren't mentioned much at the beginning but finish strong at the end of the graph.

One line that peaks around 1890 is a good example of one of these trends. Its top ten keywords are *year, government, states, congress, united, secretary, report, department, people,* and *fiscal*. Initially, it's difficult to say what this topic would be about. In fact, it is less about the addresses' subject matter per se, and more about the way that the Presidents went into the details of the topics, reporting amounts for taxation, mining, and agriculture. They tended to use a lot of phrases, such as "fiscal year". The following paragraph on sugar production from Grover Cleveland's 1894 address is typical:

> *The total bounty paid upon the production of sugar in the United States for the fiscal year was $12,100,208.89, being an increase of $2,725,078.01 over the payments made during the preceding year. The amount of bounty paid from July 1, 1894, to August 28, 1894, the time when further payments ceased by operation of law, was $966,185.84. The total expenses incurred in the payment of the bounty upon sugar during the fiscal year was $130,140.85.*

Exciting stuff.

This also illustrates how topics aren't always about the documents' subject matter, but also about rhetoric, ways of talking, and clusters of vocabulary that tend to be used together for a variety of reasons.

The topics represented in the following graph clearly describe large trends in the concerns that SOTU addresses dealt with. However, if we increase the number of topics to 200, the graph is very different, and not just because it has more lines on it:

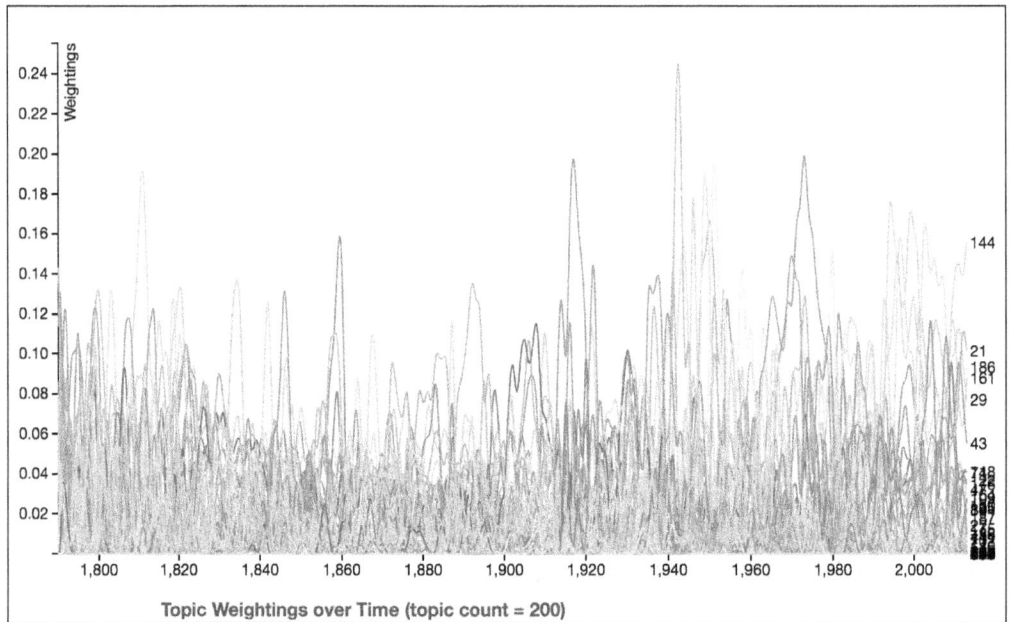

Topic Weightings over Time (topic count = 200)

Once you start looking at the topics in more detail, in general, the topics are only relevant for a smaller period of time, like for a twenty- or forty-year period, and most of the time, the documents' weightings for a given topic aren't as high. There are exceptions to this of course; however, most of the topics are more narrowly relevant and narrowly defined. For example, the third topic is largely focused on events related to the Civil War, especially those that occurred around 1862. The top ten keywords for that topic are *emancipation, insurgents, kentucky, laborers, adopted, north, hired, maryland, disloyal,* and *buy.* The following graph represents the topic of the Civil War:

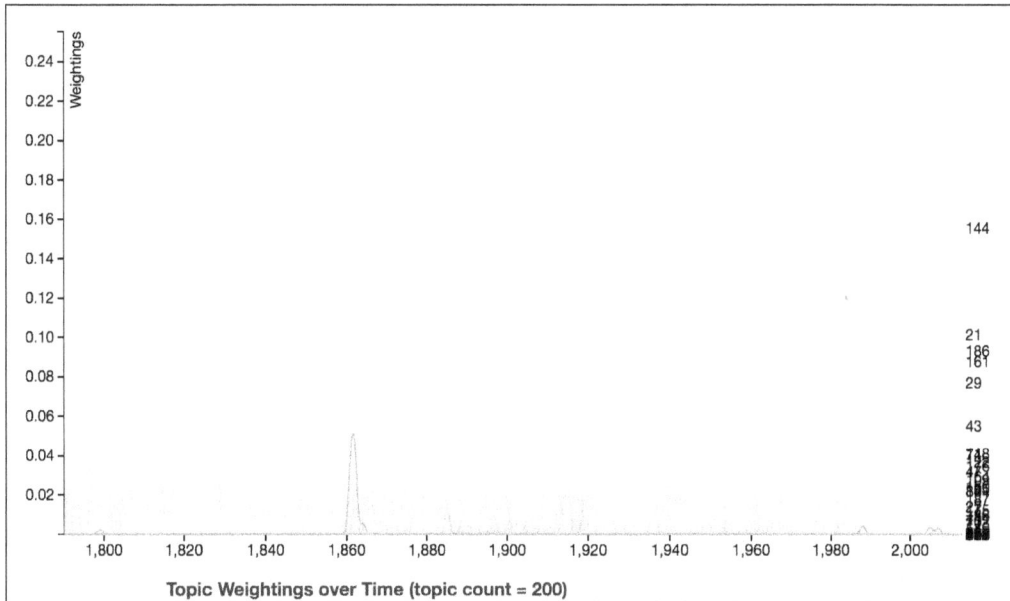

Topic Weightings over Time (topic count = 200)

The previous three graphs illustrate the role that the number of topics plays in our topic modeling. However, for the rest of this chapter, we're going to look at a run with 75 models. This graph provides a more balanced set of topics than either of the last two examples. In general, the subjects are neither too broad nor too narrow.

Visualizing with D3 and ClojureScript

Before we look at D3 or ClojureScript, we should take some time to examine how the visualizations are put together since they're such an integral part of our work. The graphs will be on a static web page, meaning that there will be no need to for any server-side component to help create them. All changes on the graph will be created through JavaScript.

The first component of this will be a standard web page that has a couple of pieces (the entire site is in the code download in the www/ directory). It needs a div tag for the JavaScript to hang the visualization on the static web page, as shown in the following code:

```
<div class="container"></div>
```

Then, it needs a few JavaScript libraries. We'll load jQuery (https://jquery.org/) from Google's **content distribution network (CDN)**. We'll load D3 (http://d3js.org/) from its website, as they suggest and then we'll load our own script. Then, we'll call an entrance function in it as shown in the following code:

```
<script src="//ajax.googleapis.com/ajax/libs/jquery/1.10.1/jquery.min.
js"></script>
<script src="http://d3js.org/d3.v3.min.js"
        charset="utf-8"></script>
<script src="js/main.js"></script>
<script type="application/javascript">
    tm_sotu.topic_plot.plot_topics();
</script>
```

The `js/main.js` file will be the output of the compiled ClojureScript. We've already set up the configuration for this in the `project.clj` file, but let's look at that again in the following code:

```
:cljsbuild {:builds [{:source-paths ["src-cljs"],
                      :compiler {:pretty-printer true,
                                 :output-to "www/js/main.js",
                                 :optimizations :whitespace}}]})
```

The preceding code specifies that ClojureScript will compile anything in the `src-cljs/` directory into the `www/js/main.js` file. We'll need to create the source directory and the directories for the namespace structure.

In ClojureScript, the files look almost exactly like regular Clojure scripts. There are slight wrinkles in importing and using macros from other libraries, but we won't need to do that today. There is also a `js` namespace always available. This is used to reference a name directly from JavaScript without requiring it to be declared.

Speaking of which, the following is the namespace declaration we'll use for the graph. You can find the `tm-sotu.utils` file along with the code that I haven't listed here in the source code for the chapter:

```
(ns tm-sotu.topic-plot
  (:require [tm-sotu.utils :as utils]
            [clojure.browser.dom :as dom]
            [clojure.string :as str]))
```

Another difference with regular JavaScript is that some functions must be exported using metadata on the function's name. This allows them to be called from regular JavaScript. The entrance function `plot-topics` is an example of this and is described in the following code:

```
(defn ^:export plot-topics []
  (let [{:keys [x y]} (utils/get-scales)
        {:keys [x-axis y-axis]} (utils/axes x y)
        color (.. js/d3 -scale category20)
        line (utils/get-line #(x (get-year %))
                             #(y (get-distribution %)))
        svg (utils/get-svg)]
    (.csv js/d3 "topic-dists.csv"
          (partial load-topic-weights
                   svg line color x x-axis y y-axis))))
```

Most of this function is concerned with calling some functions from the `tm-sotu.utils` namespace that set up boilerplate for the graphic. It's all standard D3, if you're familiar with that. The more interesting part — actually dealing with the data — we'll look at in more detail.

Before we move on, though, I'd like to pay a little more attention to the highlighted line in the previous code. This is an example of calling JavaScript directly and it illustrates a couple of things to be aware of, as follows:

- As we saw in *Chapter 1, Network Analysis – The Six Degrees of Kevin Bacon*, we can access JavaScript's global scope with the `js/` prefix, that is, `js/d3`.

- Also, we distinguish JavaScript parameters by prefixing the name with a hyphen: `(.-scale js/d3)`.

- Finally, we also see a call to a JavaScript function that takes no parameters. We've also used Clojure's standard `..` macro to make the series of calls easier to type and clearer to read: `(.. js/d3 -scale category20)`.

The last line in the preceding code is a call to another D3 function — `d3.csv` or `(.csv js/d3 …)` — as it is expressed in ClojureScript. This function makes an AJAX call back to the server for the data file `"topic-dists.csv"`. The result, along with several other pieces of data from this function, is passed to `load-topic-weights`. You may have caught that I said "back to the server." This system doesn't need any code running on the server, but it does require a web server running in order to handle the AJAX calls that load the data. If you have Python installed on your system, it comes packaged with a zero-configuration web server that is simple to use. From the command line, just change into the directory that contains the website and execute the following command:

```
$ cd www
$ python -m SimpleHTTPServer
Serving HTTP on 0.0.0.0 port 8000 …
```

At this point, we've set the stage for the chart and loaded the data. Now we need to figure out what to do with it. The `load-topic-dists` function takes the pieces of the chart that we've created and the data, and populates the chart, as follows:

```
(defn load-topic-weights [svg line color x x-axis y y-axis data]
  (let [data (into-array (map parse-datum data))]
    (.domain color (into-array (set (map get-topic data))))
    (let [topics (into-array
                    (map #(make-topic data %) (.domain color)))
          wghts (map get-weighting data)]
      (.domain x (.extent js/d3 data get-instance))
      (.domain y (array (apply min wghts) (apply max wghts)))
      (utils/setup-x-axis svg x-axis)
      (utils/setup-y-axis svg y-axis "Weightings")
      (let [topic-svg (make-topic-svg svg topics)]
        (add-topic-lines line color topic-svg)
        (add-topic-labels topic-svg x y)
        (utils/caption
          (str "Topic Weightings over Time (topic count = "
               (count topics) \))
          650)))))
```

The lines in the preceding function fall into three broad categories:

- Transforming and filtering the data
- Setting the domains for the *x* axis, the *y* axis, and the color scheme
- Adding the transformed data to the chart

The transformation and filtering of data is handled in a number of different places. Let's see what they all are. I've highlighted them in the previous code; let's break them apart in more detail as follows:

- The `(into-array (map parse-datum data))` form converts the data into its JavaScript-native types. The call to `d3.csv` returns an array of JavaScript objects, and all of the values are strings. This parses the instance string (for example, "1790-0" or "1984-1") into a decimal (1790.0 or 1984.5). This allows the years with more than one SOTU address to be sorted and displayed more naturally.

- The `(map #(make-topic data %) (.domain color))` form creates a record with a topic number and the instances for that color.

- Finally, the `(map get-weighting data)` form pulls all the weightings from the data. This is used to set the domain for the *y* axis.

This data is used to set the domains for both axes and for the color scale. All of these tasks happen in the three calls to the domain method.

Finally, in the following code, we insert the data into the chart and create the SVG elements from it. This takes place in three other functions. The first, make-topic-svg, selects the elements with the topic class and inserts data into them. It then creates a g element for each datum:

```
(defn make-topic-svg [svg topics]
  (.. svg
    (selectAll ".topic")
    (data topics)
    (enter)
    (append "g")
    (attr "class" "topic")))
```

The next function appends path elements for each line and populates it with attributes for the points on the line and for the color, as shown in the following code:

```
(defn add-topic-lines [line color topic-svg]
  (.. topic-svg
    (append "path")
    (attr "class" "line")
    (attr "id" #(str "line" (.-topic %)))
    (attr "d" #(line (.-values %)))
    (style "stroke" #(color (.-topic %)))))
```

Finally, the last function in the following code adds a label for the line to the right-hand side of the graph. The label just displays the topic number for that line. Most of these topics get layered on top of each other and are illegible, but a few of the lines that are labelled at a higher level are distinguishable, and it's useful to be able to see them:

```
(defn add-topic-labels [topic-svg x y]
  (.. topic-svg
    (append "text")
    (datum make-text)
    (attr "transform" #(str "translate(" (x (.-year (.-value %)))
                          \, (y (.-weighting (.-value %))) \)))
    (attr "x" 3)
    (attr "dy" ".35em")
    (text get-name)))
```

Put together, these functions create the graphs we've seen so far. With a few added bells and whistles (refer to the source code), they'll also create the graphs that we'll see in the rest of this chapter.

Now, let's use these graphs to explore the topics that the LDA identified.

Exploring the topics

The following is a complete set of topic weightings that we'll dig into in this chapter. This is from a run of 75 topics. This should provide a relatively focused set of topics, but not so narrow that it will not apply to more than one year:

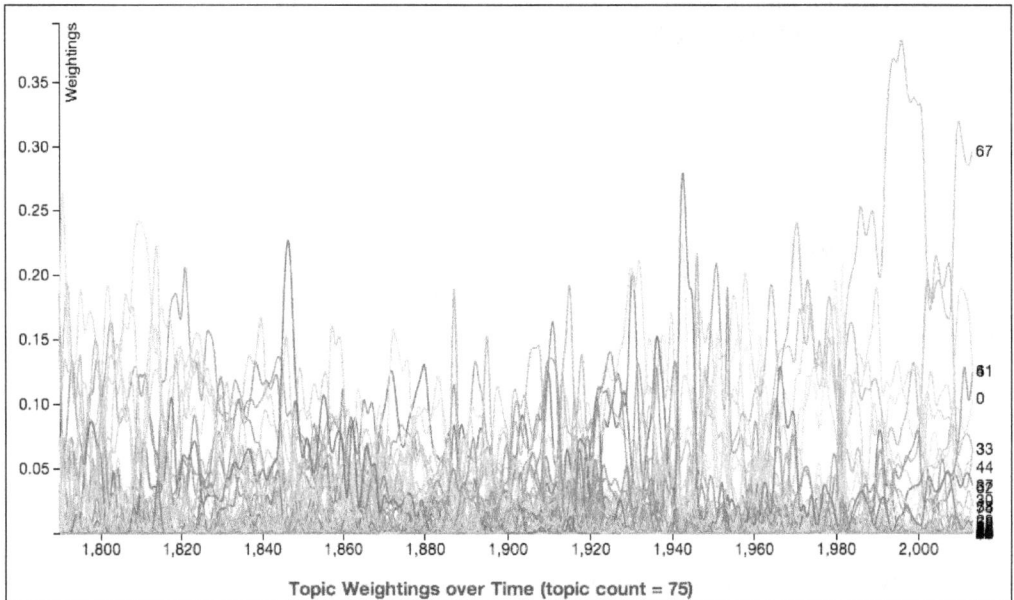

Topic Weightings over Time (topic count = 75)

The MALLET library makes it easy to get a lot of information about each topic. This includes the words that are associated with each topic, ranked by how important each word is to that topic. The following table lists some of the topics from this run along with the top five words for each:

Topic number	Top words
0	states government subject united citizens good
1	world free nations united democracy life
2	people work tonight Americans year jobs
3	years national support education rights water
4	congress government made country report united
5	present national tax great cent country
6	government congress made American foreign conditions
7	America great nation freedom free hope
8	congress president years today future ago
9	congress employment executive people measures relief

The word lists help us get an understanding of the topics and what they contain. For instance, the seventh topic seems clearly about American freedom rhetoric. However, there are still a lot of questions left unanswered. The eighth and ninth topics both have *congress* as their most important word, and some of the words listed for many topics don't have a clear relationship among each other. We'll need to dig deeper.

A better graph would help. It could make each topic's dynamics and changes through time more clear, and it would make evident the trace of each topic's relation to history, wars, expansions, and economics.

Unfortunately, as presented here, the graph is pretty confusing and difficult to read. To make it easier to pull out the weightings for a single topic, I added a feature to the graph so I could select one topic and make the others fade into the background. We'll use the graph to look at a few topics. However, we'll still need to go further and look at some of the addresses for which these topics play an important part.

Exploring topic 43

The first topic that we'll look at in more depth is number 43. The following are the top ten words for this topic and their corresponding weightings:

Word	Weighting
Great	243
War	165
Commerce	143
Powers	123
National	115
Made	113
British	103
Militia	80
Part	74
Effect	73

The following graph for topic 43 shows that this topic was primarily a concern between 1800 and 1825:

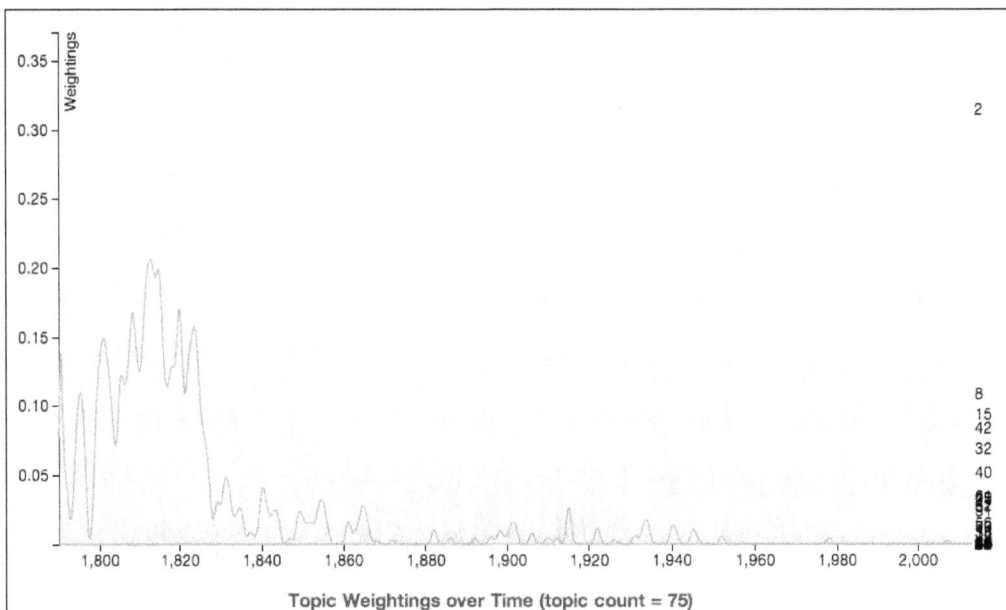

Topic Weightings over Time (topic count = 75)

The dominant theme of this topic is foreign policy and setting up the military, with a particular emphasis on the War of 1812 and Great Britain. To get an idea of the arc of this topic, we'll take a look at several SOTU addresses: one from before that War, one from the time of the War, and one from after the War.

The first address we'll look at in more depth is James Madison's 1810 address. The topic model gave the probability for this topic in the document as 11 percent. One of its concerns is trade relations with other countries and how other countries' warships are disrupting them. The following is a quote where Madison rather verbosely talks about the ongoing talks with Britain and France over blockades that were impeding the new republic's trade (I've highlighted the words in the quote that are most applicable to the topic):

> *From the **British** Government, no communication on the subject of the act has been received. To a communication from our minister at London of a revocation by the French Government of its Berlin and Milan decrees it was answered that the **British** system would be relinquished as soon as the repeal of the French decrees should have actually taken effect and the **commerce** of neutral nations have been restored to the condition in which it stood previously to the promulgation of those decrees.*

This pledge, although it does not necessarily import, does not exclude the intention of relinquishing, along with the others in council, the practice of those novel blockades which have a like **effect** *of interrupting our neutral* **commerce**, *and this further justice to the United States is the rather to be looked for, in as much as the blockades in question, being not more contrary to the established law of nations than inconsistent with the rules of blockade formally recognized by* **Great** *Britain herself, could have no alleged basis other than the plea of retaliation alleged as the basis of the orders in council.*

Later, as part of a larger discussion about enabling the state militias, Madison talks about the requirements for establishing schools of military science, even during peacetime, in the following part of the address:

Even among nations whose large standing armies and frequent **wars** *afford every other opportunity of instruction these establishments are found to be indispensable for the due attainment of the branches of military science which require a regular course of study and experiment. In a government happily without the other opportunities seminaries where the elementary principles of the art of* **war** *can be taught without actual* **war**, *and without the expense of extensive and standing armies, have the precious advantage of uniting an essential preparation against external danger with a scrupulous regard to internal safety. In no other way, probably, can a provision of equal efficacy for the public defense be* **made** *at so little expense or more consistently with the public liberty.*

Next, we'll look at Madison's 1813 address. The probability of topic 43 in this address was almost 21 percent. The War of 1812 had been going on for a year at that point, and his concerns reflect that. In the following address, Madison is concerned with the role of prisoners of war and Native Americans in the war (they sided with the British); however, there's only one mention of *commerce*, which had almost ceased because of interference by the war.

The following is a sample paragraph where Madison complains about the British trying some political prisoners in court:

The **British** *commander in that Province, nevertheless, with the sanction, as appears, of his Government, thought proper to select from American prisoners of* **war** *and send to* **Great** *Britain for trial as criminals a # of individuals who had emigrated from the* **British** *dominions long prior to the state of* **war** *between the two nations, who had incorporated themselves into our political society in the modes recognized by the law and the practice of* **Great** *Britain, and who were made prisoners of* **war** *under the banners of their adopted country, fighting for its rights and its safety.*

Finally, for topic 43, we'll take a look at James Monroe's 1820 SOTU address. The probability of topic 43 in this address was 20 percent. In this case, Monroe's looking at the United States' trade relations with the European powers. He goes through each of the major trading partners and talks about the latest happenings with them and discusses the country's military preparedness on a number of fronts.

The following is the paragraph where he talks about the trading relationship with Great Britain; he doesn't appear entirely satisfied:

> *The commercial relations between the United States and the* **British** *colonies in the West Indies and on this continent have undergone no change, the* **British** *Government still preferring to leave that* **commerce** *under the restriction heretofore imposed on it on each side. It is satisfactory to recollect that the restraints resorted to by the United States were defensive only, intended to prevent a monopoly under* **British** *regulations in favor of* **Great** *Britain, as it likewise is to know that the experiment is advancing in a spirit of amity between the parties.*

In this topic, there's a clear trend of conversations around a series of events. In this case, topic modeling has pointed out an interesting dynamic in the US government's early years.

Exploring topic 26

We'll look at a very different type of topic next. This one focuses on one event: the Japanese bombing of Pearl Harbor, which brought the United States actively and openly into World War II.

The following are the top ten words that contributed to this topic along with their weightings; as it is more narrowly focused, the subject of this topic is clear:

Word	Weighting
Production	66
Victory	48
Japanese	44
Enemy	41
United	39
Fighting	37
Attack	37
Japan	31

Word	Weighting
Pacific	28
Day	27

The narrow focus of the topic is evident in the graph as well. The spike at 1942 and 1943 in the following graph — the two years after the bombing of Pearl Harbor — lends weight to the evidence that this topic is about this particular event:

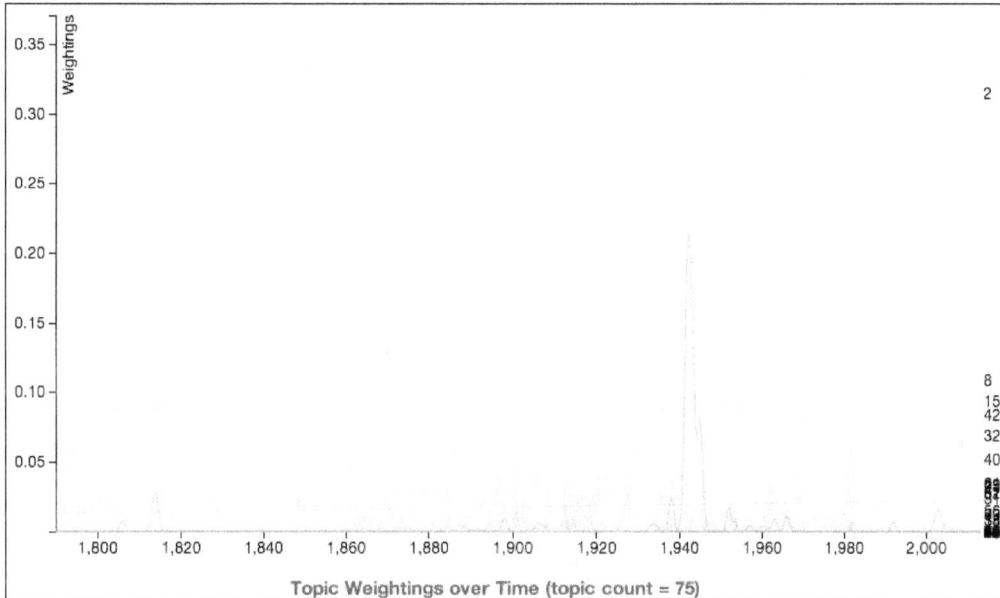

Topic Weightings over Time (topic count = 75)

For the first SOTU address that we'll examine, we'll look at the one immediately after the Pearl Harbor bombing, presented by Franklin D. Roosevelt on January 6, 1942. This topic's probability of application is 22.7 percent. This was less than one month after the attack, so its memory was still pretty raw in the minds of American citizens, and this emotion is evident in the speech.

The text of the speech itself is predictable, especially given the words listed earlier. To paraphrase: *After the attack; they're our enemy; bent on world conquest; along with the Nazis; we must have victory to maintain the cause of freedom and democracy.* Beyond this, he's also making the point that we need to enter the European theater to fight alongside the British and other ally partners, and furthermore, to do that effectively, the U.S. must increase production of military weapons, vehicles, boats, airplanes, and supplies across the board.

The following is a short paragraph in which Roosevelt outlines the steps that are already underway to work with the allied powers:

> *Plans have been laid here and in the other capitals for coordinated and cooperative action by all the* **United** *Nations – military action and economic action. Already we have established, as you know, unified command of land, sea, and air forces in the southwestern* **Pacific** *theater of war. There will be a continuation of conferences and consultations among military staffs, so that the plans and operations of each will fit into the general strategy designed to crush the* **enemy**. *We shall not fight isolated wars – each Nation going its own way. These 26 Nations are* **united** *– not in spirit and determination alone, but in the broad conduct of the war in all its phases.*

Although this particular SOTU address clearly dominates this topic, there are other addresses that have some small probability of applying. It might be interesting to see what else was categorized in this topic, even the words with a low probability percentage. One such address is James Madison's 1814 address, which has a probability of 3.7 percent for this topic.

In the following part of the address, Madison spends a lot of time talking about "the enemy," who in this case, is Great Britain. This short paragraph is typical:

> *In another recent* **attack** *by a powerful force on our troops at Plattsburg, of which regulars made a part only, the* **enemy**, *after a perseverance for many hours, was finally compelled to seek safety in a hasty retreat, with our gallant bands pressing upon them.*

This address has a number of other short descriptions of battles like this one.

Finally, a more recent SOTU address also had a relatively high probability for this topic (2 percent): George W. Bush's 2003 address. In this address, most of the mentions of words that apply to this topic are spread out and there are few quotable clusters. He spends some time referring to the United Nations, which helps this document rate more highly for this topic. He also talks quite a bit about war as he is trying to build a case for invading Iraq, which he did less than two months later.

This document is clearly weaker than the other two on this topic. However, it does contain some shared vocabulary and some discourse, so its relationship to the topic, albeit weak, is clear. It's also interesting that in both of these cases, the President is trying to make a case for war.

Exploring topic 42

Finally, we'll look at a more domestically oriented topic. The words in the following table suggest that this topic will be about childcare, schools, and healthcare:

Word	Weighting
Children	270
Health	203
Care	182
Support	164
Schools	159
School	139
Community	131
Century	130
Parents	124
Make	121

Looking at the following graph on this topic, it's clearly a late twentieth-century subject, and it really doesn't take off until after 1980. Somewhat predictably, this topic sees its zenith in the Clinton administration. We'll look at one of Clinton's speeches on this topic later in this section:

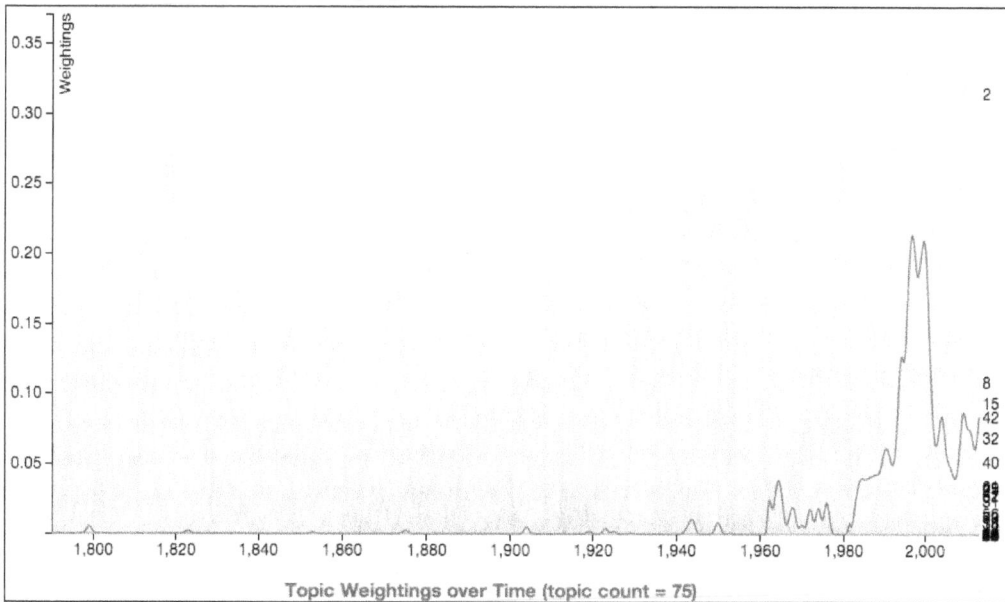

Topic Weightings over Time (topic count = 75)

Let's first look at one of the SOTU addresses from the first, smaller cluster of addresses that prove this topic. For that, we'll pick Lyndon B. Johnson's 1964 SOTU address, which shows a probability of 4.4 percent for this topic.

In this speech, Johnson lays out a proposal that includes what would become the Civil Rights Act of 1964, which outlawed major forms of racial, ethnic, religious, and gender discrimination as well as the medicare and medicaid programs, which would be created in 1965. He's obviously laying the groundwork for the "Great Society" program he would announce in May of that year at Ohio University in Athens, Ohio.

His main topic in this is combating poverty — after all, this is the speech that gave us the phrase "war on poverty" — but he saw education and healthcare as being a big part of that:

> *Our chief weapons in a more pinpointed attack will be better* **schools**, *and better* **health**, *and better homes, and better training, and better job opportunities to help more Americans, especially young Americans, escape from squalor and misery and unemployment rolls where other citizens help to carry them.*

He also saw education and healthcare as being integral to the goals of the program and the American dream itself:

> *This budget, and this year's legislative program, are designed to help each and every American citizen fulfill his basic hopes — his hopes for a fair chance to* **make** *good; his hopes for fair play from the law; his hopes for a full-time job on full-time pay; his hopes for a decent home for his family in a decent* **community**; *his hopes for a good* **school** *for his* **children** *with good teachers; and his hopes for security when faced with sickness or unemployment or old age.*

So although this particular speech has only a low probability for this topic, it clearly raises issues that will be more directly addressed later.

One of the SOTU addresses with the highest probability for this topic is Bill Clinton's 2000 address, which had a probability of 22.1 percent. This is his last SOTU address before leaving office, and although he still had one year left in his term, realistically, not much was going to happen in it.

Additionally, because it was his last chance, Clinton spends a lot of time looking back at what he's accomplished. Children, education, and healthcare were major focuses of his administration, whatever actually was passed through Congress, and this was reflected in his retrospective:

We ended welfare as we knew it, requiring work while protecting **health care** *and nutrition for* **children** *and investing more in child* **care***, transportation, and housing to help their* **parents** *go to work. We've helped parents to succeed at home and at work with family leave, which 20 million Americans have now used to* **care** *for a newborn child or a sick loved one. We've engaged 150,000 young Americans in citizen service through AmeriCorps, while helping them earn money for college.*

Clinton also spent time laying out what he saw as the major tasks ahead of the nation, and education and healthcare played a big part of them as well:

To 21st **century** *America, let us pledge these things: Every child will begin* **school** *ready to learn and graduate ready to succeed. Every family will be able to succeed at home and at work, and no child will be raised in poverty. We will meet the challenge of the aging of America. We will assure quality, affordable* **health care***, at last, for all Americans. We will* **make** *America the safest big country on Earth. We will pay off our national debt for the first time since 1835. We will bring prosperity to every American* **community***. We will reverse the course of climate change and leave a safer, cleaner planet. America will lead the world toward shared peace and prosperity and the far frontiers of science and technology. And we will become at last what our Founders pledged us to be so long ago: One Nation, under God, indivisible, with liberty and justice for all.*

In fact, even beyond these broad strokes, Clinton spends a lot of time talking specifically about education, what needs to be done to improve schools, and what works to make better schools. All of this contributes to this address's high probability for topic 42.

He also spent more time talking about healthcare, what he's done on that front, and what is still left to accomplish:

We also need a 21st **century** *revolution to reward work and strengthen families by giving every parent the tools to succeed at work and at the most important work of all, raising* **children***. That means making sure every family has* **health care** *and the* **support** *to* **care** *for aging* **parents***, the tools to bring their* **children** *up right, and that no child grows up in poverty.*

So looking at these addresses, we may wish that there was a separate topic for education and healthcare. However, it is interesting to note the ways in which the two topics are related. Not only are they often discussed together and simultaneously in two parts of a President's agenda for a year, but also have related rhetoric. Children are directly related to education, but they are also often invoked while talking about healthcare, and many laws about health insurance and healthcare try to ensure that children are still insured, even if their parents are not.

Summary

This has been an interesting dive into natural-language processing and topic modeling, and hopefully we've learned a little US history at the same time. I know I have.

However, it seems that the larger takeaway is something that we all know, but likely forget: Freeform, unstructured, text data is messy, messy, messy. In fact, what we have been working with here is exceptionally clean, as these things go. Topics don't often stand out clearly, and the relationships between subjects as opposed to the topics identified by LDA are often complex and difficult to tease apart.

However, we've also seen some interesting technologies and algorithms to help us deal with the messiness. Topic modeling doesn't—and possibly shouldn't—completely sweep the ambiguities and messiness of texts under the rug, but it does help us get a handle on what's inside large collections of documents.

In the next chapter, we'll head in a different direction and apply Bayesian classification to reports of UFO sightings.

4
Classifying UFO Sightings

In this chapter, we're going to look at a dataset of UFO sightings. Sometimes, data analysis begins with a specific question or problem. Sometimes, however, it's more nebulous and vague. We'll engage with this UFO sighting dataset, and along the way, we'll learn more about data exploration, data visualization, and topic modeling before we dive into Naïve Bayesian classification.

This dataset was collected by the **National UFO Reporting Center** (**NUFORC**), and is available at http://www.nuforc.org/. They have included dates, rough locations, shapes, and descriptions of the sightings. We'll download and pull in this dataset. We'll see how to extract more structured data from messy, free-form text. And from there, we'll see how to visualize, analyze, and gain insights into our data.

In the process, we'll discover when is the best time to look for UFOs. We'll also learn what their important characteristics are. And we'll learn how to tell a description of a possible hoax sighting from one that may be real. In the end, hopefully, we'll be better prepared for seeing one of these ourselves. After all, we'll know when to look and for what to look.

Getting the data

For this chapter, actually acquiring the data will be relatively easy. In other chapters, this step involves screen scraping, SPARQL, or other data extraction, munging, and cleaning techniques. For this dataset, we'll just download it from Infochimps (`http://www.infochimps.com/`). Infochimps is a company (and their website) devoted to Big Data and doing more with data analysis. They provide a collection of datasets that are online and freely available. To download this specific dataset, browse to `http://www.infochimps.com/datasets/60000-documented-ufo-sightings-with-text-descriptions-and-metada` and download the data from the link there, as shown in the following screenshot:

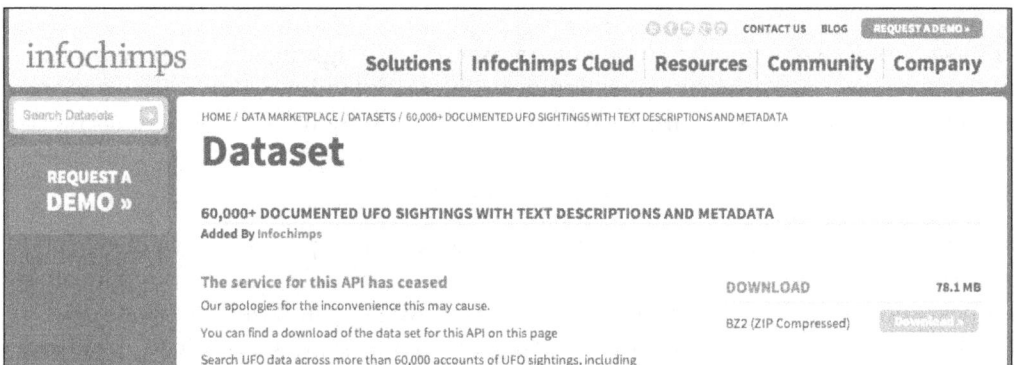

The data is in a ZIP-compressed file. This expands the files into the `chimps_16154-2010-10-20_14-33-35` directory. This contains a file that lists metadata for the dataset as well as the data itself in several different formats. For the purposes of this chapter, we'll use the **tab separated values (TSV)** file. It's similar to a **comma separated values (CSV)** file, but it uses the tab character as a delimiter instead of a comma. This works nicely, because the tab character is used less often in text files in general, so it's often possible to use this data format without escaping many, if any, fields.

If we open the `16154.yaml` file, we'll see metadata and other information about the dataset. And we learn that the fields in the dataset are as follows:

- `sighted_at`: The date (as YYYYMMDD) the sighting happened
- `reported_at`: The date the sighting was reported to NUFORC
- `location`: The city and state the event happened in
- `shape`: The shape of the object
- `duration`: The duration the event lasted
- `description`: A longer description of the sighting as a raw text string

We can get a better feel for this data by examining a row from the downloaded file. The following table represents what the fields contain for that record:

Field	Value
sighted_at	19950202
reported_at	19950203
location	Denmark, WI
shape	Cone
duration	75 min
description	Caller, and apparently several other people, witnessed multiple strange craft streaking through the night sky in the vicinity of Denmark and Mirabel, WI. Craft were seen to streak overhead, as well as to descend vertically, as fast as a meteorite, then stop suddenly just above the ground. During the last 30 minutes of the sighting, aircraft, which appeared to be US military craft, were seen either pursuing, or chaperoning, the strange craft. The objects were cone shaped, with a red nose and a green tail (sic).

Browsing through other rows, you will observe that some important fields—shape and duration—may be missing data. The description has XML entities and abbreviations such as *w/* and *repts*.

Let's see what we can do with that.

Extracting the data

Before we go further, let's look at the following Leiningen 2 (http://leiningen. org/) project.clj file that we'll use for this chapter:

```
(defproject ufo-data "0.1.0-SNAPSHOT"
  :plugins [[lein-cljsbuild "0.3.2"]]
  :profiles {:dev {:plugins [[com.cemerick/austin "0.1.0"]]}}
  :dependencies [[org.clojure/clojure "1.5.1"]
                 [org.clojure/data.json "0.2.2"]
                 [org.clojure/data.csv "0.1.2"]
                 [clj-time "0.5.1"]
                 [incanter "1.5.2"]
                 [cc.mallet/mallet "2.0.7"]
                 [me.raynes/fs "1.4.4"]]
  :cljsbuild
    {:builds [{:source-paths ["src-cljs"],
               :compiler {:pretty-printer true,
                          :output-to "www/js/main.js",
                          :optimizations :whitespace}}]})
```

The preceding code shows that over the course of this chapter, we'll parse time with the `clj-time` library (`https://github.com/clj-time/clj-time`). This provides a rich, robust date and time library. We'll also use ClojureScript (`https://github.com/clojure/clojurescript`) for the visualizations.

Our first step in working with this data is to load it from the data file. To facilitate this, we'll read it into a record type that we'll define just to store the UFO sightings. We'll work with the `model.clj` file placed at `src/ufo_data/`. The following is a namespace declaration with the imports and requirements that we'll use in this module:

```clojure
(ns ufo-data.model
  (:require [clojure.java.io :as io]
            [clojure.core.reducers :as r]
            [clojure.string :as str]
            [clojure.data.json :as json]
            [clj-time.format :as tf]
            [ufo-data.text :as t]
            [ufo-data.util :refer :all]
            [me.raynes.fs :as fs])
  (:import [java.lang StringBuffer]))
```

Now we'll define the record. It simply lists the same fields that we walked through earlier. We also include a few new fields. We'll use these to parse the year, month, and season from the `reported_at` field as follows:

```clojure
(defrecord UfoSighting
  [sighted-at reported-at location shape duration description
   year month season])
```

Now, when we take a row from the TSV file, we'll need to parse it into one of these structures. Because each line of input only has six fields, we'll make sure that it's padded out to nine fields. We'll also verify that there are exactly six input fields. If there are more or less, we'll take steps to either further pad the fields or to join some of the fields, as shown in the following code:

```clojure
(defn ->ufo [row]
  (let [row (cond
              (> (count row) 6)
                (concat (take 5 row)
                  [(str/join \t (drop 5 row))])
              (< (count row) 6)
                (concat row (repeat (- 6 (count row)) nil))
              :else row)]
    (apply ->UfoSighting (concat row [nil nil nil]))))
```

Some of the fields (the most important ones, actually) are dates, and we'll want to parse them into valid date objects. To do this, we'll use the excellent clj-time library (https://github.com/clj-time/clj-time). This provides a more "Clojuresque" interface for the Joda time library (http://joda-time.sourceforge.net/). The code that does this takes a custom date format and attempts to parse the dates. If any fail, we just fall back on using nil. Look at the following code:

```
(def date-formatter (tf/formatter "yyyyMMdd"))
(defn read-date [date-str]
  (try
    (tf/parse date-formatter date-str)
    (catch Exception ex
      nil)))
```

We use the following function to coerce the raw string date fields into the more useful date objects that Joda time provides:

```
(defn coerce-fields [ufo]
  (assoc ufo
         :sighted-at (read-date (:sighted-at ufo))
         :reported-at (read-date (:reported-at ufo))))
```

That's all that we need to load the data. Now we can write the function that will actually take care of reading the data from the file on disk into a sequence of records, as follows:

```
(defn read-data
  [filename]
  (with-open [f (io/reader filename)]
    (->> (csv/read-csv f :separator \tab)
      vec
      (r/map ->ufo)
      (r/map coerce-fields)
      (into []))))
```

Now that we can read in the data, we can start picking it apart and learn about the data that we have.

Dealing with messy data

The first thing that we need to deal with is qualitative data from the shape and description fields.

The `shape` field seems like a likely place to start. Let's see how many items have good data for it:

```
user=> (def data (m/read-data "data/ufo_awesome.tsv"))
user=> (count (remove (comp str/blank? :shape) data))
58870
user=> (count (filter (comp str/blank? :shape) data))
2523
user=> (count data)
61393
user=> (float 2506/61137)
0.04098991
```

So 4 percent of the data does not have the `shape` field set to meaningful data. Let's see what the most popular values for that field are:

```
user=> (def shape-freqs
            (frequencies
              (map str/trim
                (map :shape
                  (remove (comp str/blank? :shape) data)))))
#'user/shape-freqs
user=> (pprint (take 10 (reverse (sort-by second shape-freqs))))
(["light" 12202]
 ["triangle" 6082]
 ["circle" 5271]
 ["disk" 4825]
 ["other" 4593]
 ["unknown" 4490]
 ["sphere" 3637]
 ["fireball" 3452]
 ["oval" 2869]
 ["formation" 1788])
```

Interesting! The most frequent shape isn't a shape at all. The values `other` and `unknown` also rank pretty high. We can use the `shape` field, but we need to keep these things in mind.

Visualizing UFO data

We'll spend a good bit of time visualizing the data, and we'll use the same system that we have in the previous chapters: a bit of HTML, a splash of CSS, and a lot of JavaScript, which we'll generate from ClojureScript.

We've already taken care of the configuration for using ClojureScript in the `project.clj` file that I mentioned earlier. The rest of it involves a couple of more parts:

- The code to generate the JSON data for the graph. This will be in the `src/ufo_data/analysis.clj` file. We'll write this code first.

- An HTML page that loads the JavaScript libraries that we'll use—jQuery (`https://jquery.org/`) and D3 (`http://d3js.org/`)—and creates a `div` container in which to put the graph itself.

- The source code for the graph. This will include a namespace for utilities in `src-cljs/ufo-data/utils.cljs` and the main namespace at `src-cljs/ufo-data/viz.cljs`.

With these prerequisites in place, we can start creating the graph of the frequencies of the different shapes.

First, we need to make sure we have what we need for this namespace. This will be in the `src/ufo_data/analysis.clj` file. The following code gives the `ns` declaration. Most of these dependencies won't be needed immediately, but we will use them at some point in this chapter:

```
(ns ufo-data.analysis
  (:require [ufo-data.text :as t]
            [clj-time.core :as time]
            [clj-time.coerce :as coerce]
            [clojure.string :as str]
            [incanter.core :as i]
            [incanter.stats :as s]))
```

Now, we'll define a rather long function that takes the input data. It will pull out the `shape` field, remove blanks, break it into words, and count their frequencies. A few of the functions that this function uses aren't listed here, but they're available in the code download for this chapter. Then, the following function will remove any shapes that don't occur at least once, reverse-sort them by their frequencies, and finally turn them into map structures in a vector:

```
(defn get-shape-freqs
  "This computes the :shape field's frequencies. This also
```

```
       removes any items with a frequency less than min-freq."
   [coll min-freq]
   (->> coll
      (map :shape)
      (remove str/blank?)
      (map normalize)
      (mapcat tokenize)
      frequencies
      (remove #(< (second %) min-freq))
      (sort-by second)
      reverse
      (map #(zipmap [:shape :count] %))
      (into []))))
```

We can then use the `clojure.data.json` package (`https://github.com/clojure/data.json`) to save it to disk. I saved it to www/term-freqs.json. The following is a small sample of the first two records:

```
[{"count":12202,"shape":"light"},
 {"count":6082,"shape":"triangle"},
 ...]
```

Now we need a web page in which to draw the graph. I downloaded a template from the HTML 5 Boilerplate project (`http://html5boilerplate.com/`) and saved it as www/term-freqs.html. I removed almost everything inside the `body` tag. I left only the following `div` tag and a string of `script` tags:

```
<div class="container"></div>
```

This takes care of the HTML page, so we can move on to the ClojureScript that will create the graph.

All of the ClojureScript files for this chapter will be in the `src-cljs` directory. Under this directory is a tree of Clojure namespaces, similar to how the code in `src` is organized for Clojure. Most of the ClojureScript for this chapter will be in the `src-cljs/ufo-data/viz.cljs` file. There are a number of utility functions in another namespace, but those are primarily boilerplate, and you can find them in the code download for this chapter. The following function loads the data and creates the graph. We'll walk through it step-by-step.

```
(defn ^:export term-freqs []
  (let [{:keys [x y]} (u/get-bar-scales)
        {:keys [x-axis y-axis]} (u/axes x y)
        svg (u/get-svg)]
```

```
(u/caption "Frequencies of Shapes" 300)
(.json js/d3 "term-freqs.json"
  (fn [err json-data]
    (u/set-domains json-data [x get-shape] [y get-count])
    (u/setup-x-axis svg x-axis)
      (u/setup-y-axis svg y-axis "")
  (.. svg
    (selectAll ".bar") (data json-data)
    (enter)
    (append "rect")
    (attr "id" #(str "id" (get-shape %)))
    (attr "class" "bar")
    (attr "x" (comp x get-shape))
    (attr "width" (.rangeBand x))
    (attr "y" (comp y get-count))
    (attr "height"
          #(- u/height (y (get-count %)))))))))))))
```

The part of the function before the highlighting sets up the axes, the scales, and the parent SVG element. Then, we load the data from the server. Once it's loaded, we set the domains on the axes and draw the axes themselves.

The main part of the function is highlighted. This creates the bars in the SVG element. All these tasks take place in the following manner:

- `(selectAll ".bar") (data data)`: This command selects all elements with the `bar` class. Currently, there aren't any elements to select because we haven't created any, but that's all right. Then it joins those elements with the data.

- `(enter)`: This command starts processing any data rows that don't have previously created `.bar` elements.

- `(append "rect")`: For each row of data with no `.bar` elements, this command appends a `rect` tag to the element.

- `(attr "id" #(str "id" (get-shape %))) (attr "class" "bar")`: This line of code adds the ID and `class` attributes to the rectangle.

- `(attr "x" (comp x get-shape)) (attr "y" (comp y get-count))`: This line of code populates the *x* and *y* attributes with values from each data row, projected onto the graph's pixel grid.

- `(attr "width" (.rangeBand x)) (attr "height" #(- u/height (y (get-count %)))))`: This line of code finally sets the height and width for each rectangle.

These commands together create the graph. There's a little bit of CSS involved, also. Refer to the code download for all the details. But in the end, the graph looks as follows:

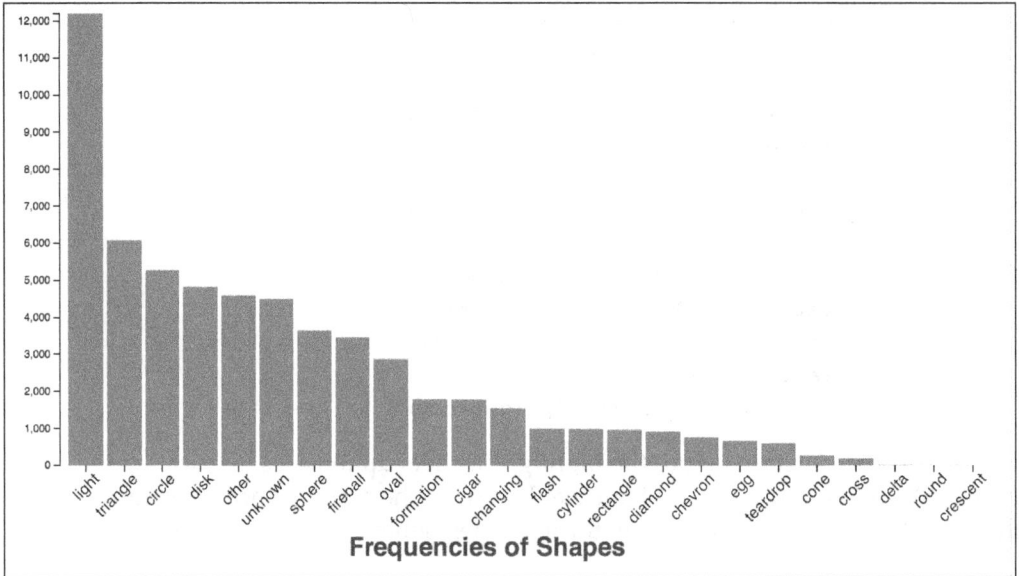

Frequencies of Shapes

This set of files acts as a framework for all of the visualizations and charts that we'll see in this chapter. Although bar charts are simple, once in place, this framework can be used for much more complex and sophisticated types of graphs.

This graph shows us more clearly what the quick frequency dump at the REPL also showed us: most of the people listed the shape as *light*. More than twice as many people listed the shape of *light* as listed the runner-up, *triangle*. In fact, almost one in five observations listed that as the shape.

Now let's try to get a feel for some other facts about this data.

First, when have UFOs been observed? To find this out, we have to group the observations by the year from the `sighted-at` field. We group the items under each year, and then we save that to graph it. The following are the functions in `ufo-data. analysis` that will take care of getting the right data for us:

```
(defn group-by-year [coll]
  (group-by #(timestamp->year (:sighted-at %)) coll))
```

```
(defn get-year-counts [by-year]
  (map #(zipmap [:year :count] %)
    (map (on-second count)
      by-year)))
```

Once we've created the graph from this data, the following is the output:

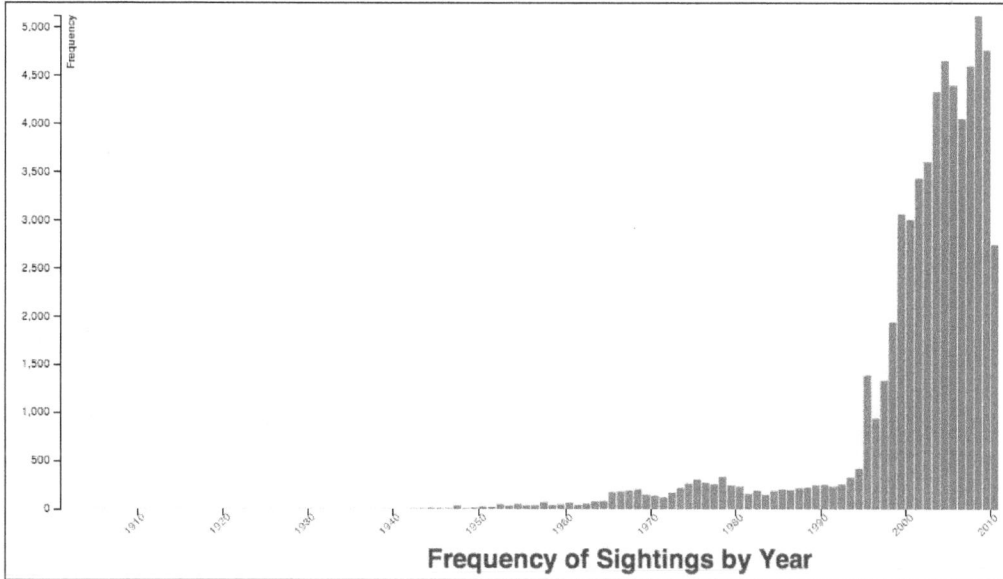

Frequency of Sightings by Year

This graph suggests that the number of observations in the dataset increased dramatically in the mid-1990s, and that they have continued to increase. NUFORC, the organization that collects the data, was established in 1974. I was unable to discover when they began collecting data online, but the increased widespread use of the Internet could also be a factor in the increase in reported sightings. Also, wider cultural trends, such as the popularity of X-Files, may have contributed to a greater awareness of UFOs during this time period.

As we continue to get to know our data, another interesting distribution is looking at the number of sightings each month. The process for getting this data is very similar to the process for getting the number of sightings by year, so we won't go into that now.

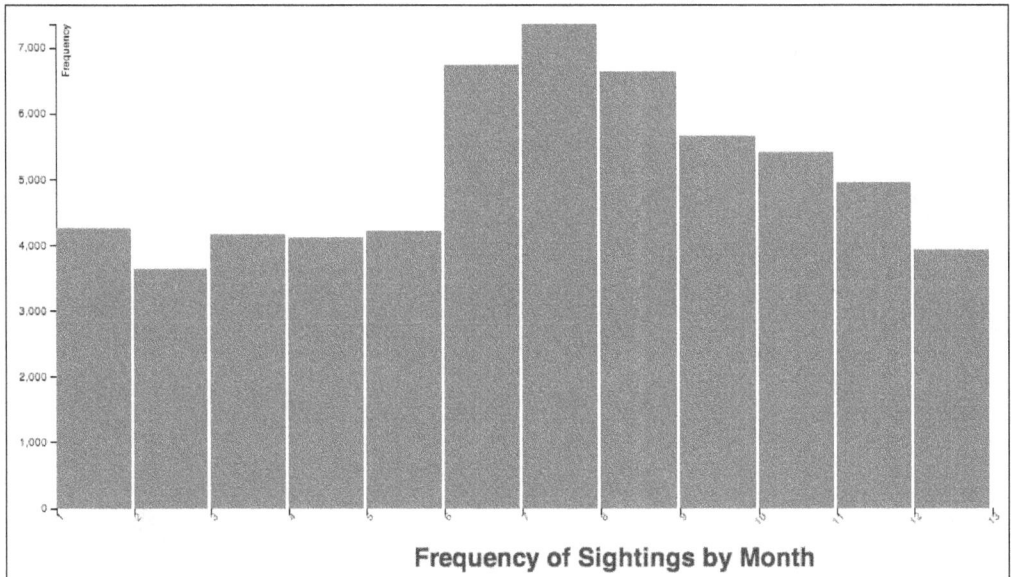

Frequency of Sightings by Month

The preceding graph shows that the summer, starting in June, is a good time to see a UFO. One explanation for this is that during these months, people are outside more in the evenings.

Description

While the *shape* field is important, the *description* has more information. Let's see what we can do with it.

First, let's examine a few and see what some of them look like. The following example is one that I selected randomly:

> *Large boomerang shaped invisible object blocked starlight while flying across sky. I have a sketch and noted the year was 1999, but did not write down the day. The sighting took place in the late evening when it was completely dark and the sky was clear and full of stars. Out of the corner of my eye, I noticed movement in the sky from the north moving to the south. When I looked closer, however, it wasn’t an object that I was seeing move, rather it was the disappearance and reappearance of stars behind an object. The object itself was black or invisible with no lights. Given the area of stars that were blocked out, I would say the object was five times larger than a jet. It was completely silent. It was shaped like a boomerang only a little more rounded in front rather than triangle and a slightly sharper points on the “wing” tips. Since the object was invisible, I can only suggest the shape based on the black area absent of stars like a silhouette as it moved across the sky. If the object was indeed five times the size of a jet and flying at about the attitude of a jet, then it was moving much faster than a jet. I blinked a couple times, looked away and looked back, and then followed the object across the remainder of the horizon until it was out of sight. In all it took about 8-10 seconds to span the sky and flew at the same altitude the whole time. Given the triangular shape, I suppose it could have been a low-flying Stealth Bomber that just appeared much larger if flying low. But is a Stealth completely silent? Also, Stealth Bombers have three triangles pointing backwards from the mid section. The object I saw did not seem to have any mid section as such.((NUFORC Note: Witness indicates that date of incident is approximate. PD))*

So we can see that some examples are fairly long, and they may have characters encoded as HTML/XML entities (`&ldquo;` and `&rdquo;` in this example). And this quote is relatively clean: some have two or more words jammed together with just punctuation—often several periods—stuck between the words.

In order to deal with this data, we'll need to clean it up some and break the words out, or tokenize it. You can see the details of this in the code download, most of which is just pasting together a lot of string manipulation methods, but it's helpful to remind ourselves with what we're working and how we need to deal with it. I also filtered on a standard English stop-words list, which I augmented by adding a few words that are specific to the *description* fields, such as *PD* and *NUFORC*.

Let's see what the most frequent words are in the description fields:

```
user=> (def descr-counts (a/get-descr-counts data 50))
#'user/descr-counts
user=> (take 10 descr-counts)
({:count 85428, :descr "object"}
 {:count 82526, :descr "light"}
 {:count 73182, :descr "lights"}
 {:count 72011, :descr "sky"}
 {:count 58016, :descr "like"}
 {:count 47193, :descr "one"}
 {:count 40690, :descr "bright"}
 {:count 38225, :descr "time"}
 {:count 37065, :descr "could"}
 {:count 35953, :descr "looked"})
```

This seems more like what we'd expect. The most frequent word is *object*, which seems appropriate for a corpus made up of people talking about things that they can't identify. The next two words are *light* and *lights*, which would be expected, especially since *light* is the most common item in the *shape* field.

Let's graph these terms too. We won't be able to see the details of the words' frequencies but it will give us a better feel for their distribution. There are enough tokens; however, we'll only look at the 75 most frequent ones in the following graph:

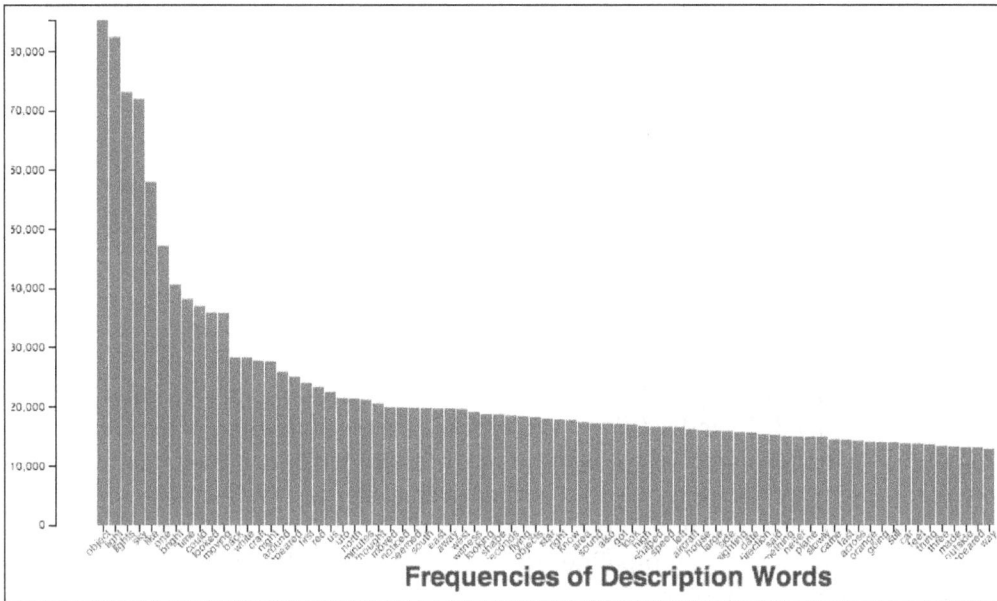

Frequencies of Description Words

The distribution of these words seems very similar. In fact, it very roughly conforms to Zipf's law, which predicts the power-law distribution of many types of physical and social data, including language frequencies.

Topic modeling descriptions

Another way to gain a better understanding of the descriptions is to use topic modeling. We learned about this text mining and machine learning algorithm in *Chapter 3, Topic Modeling – Changing Concerns in the State of the Union Addresses*. In this case, we'll see if we can use it to create topics over these descriptions and to pull out the differences, trends, and patterns from this set of texts.

First, we'll create a new namespace to handle our topic modeling. We'll use the src/ufo_data/tm.clj file. The following is the namespace declaration for it:

```clojure
(ns ufo-data.tm
  (:require [clojure.java.io :as io]
            [clojure.string :as str]
            [clojure.pprint :as pp])
```

```
(:import [cc.mallet.util.*]
         [cc.mallet.types InstanceList]
         [cc.mallet.pipe
          Input2CharSequence TokenSequenceLowercase
          CharSequence2TokenSequence SerialPipes
          TokenSequenceRemoveStopwords
          TokenSequence2FeatureSequence]
         [cc.mallet.pipe.iterator ArrayIterator]
         [cc.mallet.topics ParallelTopicModel]
         [java.io FileFilter]
         [java.util Formatter Locale]))
```

The process for generating the topic model is very similar to the process that
we used in *Chapter 3, Topic Modeling – Changing Concerns in the State of the Union
Addresses*. The first change that we need to make is that we'll load the instances
from the in-memory data that we read earlier in this chapter. We'll create a function
that pushes an input collection into an array and uses ArrayIterator to then feed
that array into the processing pipeline. The function to train the data is the same as
it was in the previous chapter.

In this chapter, we'll look at more functions that help us introspect on the trained
model, the instances, and the probabilities and keywords that are important to each
topic. The first function returns the words that apply to a topic and their weights.
We get the feature vectors from the model, and the words themselves from the
instance list as follows:

```
(defn get-topic-words [model instances topic-n]
  (let [topic-words (.getSortedWords model)
        data-alpha (.getDataAlphabet instances)]
    (map #(vector (.lookupObject data-alpha (.getID %))
                  (.getWeight %))
         (iterator-seq (.. topic-words (get topic-n)
                           iterator)))))
```

The other reporting function that we'll use ranks the instances by their probabilities
for each topic. We can use this to look at the documents that are most likely to apply
to any particular topic:

```
(defn rank-instances [model data topic-id]
  (let [get-p (fn [n]
                [(aget (.getTopicProbabilities model n) topic-id)
                 (nth data n)])]
    (->> data count range (map get-p) (sort-by first) reverse)))
```

We can use these functions—as well as a few others based on these—from the REPL
to explore our data.

Generally, when deciding how many topics to use, we'll want to use some kind of objective metric to find a good definition of the sets. However, for exploring in an off-the-cuff way, we'll use something more subjective. First, after playing around with the number of topics, I chose to use a topic count of twelve. Since all of these are really about just one thing, UFO sightings, I didn't expect there to be too many meaningful topics, even at a fairly detailed, narrow level. At twelve topics, there still seemed to be some vague, less helpful topics, but the more interesting topics that I'd seen before were still there. When I attempted fewer topics, some of those interesting topics disappeared.

So to get started, let's see the topics and the top 10 words for each. Remember that the topic descriptions here aren't generated by the computer. I came up with them after looking at the top words and the top few descriptions for those topics. Some of these are not obvious, given the small sample of terms included here. However, diving further into the topic terms, the documents themselves gave these categorizations. In some cases, I've included notes in parentheses as follows:

- **Remembering childhood experiences**: back time house craft car looked years remember road home

- **Lots of NUFORC notes, thanks to other organizations or local chapters**: report witness nuforc note ufo sighting pd date reported object

- **Bright, silent objects in the sky**: light sky bright lights white star object red moving looked

- **Visual descriptions**: lights sky light time night red minutes objects back bright (this one doesn't have a clear topic as it's commonly defined)

- **White, red, and reddish-orange lights**: light sky lights looked bright moving object back red white

- **Very fast, bright objects in the sky, compared to airplanes and meteors**: lights sky object aircraft light west north appeared flying south

- **NUFORC notes. "Witness elects to remain totally anonymous"**: nuforc note pd witness date sky light anonymous remain approximate

- **Vague**: ufo camera air object picture time pictures photo photos day (again, the subject of this topic isn't clear)

- **Objects in the sky, no lights, or not mentioned**: object driving road car lights shaped craft looked side feet

- **Abductions, visitations, fear. Close encounters of the fourth kind**: time night back looked light house thing window lights sound

- **Sightings. Moving in different directions**: lights object craft light flying white north south east moving

- **Technical descriptions**: object sky light moving objects appeared bright time high north

Several of these topics, for instance, the third, fifth, sixth, and ninth bullet, seem to be pretty generic descriptions of sightings. They describe lots of moving lights in the sky.

Other topics are more interesting. Topic one contained a number of descriptions written by people looking back at their childhood or college years. For instance, in the following paragraph, someone describes having a close encounter when they were about six years old. There are a number of spelling mistakes, and part of the reason I've kept it in is to illustrate just how messy this data can be:

> *Blus light, isolated road, possible missing timeI was six years old at the time, and even now, if I concentrate, I can recall what happened. My mother, her best friend, and myself were driving on a section of road called "Grange Road." Today, there are a lot of houses, but at the time, it was all farmland with maybe one or two houses. It was just after midnight, and I remember waking up. I was alseep in the back seat, and I woke up feeling very frightened. I sat up, and my mother and her friend were obviously worried. The car we were in was cutting in-and-out, and finally died. As soon as the car stopped, we all saw a blue light directly ahead, maybe about 20 feet off of the ground, and about a football field legnth away. It glided towards us, made no noise, and as it got to within 15 feet, it stopped in midair, hoovering. My mom grabbed me from the backseat and held on, and her friend was crying. I was crying, too, because whatever it was, it was making us all upset. After about five minutes, I don't recall what happened, because for whatever reason, I fell alseep. Weird, I know, but I swear it happened. I woke up sometime later, and we three were sitting there, shocked, and the light was gone. My mom and her friend - to this day - swear they had missing time, about 10 minutes worth. I hope this helps...((NUFORC Note: Witness indicates that date of sighting is approximate. PD))*

And some topics are puzzling, number eight, for instance. The top 10 documents for it had nothing obvious that appeared to make them a coherent subject. There may be something about some of the subtler vocabulary selection that was getting identified, but it wasn't readily apparent.

Hoaxes

One of the most interesting finds in this was topic seven. This topic was focused on annotations added to the descriptions for which the witnesses wished to remain anonymous. But its most likely document was the following:

Round, lighted object over Shelby, NC, hovered then zoomed away. It was my birthday party and me and my friends were walking around the block about 21:30. I just happened to look up and I saw a circular object with white and bright blue lights all over the bottom of it. It hovered in place for about 8 seconds then shot off faster than anything I have ever seen.((NUFORC Note: Witness elects to remain totally anonymous; provides no contact information. Possible hoax?? PD))((NUFORC Note: Source of report indicates that the date of the sighting is approximate. PD))

What caught my attention was the note "Possible hoax??" Several other descriptions in this topic had similar notes, often including the word *hoax*.

Finding this raised an interesting possibility: could we train a classifier to recognize possible hoaxes? My initial reaction was to be skeptical. But I still thought it would be an interesting experiment.

Eventually, we'll want to load this data and process it with MALLET (http://mallet.cs.umass.edu/). MALLET works a little easier with data that's kept in a particular directory format. The template for this is base-directory/tag/data-file.txt. In fact, we'll include a directory above these, and for base-directory, we'll define a directory for training data and one for test data.

The training group is used to train the classifier, and the test group is used to evaluate the classifier after it's been trained in order to determine how successful it is. Having two different groups for these tasks helps to find whether the classifier is over-fitting, that is, whether it has learned the training group so well that it performs poorly on new data.

Preparing the data

So before we get started, we'll preprocess the data to put it into a directory structure such as src/ufo_data/. All the code for this will go into the model.clj file. The namespace declaration for this is as follows:

```
(ns ufo-data.model
  (:require [clojure.java.io :as io]
            [clojure.core.reducers :as r]
            [clojure.string :as str]
            [clojure.data.json :as json]
            [clj-time.format :as tf]
            [ufo-data.text :as t]
            [ufo-data.util :refer :all]
            [me.raynes.fs :as fs])
  (:import [java.lang StringBuffer]))
```

Now, to process this dataset into a form that MALLET can deal with easily, we're going to put it through the following steps:

1. Read the data into a sequence of data records.
2. Split out the NUFORC comments.
3. Categorize the documents based on the comments.
4. Partition them into directories based on the categories.
5. Divide them into training and test sets.

Let's see how we'll put these together.

Reading the data into a sequence of data records

The data in the downloaded file has a number of problems with values that can't be escaped properly. I've cleaned this up and made a new data file, available at http://www.ericrochester.com/clj-data-master/data/ufo.json. I've saved this into my data directory and bound that path to the name *data-file*. You can find this and a few other definitions in the code download for this chapter.

But primarily, I'd like to focus on the data record for a minute. This just contains the fields from the JSON objects being read in. The following definition will serve as documentation of our data and make working with the rows a little easier:

```
(defrecord UfoSighting
  [sighted-at reported-at location shape duration description
   year month season])
```

The data as we read it in from the JSON file won't be quite right, however. We'll still need to convert date strings into data objects. We'll do that with read-date, which parses a single date string, and with coerce-fields, which coordinates the calling of read-date on the appropriate fields in UfoSighting, as shown in the following code:

```
(def date-formatter (tf/formatter "yyyyMMdd"))
(defn read-date [date-str]
  (try
    (tf/parse date-formatter date-str)
    (catch Exception ex
      nil)))
(defn coerce-fields [ufo]
  (assoc ufo
         :sighted-at (read-date (:sighted-at ufo))
         :reported-at (read-date (:reported-at ufo)))))
```

Now we can use these functions to read and parse each line of the input data file. As shown in the following code, each line is a separate JSON object:

```
(defn read-data
  ([] (read-data *data-file*))
  ([filename]
   (with-open [f (io/reader filename)]
     (->> f
       line-seq
       vec
       (r/map #(json/read-str % :key-fn keyword))
       (r/map map->UfoSighting)
       (r/map coerce-fields)
       (into [])))))
```

Now we can use these on the REPL to load the data file. As shown in the following code, in this session, model is bound to ufo-data.model:

```
user=> (def data (model/read-data))
user=> (count data)
61067
user=> (first data)
{:sighted-at nil,
 :reported-at nil,
 :location " Iowa City, IA",
 :shape "",
 :duration "",
 :description
 "Man repts. witnessing &quot;flash, followed by a classic UFO, w/
a tailfin at back.&quot; Red color on top half of tailfin. Became
triangular.",
 :year nil,
 :month nil,
 :season nil,
 :reported_at "19951009",
 :sighted_at "19951009"}
```

Looks good. We're ready to start processing the descriptions further.

Splitting the NUFORC comments

Many of the descriptions contain comments by NUFORC (`http://www.nuforc.org/`). These contain editorial remarks – some of them about the authenticity of the report. The following is a sample description with NUFORC commentary:

> *Telephoned Report:Husband and wife were awakened by a very bright light outside their house in Rio Vista area of McCall. It was so bright, it was "like being inside a football stadium." No sound. Ground was covered with snow at the time. It lasted for 10 seconds.((NUFORC Note: We spoke with the husband and wife, and found them to be quite credible and convincing in their description of what they allegedly had seen. Both have responsible jobs. PD))*

This is a standard format for these comments: They're enclosed in double parentheses and begin with "NUFORC." We can leverage this information, and a regular expression, to pull all the notes out of the document.

To do this, we'll go a little deeper into the Java regular expression API than Clojure has utility functions defined to do. Let's see what we need to do, and then we can take it apart after the following code listing:

```clojure
(defn split-nuforc [text]
  (let [m (.matcher #"\(\(.*?\)\)" text), sb (StringBuffer.)]
    (loop [accum []]
      (if (.find m)
        (let [nuforc (.substring text (.start m) (.end m))]
          (.appendReplacement m sb "")
          (recur (conj accum nuforc)))
        (do
          (.appendTail m sb)
          [(str sb) (str/join " " accum)])))))
```

So first we create a regular expression that picks out text enclosed in double parentheses. We also create `java.lang.StringBuffer`. We'll use this to accumulate the description of the UFO sighting, with the NUFORC comments stripped out.

The body of the function is a loop that has a single parameter, a vector named `accum`. This will accumulate the NUFORC comments.

Inside the loop, every time the regular expression finds a match, we extract the NUFORC comment out of the original string and replace the match with an empty string in `StringBuffer`. Finally, when there are no more matches on the regular expression, we append the rest of the string onto `StringBuffer`, and we can retrieve its contents and the comments, joined together.

Let's see what happens when we strip the NUFORC comments from the description quoted earlier:

```
user=> (def split-descr (model/split-nuforc description))
user=> (first split-descr)
"Telephoned Report:Husband and wife were awakened by a very bright light
outside their house in Rio Vista area of McCall.  It was so bright, it
was &quot;like being inside a football stadium.&quot;  No sound.  Ground
was covered with snow at the time.  It lasted for 10 seconds."
user=> (second split-descr)
"((NUFORC Note:  We spoke with the husband and wife, and found them to be
quite credible and convincing in their description of what they allegedly
had seen.   Both have responsible jobs.   PD))"
```

So we can see that the first item in the pair returned by split-nuforc contains the description by itself, and the second item is the comments.

Now we can use the comments to categorize the descriptions in the first part. And we'll use that to figure out where to save the cleaned-up descriptions.

Categorizing the documents based on the comments

Categorizing the documents is relatively easy. We'll use a tokenize function, which can be found in the code download for this chapter, in the namespace ufo-data. text (which is aliased to t in the code). We can convert the words in the comment to a set of tokens and then look for the word "*hoax*". If found, we'll categorize it as follows:

```
(defn get-category [tokens]
  (if (contains? (set tokens) "hoax")
    :hoax
    :non-hoax))
```

When called with the tokens of a comment, it returns the category of the description as follows:

```
user=> (model/get-category
         (map t/normalize (t/tokenize (second split-descr))))
:non-hoax
```

Of course, this is very rough, but it should be all right for this experiment.

Partitioning the documents into directories based on the categories

Now that they're in categories, we can use those categories to save the descriptions into files. Each description will be in its own file.

Initially, we'll put all of the files into one pair of directories. In the next step, we'll divide them further into test and training sets.

The first function for this section will take a base directory, a number, and the document pair, as returned by `ufo-data.model/split-nuforc`. From there, it will save the text to a file and return the file's category and filename, as shown in the following code:

```
(defn save-document [basedir n doc]
  (let [[text category] doc
        filename (str basedir \/ (name category) \/ n ".txt")]
    (spit filename text)
    {:category category, :filename filename}))
```

The next function, `make-dirtree-sighting`, will do a lot of the work. It will take an instance of `UfoSighting` and will split out the NUFORC commentary, tokenize both parts, get the category, and use it to save the filename, as shown in the following code:

```
(defn make-dirtree-sighting
  ([basedir]
   (fn [sighting n]
     (make-dirtree-sighting basedir sighting n)))
  ([basedir sighting n]
   (->> sighting
        :description
        split-nuforc
        (on-both #(map t/normalize (t/tokenize %)))
        (on-second get-category)
        (on-first #(str/join " " %))
        (save-document basedir n))))
```

This will handle saving each file individually into one pair of directories: one for hoaxes and one for non-hoaxes. We'll want to process all of the UFO sightings, however, and we'll want to divide the two sets of documents into a test set and a training set. We'll do all of this in the next section.

Dividing them into training and test sets

Now, we can divide the data that we have into a training set and a test set. We'll need the following two utility functions to do this:

1. We'll need to create subdirectories for the categories several times. Let's put that into the following function:

```
(defn mk-cat-dirs [base]
  (doseq [cat ["hoax" "non-hoax"]]
    (fs/mkdirs (fs/file base cat))))
```

2. We'll also need to divide a collection into two groups by ratio, as shown in the following code. That is, one subgroup will be 80 percent of the original and the other subgroup will be 20 percent of the original.

```
(defn into-sets [ratio coll]
  (split-at (int (* (count coll) ratio)) coll))
```

Now, the function to move a collection of files into a stage's subdirectory (testing or training) will be `mv-stage`. The collection of files is generated by `save-document`, so it's a collection of maps, each containing the category and filename of the file, as shown in the following code:

```
(defn mv-stage [basedir stage coll]
  (let [stage-dir (fs/file basedir stage)]
    (doseq [{:keys [category filename]} coll]
      (fs/copy filename
               (fs/file stage-dir (name category)
                        (fs/base-name filename))))))
```

To control this whole process, we'll use `make-dirtree`. This will take a collection of instances of `UfoSighting` and process them into separate text files. All of the files will be in the `basedir` directory, and then they'll be divided into a training set and a test set. These will be put into sibling directories under `basedir` as shown in the following code:

```
(defn make-dirtree [basedir training-ratio sightings]
  (doseq [dir [basedir (fs/file basedir "train")
               (fs/file basedir "test")]]
    (mk-cat-dirs dir))
  (let [outputs (map (make-dirtree-sighting basedir)
                     sightings (range))
        {:keys [hoax non-hoax]} (group-by :category
                                          (shuffle outputs))
```

```
        [hoax-train hoax-test] (into-sets training-ratio hoax)
        [nhoax-train nhoax-test] (into-sets
                                   training-ratio non-hoax)]
  (mv-stage basedir "train" (concat hoax-train nhoax-train))
  (mv-stage basedir "test" (concat hoax-test nhoax-test))))
```

Now, let's use this to divide out sightings data into groups and save them into the bayes-data directory as follows:

```
user=> (model/make-dirtree "bayes-data" 0.8 data)
```

We have the data now, and it's in a shape that MALLET can use. Let's look at how we're going to leverage that library for Naïve Bayesian classification.

Classifying the data

Bayesian inference can seem off-putting at first, but at its most basic level, it's how we tend to deal with the world. We start out with an idea of how likely something is, and then we update that expectation as we receive more information. In this case, depending on our background, training, history, and tendencies, we may think that all UFO reports are hoaxes or that most of them are. We may think that few UFO reports are hoaxes, or we may be completely undecided and assume that about half of them are hoaxes and half are true. But as we hear reports that we know the truth of, we change our opinions and expectations of the other reports. We may notice patterns, too. Hoaxes may talk about green men, while true reports may talk about grays. So you may also further refine your intuition based on that. Now, when you see a report that talks about little green men, you're more likely to think it's a hoax than when you see a report that talks about little gray men.

You may also notice that triangular UFOs are considered hoaxes, while circular UFOs are not. Now, when you read another document, this observation then further influences your beliefs about whether that document is a hoax or not.

In Bayesian terms, our original expectation that a document is a hoax or not is called the **prior or assumed probability**, and its notation is $P(H)$, where H is the probability that the document is considered a hoax. The updated expectation after seeing the color of the aliens in the description, C, is called the **conditional probability**, and its notation is $P(C \mid H)$, which is read as *the probability of C given H*. In this case, it's the probability distribution over the alien's color, given that the document is a hoax.

Bayes' theorem is a way of swapping the conditions for a set of conditional probabilities. That is, we can now find $P(H \mid C)$, or the probability distribution over the document's being a hoax, given that the alien is green or gray.

The formula to do this is pretty simple. To compute the probability that the document is a hoax, given the aliens' color, consider the following conditions:

- The probability of the aliens' color, given that the document is a hoax or not
- The probability that the document is a hoax
- The probability of the aliens' color.

For Naïve Bayesian classification, we make an important assumption: we assume that the features in a document are independent. This means that the probability that whether aliens are green or gray in a document is independent of whether the UFO is a disk or a triangle.

In spite of this assumption, Naïve Bayesian classifiers often work well in the real world. We can train them easily and quickly, and they classify new data quickly and often perform well enough to be useful.

So with that understanding, let's look at how MALLET handles Naïve Bayesian classification.

Coding the classifier interface

Before we begin the next part of this chapter, it's probably a good time to start a new namespace for the following code to live in. Let's put it into the src/ufo_data/ bayes.clj file. The ns declaration is as follows:

```
(ns ufo-data.bayes
  (:require [clojure.java.io :as io])
  (:import [cc.mallet.util.*]
           [cc.mallet.types InstanceList]
           [cc.mallet.pipe Input2CharSequence
            TokenSequenceLowercase
            TokenSequenceRemoveStoplist
            CharSequence2TokenSequence SerialPipes
            SaveDataInSource Target2Label
            TokenSequence2FeatureSequence
            FeatureSequence2AugmentableFeatureVector]
           [cc.mallet.pipe.iterator FileIterator]
           [cc.mallet.classify NaiveBayesTrainer]
           [java.io ObjectInputStream ObjectOutputStream]]))
```

With the preceding code in place, let's see what we need to do.

Setting up the Pipe and InstanceList

MALLET processes all input through `Pipe`. Pipes represent a series of transformations over the text. When you're working with a classifier, the data that's used for training, testing, and later for classifying new documents, all need to be put through the same pipe of processes. Also, all of them must use the same set of features and labels. MALLET calls these *alphabets*.

Each data document, at whatever stage of processing, is stored in an `Instance` object, and corpora of these are kept in `InstanceList`. `Pipe` objects are associated with `InstanceList` objects. This makes sure that all `Instance` objects in a collection are processed consistently.

In order to keep things straight, we'll define `make-pipe-list`. This will create the `Pipe` object as shown in the following code:

```
(defn make-pipe-list []
  (SerialPipes.
    [(Target2Label.)
     (SaveDataInSource.)
     (Input2CharSequence. "UTF-8")
     (CharSequence2TokenSequence. #"\p{L}[\p{L}\p{P}]+\p{L}")
     (TokenSequenceLowercase.)
     (TokenSequenceRemoveStoplist.)
     (TokenSequence2FeatureSequence.)
     (FeatureSequence2AugmentableFeatureVector. false)]))
```

This processing pipeline performs the following steps:

1. `Target2Label` takes the category from the directory path and assigns it to the `Instance` object's label. Labels are the categories or classes used for classification.

2. `SaveDataInSource` takes the path name, which is currently in the data property, and puts it into the `Instance` object's source property.

3. `Input2CharSequence` reads the data from the filename and replaces it with the file's contents.

4. `CharSequence2TokenSequence` tokenizes the file's contents.

5. `TokenSequenceLowercase` converts all uppercase characters in the tokens to lowercase.

6. `TokenSequenceRemoveStoplist` removes common English words so that the classifier can focus on content words.

7. `TokenSequence2FeatureSequence` categorizes the tokens as sequences. Each unique word is assigned a unique integer identifier.

8. `FeatureSequence2AugmentableFeatureVector` converts the sequence of tokens into a vector. The token's feature identifier is that token's index in the feature vector.

MALLET's classifier expects feature vectors as input, so this is the appropriate pipeline to use.

Now we need to take an input directory, generate `Instance` objects from it, and associate their processing with a pipeline. In the following code, we'll use the `add-input-directory` function to do all of that:

```
(defn add-input-directory [dir-name pipe]
  (doto (InstanceList. pipe)
    (.addThruPipe
      (FileIterator. (io/file dir-name)
                     #".*/([^/]*?)/\d+.txt$"))))
```

The regular expression in the last line takes the name of the file's directory and uses that as the `Instance` object's classification. We can use these two functions to handle the loading and processing of the inputs.

Training

Training is pretty simple. We create an instance of `NaiveBayesTrainer`. Its `train` method returns an instance of `NaiveBayes`, which is the classifier. We'll wrap this in the following function to make it slightly easier to use:

```
(defn train [instance-list]
  (.train (NaiveBayesTrainer.) instance-list))
```

Wrapping it in this way provides a Clojure-native way of dealing with this library. It also keeps users of our module from needing to import `NaiveBayesTrainer` and the other classes from MALLET directly.

Classifying

Just like training, classifying is also easy. The classifier returned by the `train` function just defers to the `classify` method as follows:

```
(defn classify [bayes instance-list]
  (.classify bayes instance-list))
```

The preceding code will return an instance of type `cc.mallet.classify.Classification`. This returns not only the best label and the probabilities associated with it, but also the probabilities of the other labels and the classifier and document instance involved.

Validating

We can now train a classifier and run it on new documents. We'd like to be able to test it as well, by comparing our expectations from preclassified documents with how the classifier actually performs.

At the lowest level, we'll want to compare the expected classification with the actual classification and keep a count of each pairing of these values. We can do that with validate1. This gets the expected and actual labels, and it creates a vector pair of them. The confusion-matrix function then gets the frequency of those pairs as follows:

```
(defn validate1 [bayes instance]
  (let [c (.classify bayes instance)
        expected (.. c getInstance getTarget toString)
        actual (.. c getLabeling getBestLabel toString)]
    [expected actual]))
(defn confusion-matrix [classifier instances labels]
  (frequencies (map #(validate1 classifier %) instances)))
```

A confusion matrix is a table with the counts of the correctly classified instances (expected and actual match), the false positives (expected is to not classify, but the actual is to classify it), and the false negatives (expected is to classify the instance, but the actual is to not classify it). This provides an easy-to-comprehend overview of the performance of a classifier.

Tying it all together

In the following code, we'll create a bayes function that creates, trains, and tests a classifier on a directory of data. It will take the hash map of information returned by validate and add the classifier and the Pipe object to it. Having the pipe object available later will be necessary to run the classifier on more data in the future.

```
(defn bayes [training-dir testing-dir]
  (let [pipe (make-pipe-list)
        training (add-input-directory training-dir pipe)
        testing (add-input-directory testing-dir pipe)
        classifier (train training)
        labels (iterator-seq
                 (.iterator (.getLabelAlphabet classifier)))
        c-matrix (confusion-matrix classifier testing labels)]
    {:bayes classifier
     :pipe pipe
     :confusion c-matrix}))
```

Now that we have all the pieces in place, let's see how to run the classifier.

Running the classifier and examining the results

For this section, I've loaded the `ufo-data.bayes` namespace into the REPL and aliased it with the name `bayes`.

We can pass to the `bayes` function the test and training directories that we created from the sightings as shown in the following code:

```
user=> (def bayes-out
          (bayes/bayes "bayes-data/train" "bayes-data/test"))
user=> (:confusion bayes-out)
{["hoax" "non-hoax"] 83, ["non-hoax" "non-hoax"] 12102,
["non-hoax" "hoax"] 29}
```

Let's put this into a more traditional form for this information. The expected values have their labels across the top of the table. The actual values have theirs down the side. Look at the following table:

	Hoax	Non-hoax
Hoax	0	31
Non-hoax	83	12100

Well, that seems pretty useless. Evidently, my previous skepticism was warranted. The classifier managed to identify no hoaxes correctly, and it incorrectly identified 31 non-hoaxes as hoaxes (false positives).

But that's not all that we can learn about this. Instances of `NaiveBayes` also include a way to print out the top-weighted words for each category. Let's see what the top 10 words for each classification are:

```
user=> (.printWords (:bayes bayes-out) 10)

Feature probabilities hoax
apos 0.002311333180377461
lights 0.0022688454380911096
light 0.00217537240506114
object 0.0020988944689457082
sky 0.002081899372031169
quot 0.0015295587223086145
looked 0.0014360856892786434
craft 0.0011556665901887302
```

```
red 0.0011301739448169206
back 0.0010961837509878402
```

```
Feature probabilities non-hoax
object 0.016553223428401043
light 0.016198059821948316
apos 0.015460989114397925
lights 0.014296272431730976
sky 0.014028337606877127
```

quot 0.010350232305991571

bright 0.007963812802535785

time 0.007237239541481537

moving 0.007063281856688359

```
looked 0.007037538118852588
```

So the terms are in slightly different order, but the vocabulary describing hoaxes and non-hoaxes is almost identical. Both mention *object*, *light*, *lights*, *sky*, and *looked*. So, based on the features we've selected here (single-word tokens), it's not surprising that we didn't get good results.

However, the primary thing that we can learn is that hoaxes are considered to be extremely rare, and the decision that a sighting is a hoax or not is often based on external data. Consider the sighting quoted earlier. To support the judgment that the sighting is not a hoax, the commenter mentions that they have a stable job, even though that's not mentioned in the description itself.

Summary

This has been a wandering and hopefully fun trip through the UFO sightings dataset. We've learned something about the language used in describing close encounters, and we've learned about how to use visualizations, exploratory data analysis, and Naïve Bayesian classification to learn more about the data.

But the primary impression I have of this is the feedback analysis, visualization, and exploration. The visualization led us to topic modeling, and something we discovered there led us to Bayesian classification. This is typical of data analysis, where one thing we learn informs and motivates the next stage in the analysis. Each answer can raise further questions and drive us back into the data.

5
Benford's Law – Detecting Natural Progressions of Numbers

In this chapter, we'll look at **Benford's Law**; an interesting set of properties that are inherent in many naturally occurring sequences of numbers. For these sets of numbers, this observation predicts the distribution of initial digits.

The odd rule captures an interesting observation about the way numbers are distributed, and it's useful too. Benford's Law has been used as an evidence of fraud. If a sequence of numbers should be naturally occurring but Benford's Law indicates that they are not, then the sequence is likely to be fraudulent. For example, the daily balances in your bank account should follow Benford's Law, but if they don't, that may be evidence that someone is cooking the books.

Learning about Benford's Law

Originally, Benford's Law was observed by the astronomer Simon Newcomb in 1881. He was referencing the logarithm tables, which were tomes listing the values for logarithms of different numbers. He noticed that the pages of the books were more worn out and discolored at the beginning than they were at the end. In fact, the pages that deal with numbers that begin with *1* were significantly more worn out than pages that begin with *9*. As the initial digits climbed, the pages were less and less worn.

This phenomenon was noticed again in 1938 by the physicist Frank Benford. He tested this against data in a number of domains, and the principle now bears his name.

In practical terms, this means that about one-third of the numbers in the sequence begin with the digit *1*, a little more than 15 percent begin with *2*, about 12 percent begin with *3*, and the rest until the digit *9* are all below 10 percent. Five percent of the numbers begin with *9*. The following is a graphical representation of Benford's law:

Benford's Law

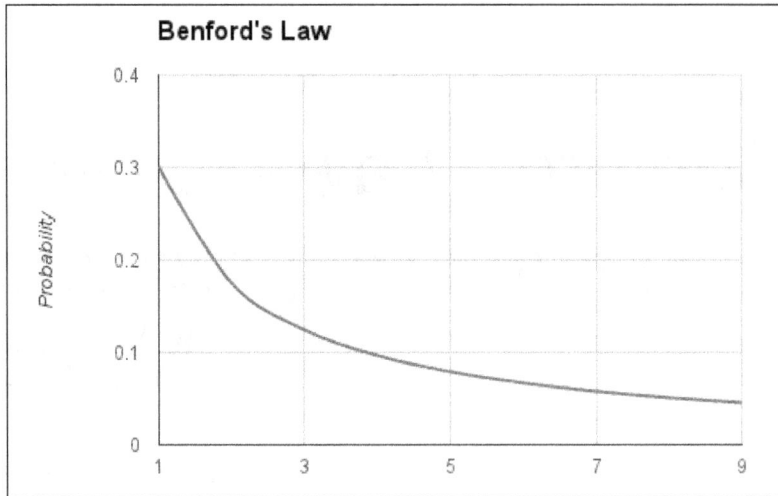

So what's the logic behind this? Although the observation itself is surprising, understanding it is really not that difficult. Let's walk through an example to see what we can learn.

First, we'll take the example of putting a 100 dollars in the bank and earning an unheard-of 10 percent interest per year, compounded monthly, where the annual interest rate is divided evenly by the number of times it is compounded (in this case, 12), and that is the effective interest rate used each for compounding period. This behavior is evident in more typical interest rates too, but it takes a longer span of time. Let's look at a table of the end-of-year reports for this account:

Year	Amount in dollars
0	100.00
1	110.47
2	122.04
3	134.82
4	148.94
5	164.53
6	181.76
7	200.79

Year	Amount in dollars
8	221.82
9	245.04
10	270.70
11	299.05
12	330.36
13	364.96
14	403.17
15	445.39
16	492.03
17	543.55
18	600.47
19	663.35
20	732.81
21	809.54
22	894.31
23	987.96
24	1,091.41

When the money in a bank account is compounded, the amount of money increases nonlinearly. That is, as the 0.30 dollars of interest that I accrued last month is now earning interest, this month, I'll earn 0.32 dollars. As each month's interest is rolled back into the balance, the amount increases faster and faster.

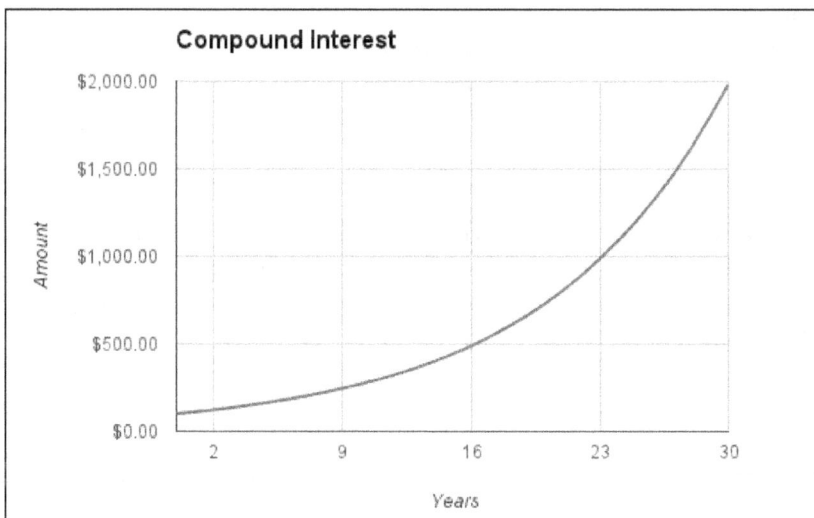

Looking at the balances, we can see that the amount stays in the 100s longer than it does in any other number (seven years). It only stays five years in the 200s. Finally, it stays in the 900s for only one year, at which point it rolls over, and the process starts all over again. Because there is less to work with and grow on, the lower the number (that is, in the 100s), the longer the graph will take to grow out of that range.

This pattern is common in any geometrically increasing amounts. Populations increase in this way, as do many other sequences.

However, concrete examples are always good. In this chapter, we'll work through several concrete examples. Then, we'll see what a failure of Benford's Law looks like, and finally, we'll look at an example of its use in life.

Applying Benford's law to compound interest

For the first illustration, let's keep working with the example we just started with.

There are good implementations of analyses using Benford's Law already in a number of libraries — we'll use **Incanter** (http://incanter.org/) for the examples later in the chapter — but to better understand what's going on, we'll write our own implementation first. To get started, the project.clj file for this chapter is as follows:

```
(defproject benford "0.1.0-SNAPSHOT"
  :dependencies [[org.clojure/clojure "1.5.1"]
                 [org.clojure/data.csv "0.1.2"]
                 [incanter "1.5.2"]]])
```

The namespace declaration is as follows:

```
(ns benford.core
  (:require [clojure.string :as str]
            [clojure.java.io :as io]
            [clojure.pprint :as pp]
            [clojure.data.csv :as csv]
            [incanter.stats :as s]))
```

First, we need a way to take a sequence of numbers and pull the first digit out of each. There are a couple of ways to do this. We could do this mathematically by repeatedly dividing by ten until the value is less than ten. At that point, we take the integer portion of the result.

However, we'll do something simpler for this. We'll convert the number to a string and use a simple regular expression to skip over any signs or prefixes and just take the first digit. We'll convert that single digit back into an integer as follows:

```
(defn first-digit [n]
  (Integer/parseInt (re-find #"\d" (str n))))
```

Now, extracting the first digits for each item in a sequence of numbers becomes simple:

```
(defn first-digit-freq [coll]
  (frequencies (map first-digit coll)))
```

Let's use these to pull the first digit from the yearly balances of the compound interest data, and we can graph them against the expected probabilities for Benford's Law.

The graph that is the result of this analysis is shown as follows. It looks at 25 years of accumulated interest, which is enough to go from 100 dollars to more than 1,000 dollars.

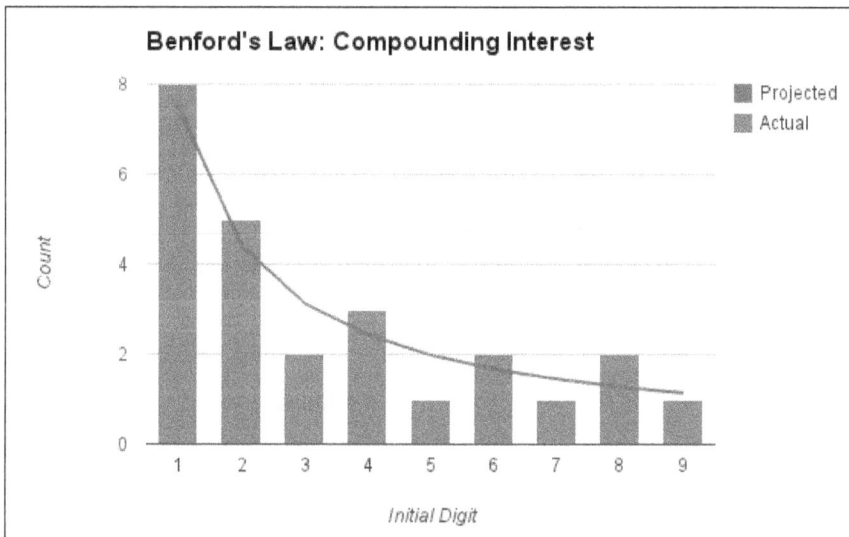

This gives us an idea of just how close the number sequence is. However, while the bars appear to match the line, they don't quite match. Are they close enough? We need to apply a simple statistical test to find out the answer.

First, we'll need a function that computes the expected value for sequences that conform to Benford's Law. This will take a digit and return the expected proportion for the number of times that digit starts the sequence:

```
(defn benford [d]
  (Math/log10 (+ 1.0 (/ 1.0 (float d)))))
```

We can use this to produce the full sequence of ratios for Benford's Law. We can see that the blue line in the preceding graph tracks the following values:

```
user=> (map benford (range 1 10))
(0.3010299956639812 0.17609125905568124 0.12493873660829993
   0.09691001300805642 0.07918124604762482 0.06694678963061322
   0.05799194697768673 0.05115252244738129 0.04575749056067514)
```

Next, we'll need a statistical function to test whether the frequencies of digits in a sequence match these values or not. As this is categorical data, Pearson's X^2 (**chi-squared**) test is commonly used to test for conformance with Benford's Law.

The formula for the X^2 test is simple. This uses o for the observed data and e for the expected data. n is the number of the categories of data. For example, numbers that begin with 1 are one category. In the case of testing against Benford's law, n will always be 9.

The formula for an X^2 test looks like what is shown in the following figure:

$$X^2 = \sum_{i=1}^{N} \frac{(O_i - E_i)^2}{E_i}$$

This translates directly into Clojure. The only wrinkle here is that we need to compare the same quantities. This uses ratios for the expected values but raw frequencies for the observed data. So we take the total number of observations and scale the expected ratios to match it:

```
(defn x-sqr [expected-ratios observed]
  (let [total (sum observed)
        f (fn [e o]
            (let [n (- o e)]
              (/ (* n n) e)))]
    (sum (map f (map #(* % total) expected-ratios) observed)))))
```

We can tie together the X^2 function to the expected values from Benford's Law:

```
(defn benford-test [coll]
  (let [freqs (first-digit-freq coll)
        digits (range 1 10)]
    (x-sqr (map benford digits) (map freqs digits)))))
```

Let's see what kind of results it gives out:

```
user=> (benford-test data)
1.7653767101950812
```

What does this number mean? The way this test is set up, values close to zero indicate that the sequence conforms to Benford's Law.

The value we obtained here, `1.8`, is fairly close to zero, given the range of this function, so this looks good. However, we still need to know whether it's statistically significant or not. To find that, we need to find the `p-value` for this X^2. There is the probability that this would happen by chance.

However, before we can find that information for an X^2 test, we have to know the degrees of freedom in our experiment. This is the number of variables that are free to vary. Generally, for X^2, the degree of freedom is one less than the number of cells in the test, so for Benford's Law, the degrees of freedom will be eight.

We use this information to find the value's probability of occurring in a X^2 cumulative distribution. A cumulative distribution is the probability that a value or lesser value would occur. While a probability distribution gives the probability of x having a given value, a cumulative distribution gives the probability that x is less than or equal to that value. Incanter has a CDF for X^2 in `incanter.stats/cdf-chisq`. We can use this to find p for any output of the X^2 test:

```
user=> (s/cdf-chisq 1.7653 :df 8 :lower-tail? false)
0.9873810658453659
```

This is a very high p-value. We'd like it to be above 0.05; any value below that would indicate that this data did not follow Benford's law. (We'll get into the reasons for this in *Chapter 7, Null Hypothesis Tests – Analyzing Crime Data* when we discuss the null-hypothesis testing.) As it's higher, it's clear that this sequence of numbers tracks the predications of Benford's Law. There is no evidence of tampering here.

Looking at the world population data

For the next example, let's look at the world population data. I downloaded this from **World DataBank** (`http://databank.worldbank.org/`). To download it to your computer, use the following steps:

1. Navigate to the **World Development Indicators** database.
2. Select all countries.
3. Select **Population (Total)**.

4. Select all years.

5. Click on **Download** and download the data as a CSV file.

6. To make it easier to reference later, I moved and renamed this file `data/population.csv`.

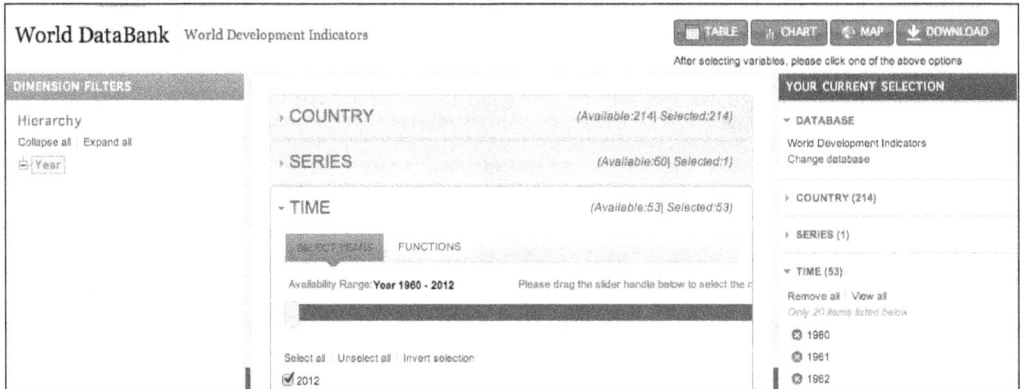

Now, let's read in this data. To make this easier, we'll write a function that reads in a CSV file, and from each row, create a map that uses the values from the header row as keys. The data for this looks like the following code snippet, which lists the header row and one data row:

```
Country Name,Country Code,Indicator Name,Indicator Code,1960
[YR1960],1961 [YR1961],1962 [YR1962],1963 [YR1963],1964 [YR1964],1965
[YR1965],1966 [YR1966],1967 [YR1967],1968 [YR1968],1969 [YR1969],1970
[YR1970],1971 [YR1971],1972 [YR1972],1973 [YR1973],1974 [YR1974],1975
[YR1975],1976 [YR1976],1977 [YR1977],1978 [YR1978],1979 [YR1979],1980
[YR1980],1981 [YR1981],1982 [YR1982],1983 [YR1983],1984 [YR1984],1985
[YR1985],1986 [YR1986],1987 [YR1987],1988 [YR1988],1989 [YR1989],1990
[YR1990],1991 [YR1991],1992 [YR1992],1993 [YR1993],1994 [YR1994],1995
[YR1995],1996 [YR1996],1997 [YR1997],1998 [YR1998],1999 [YR1999],2000
[YR2000],2001 [YR2001],2002 [YR2002],2003 [YR2003],2004 [YR2004],2005
[YR2005],2006 [YR2006],2007 [YR2007],2008 [YR2008],2009 [YR2009],2010
[YR2010],2011 [YR2011],2012 [YR2012],2013 [YR2013]

Afghanistan,AFG,Population (Total),SP.POP.TOTL,8774440,8953544,9141783
,9339507,9547131,9765015,9990125,10221902,10465770,10729191,11015621,1
1323446,11644377,11966352,12273589,12551790,12806810,13034460,13199597
,13257128,13180431,12963788,12634494,12241928,11854205,11528977,112624
39,11063107,11013345,11215323,11731193,12612043,13811876,15175325,1648
5018,17586073,18415307,19021226,19496836,19987071,20595360,21347782,22
202806,23116142,24018682,24860855,25631282,26349243,27032197,27708187,
28397812,29105480,29824536,..
```

The first function for this is `read-csv`:

```
(defn read-csv [filename]
  (with-open [f (io/reader filename)]
    (let [[row & reader] (csv/read-csv f)
          header (map keyword
                      (map #(str/replace % \space \-) row))]
      (doall
        (map #(zipmap header %) reader)))))
```

From this, we can create another function that reads in the population file and pulls out all the year columns and returns all the populations for all countries for all years in one long sequence:

```
(defn read-databank [filename]
  (let [year-keys (map keyword (map str (range 1960 2013)))]
    (->> filename
      read-csv
      (mapcat #(map (fn [f] (f %)) year-keys))
      (remove empty?)
      (map #(Double/parseDouble %))
      (remove zero?))))
```

One of the problems with the X^2 test is that it is very sensitive to the sample size. Small samples (less than 50) will almost always have a high `p-value`. Likewise, large samples incline toward low `p-values`. In general, samples between 100 and 2,500 observations are a good range, but even in this range, we can see some variance. It's easy to create a function that returns a random subset of a collection. The only problem with using it is that the value of the statistical tests is dependent on the nature of the sample returned. However, that is always the problem with samples:

```
(defn sample [coll k]
  (if (<= (count coll) k)
    coll
    (let [coll-size (count coll)]
      (loop [seen #{}]
        (if (>= (count seen) k)
          (map #(nth coll %) (sort seen))
          (recur (conj seen (rand-int coll-size))))))))
```

Now we can put all of this together. For the last example, we used our own functions to perform the Benford's test and the X^2 on the output. This time, we'll use Incanter's function for this purpose from `incanter.stats`. This also looks up the p-value from the X^2 distribution, so it's a bit handier than doing it in two steps:

```
user=> (def population (b/read-databank "data/population.csv"))
#'user/population
user=> (def pop-test (s/benford-test (b/sample population 100)))
#'user/pop-test
user=> (:X-sq pop-test)
7.926272852944953
user=> (:p-value pop-test)
0.4407050181730324
```

As the value of p is greater than 0.05, this appears to conform to Benford's Law. Graphing this makes the p-Benford's Law relationship clearer. If anything, this seems a better fit than the preceding compounding interest data:

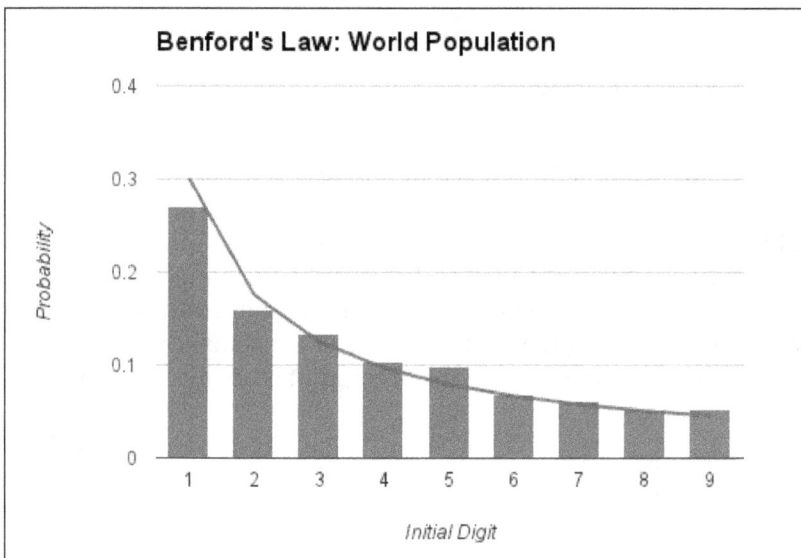

Again, it appears that this data also conforms to Benford's Law.

Failing Benford's Law

So far, we've seen several datasets, all of which conform to Benford's Law, most of them quite strongly. We haven't yet seen a dataset that does not conform to this distribution of initial digits. What would a failing dataset look like?

There are many ways in which we could get data that doesn't conform. Any linear data, for example, would have a more uniform distribution of the initial digits. However, we can also simulate fraudulent data easily, and in the process, we can learn just how much noise a dataset can handle before Benford's Law begins to have trouble with it.

We'll start this experiment with the population data that we looked at earlier. We'll progressively introduce more and more junk into the dataset. We'll randomly replace items in the dataset with a random value and re-run `incanter.stats/benford-test` on it. When it finally fails, we can note how many items we've replaced and how far off the new distribution is.

The primary function is shown as follows. There are a few utilities, and you can look into the code download for their definitions:

```
(defn make-fraudulent
  ([data] (make-fraudulent data 1 0.05 1000))
  ([data block sig-level k]
   (let [get-rand (make-rand-range-fn data)]
     (loop [v (vec (sample data k)), benford (s/benford-test v),
            n 0, ps [], swapped #{}]
       (println n \. (:p-value benford))
       (if (< (:p-value benford) sig-level)
         {:n n, :benford benford, :data v, :p-history ps,
          :swapped swapped}
         (let [[new-v new-swapped]
               (swap-random
                 v swapped #(rand-int k) get-rand block)
               benford (s/benford-test new-v)]
           (recur new-v benford (inc n)
                  (conj ps (:p-value benford))
                  new-swapped)))))))
```

This function is primarily a loop. At each step, it checks whether the p-value is low enough to declare the job as finished. If so, it returns the information it has collected so far.

If this isn't done, it swaps out `block` indexes, recomputes a new p-value, and stores the information it tracks.

This isn't a particularly efficient process. It is essentially a random walk over the data space. Sometimes, it actually improves the sequence's fit. However, because there's more space that isn't close to the probabilities that Benford's Law predicates for the digits, the values eventually wander off into areas with worse fit and lower `p-values`. The following is a graph from one run that began with a `p-value` around 0.05. Instead of immediately dropping below 0.05, it goes up to about 0.17 before finally and gradually, dropping below 0.05 around the iteration number 160.

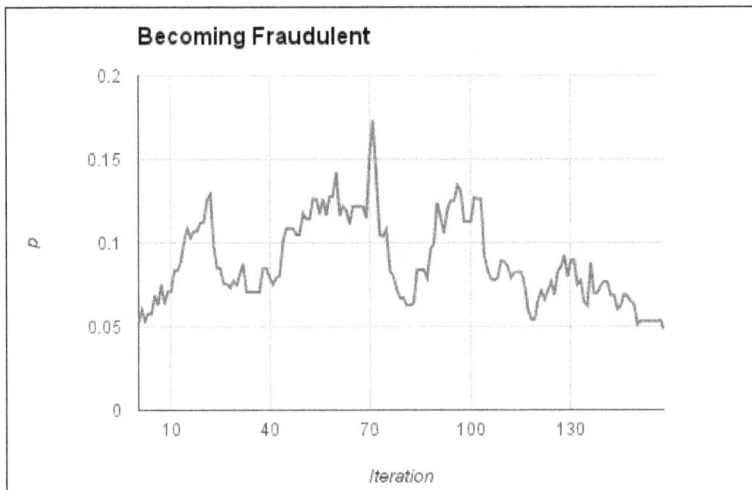

Looking at the final data from this process is also interesting. It's really not as different from the regular Benford's curve as you might expect it to be. It appears that the problem has too few twos and too many eights and nines.

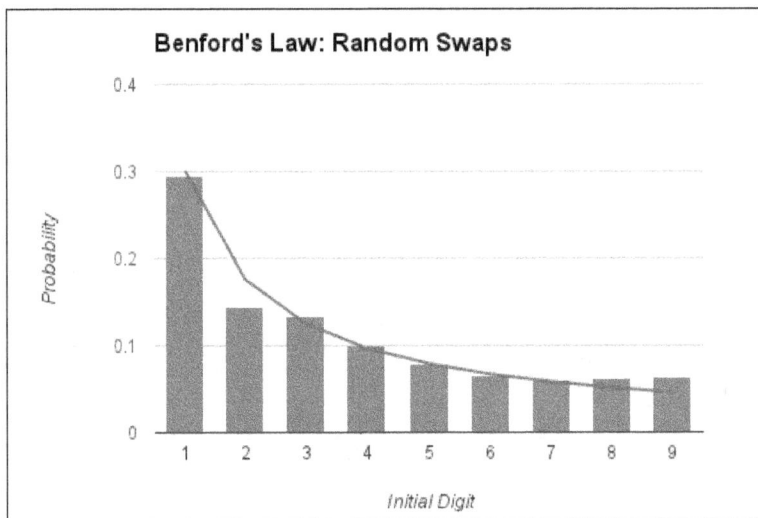

Case studies

This has all been very interesting but not exactly useful. So, can Benford's Law be useful? The answer is *yes*. In fact, analyses using Benford's Law is admissible in the United States courts. To get an idea for some uses of this analysis, let's take a look at a moderately well-publicized case where Benford's law was used.

The 2009 Iranian presidential election committee gathered analyses into whether the elections were fraudulent or not. Some of these used Benford's Law. One major article on this was *A first-digit anomaly in the 2009 Iranian presidential election* by Boudewijn F. Roukema (http://arxiv.org/abs/0906.2789). In this study, the author analyzes the first digit of vote counts in the election results publicized by the Iranian Ministry of the Interior on June 14, 2009. First, he analyzed first-round results for elections in immediately preceding years in other countries. This established a baseline or control to compare with. He also took into account the pre-election polls. This allowed him to establish the immediate political landscape in which the election was conducted.

Roukema then used a bootstrap to obtain a sample of the votes. In applying an analysis of the votes using Benford's Law, he found that there was a significant number of more vote counts beginning with the digit 7 than could be predicated by Benford's Law. In fact, the frequency of 7 was more in line with the frequency of the digit 3.

In another study of the 2009 Iranian elections, Walter R. Mebane, a forensics expert, used Benford's Law to analyze the first and second digits of the vote counts. Based particularly on the second digits, he also found evidence of fraud, especially in the counts of two of the candidates.

This seems like it should be clear-cut. However, several other people looked at this situation with varying degrees of thoroughness and failed to find anything. Several people wrote blog posts about doing cursory inspections of the data using Benford's Law, without finding evidence of any problems.

The Carter Center also questioned whether Benford's Law applied to election data at all, and in *The Irrelevance of Benford's Law for Detecting Fraud in Elections*, Joseph Deckert, Mikhail Myagkov, and Peter C. Ordenshook looked at election data from Ohio, Massachusetts, and Ukraine as well as at simulations of elections and concluded that Benford's Law does not, in fact, indicate election fraud well. Deviations in the frequencies of first and second digits do not reliably indicate fraud, and actual fraud may push the distributions into more compliance with Benford's Law. Thus, for a number of reasons, Benford's Law may not work well with the election data.

Summary

In many ways, Benford's Law seems like the perfect test for fraud and other misdeeds. It's intriguing, simple, and computationally cheap. However, as we've seen, it's not always reliable; X^2 tests can be finicky, and as evidence, it doesn't stand on its own. It really needs to be buttressed by other data and helps to support cases of fraud.

However, it is a piece of evidence. It provides a distribution that is difficult to mimic, and it describes a wide class of number sequences accurately. In combination with other information and evidences, it can provide support in the cases of misdeed.

We've also learned about X^2 tests, a very useful statistical procedure. Although they are sensitive to the sample size, these tests still have a lot to offer and are highly recommended. They're cheap to perform., and they work well with the categorical data or data that counts a limited, fixed number possibilities, such as sex or color. When used with appropriate sample sizes, they're straightforward to interpret.

In the end, we're again reminded that working with data is messy. Having a wide range of tools and techniques that we can apply to our researches and questions is critical to being able to successfully track down the information and analyses that we need.

In the next chapter, we'll look at using sentiment analysis to find positive and negative hotel reviews automatically. This turns out to be a more problematic and a more interesting problem than you might suspect at first.

6

Sentiment Analysis – Categorizing Hotel Reviews

People talk about a lot of things online. There are forums and communities for almost everything under the sun, and some of them may be about your product or service. People may complain, or they may praise, and you would want to know which of the two they're doing.

This is where sentiment analysis helps. It can automatically track whether the reviews and discussions are positive or negative overall, and it can pull out items from either category to make them easier to respond to or draw attention to.

Over the course of this chapter, we'll cover a lot of ground. Some of it will be a little hazy, but in general, here's what we'll cover:

- Exploring and preparing the data
- Understanding the classifiers
- Running the experiment
- Examining the error rates

Before we go any further, let's learn what sentiment analysis is.

Understanding sentiment analysis

Sentiment analysis is a form of text categorization that works on opinions instead of topics. Often, texts are categorized according to the subject they discuss. For example, sentiment analysis attempts to categorize texts according to the opinions or emotions of the writers, whether the text is about cars or pets. Often, these are cast in binary terms: good or bad, like or dislike, positive or negative, and so on. Does this person love Toyotas or hate them? Are Pugs the best or German Shepherds? Would they go back to this restaurant? Questions like these have proven to be an important area of research, simply because so many companies want to know what people say about their goods and services online. This provides a way for companies' marketing departments to monitor people's opinions about their products or services as they talk on Twitter and other online public forums. They can reach out to unhappy customers to provide better, more proactive customer service or reach out to satisfied ones to strengthen their relationships and opinions.

As you can imagine, categorizing based on opinion than on topics is much more difficult. Even basic words tend to take on multiple meanings that are very dependent on their contexts.

For example, take the word *good*. In a review, I can say that something is *good*. I can also say that it's not good, no good, or so far from good that It can almost see it on a clear day. On the other hand, I can say that something's *bad*. Or can I say that it's *not bad*. Or, if I'm stuck in the '80s, I can say that "I love it, it's so bad."

This is a very important and interesting problem, so people have been working on it for a number of years. An early paper on this topic came in 2002, *Thumbs up? Sentiment classification using machine learning techniques*, published by *Bo Pang, Lillian Lee*, and *Shivakumar Vaithyanathan*. In this paper, they compared movie reviews using naive Bayes' maximum entropy and support vector machines to categorize movie reviews into positive and negative. They also compared a variety of feature types such as unigrams, bigrams, and other combinations. In general, they found that support vector machines with single tokens performed best, although the difference wasn't usually huge.

Together and separately, *Bo Pang, Lillian Lee*, and many others have extended sentiment analysis in interesting ways. They've attempted to go beyond simple binary classifications toward predicting finer-grained sentiments. For example, they've worked on systems to predict from a document the number of stars the author of the review would give the reviewed service or object on a four-star or five-star rating system.

Part of what makes this interesting is that the baseline is how well the system explicitly agrees with the judgment of the human raters. However, in research, human raters only agree about 79 percent of the time, so a system that agrees with human raters 60 or 70 percent of the time is doing pretty well.

Getting hotel review data

For this chapter, we'll look at the **OpinRank Review** dataset (`http://archive.ics.uci.edu/ml/datasets/OpinRank+Review+Dataset`). This is a dataset that contains almost 260,000 reviews for hotels (`http://tripadvisor.com/`) from around the world on **TripAdvisor** as well as more than 42,000 car reviews (`http://edmunds.com/`) from 2007, 2008, and 2009 on **Edmunds**.

Exploring the data

If we look at some of these reviews, we can see just how difficult categorizing the reviews as positive or negative is, even for humans.

For instance, some words are used in ways that aren't associated with their straightforward meaning. For example, look at the use of the term *greatest* in the following quote from a review for a Beijing hotel:

> *"Not the greatest area but no problems, even at 3:00 AM."*

Also, many reviews recount both good and bad aspects of the hotel that they're discussing, even if the final review decidedly comes down one way or the other. This review of a London hotel starts off listing the positives, but then it pivots:

> *"… These are the only real positives. Everything else was either average or below average…."*

Another reason why reviews are difficult to classify is that many reviews just don't wholeheartedly endorse whatever it is they're reviewing. Instead, the review will be tepid, or the reviewers qualify their conclusions as they did in this review for a Las Vegas hotel:

> *"It's faded, but it's fine. If you're on a budget and want to stay on the Strip, this is the place. But for a really great inexpensive experience, try the Main Street Station downtown."*

All of these factors contribute toward making this task more difficult than standard document classification problems.

Preparing the data

For this experiment, I've randomly selected 500 hotel reviews and classified them manually. A better option might be to use Amazon's Mechanical Turk (https://www.mturk.com/mturk/) to get more reviews classified than any one person might be able to do easily. Really, a few hundred is about the minimum that we'd like to use as both the training and test sets need to come from this. I made sure that the sample contained an equal number of positive and negative reviews. (You can find the sample in the data directory of the code download.)

The data files are **tab-separated values** (**TSV**). After being manually classified, each line had four fields: the classification as a + or - sign, the date of the review, the title of the review, and the review itself. Some of the reviews are quite long.

After tagging the files, we'll take those files and create feature vectors from the vocabulary of the title and create a review for each one. For this chapter, we'll see what works best: unigrams (single tokens), bigrams, trigrams, or part-of-speech annotated unigrams. These features comprise several common ways to extract features from the text:

- Unigrams are single tokens, for example, features from the preceding sentence
- Bigrams are two tokens next to each other, for example, *features comprise*
- Trigrams are three tokens next to each other, for example, *features comprise several*
- Part-of-speech annotated unigrams would look something like features_N, which just means that the unigram features is a noun.

We'll also use these features to train a variety of classifiers on the reviews. Just like *Bo Pang* and *Lillian Lee* did, we'll try experiments with naive Bayes maximum entropy classifiers. To compare how well each of these does, we'll use cross validation to train and test our classifier multiple times.

Tokenizing

Before we get started on the code for this chapter, note that the Leiningen 2 project. clj file looks like the following code:

```
(defproject sentiment "0.1.0-SNAPSHOT"
:plugins [[lein-cljsbuild "0.3.2"]]
:dependencies [[org.clojure/clojure "1.5.1"]
               [org.clojure/data.csv "0.1.2"]
               [org.clojure/data.json "0.2.3"]
               [org.apache.opennlp/opennlp-tools "1.5.3"]
```

```
                [nz.ac.waikato.cms.weka/weka-dev "3.7.7"]]
:jvm-opts ["-Xmx4096m"])
```

First, let's create some functions to handle tokenization. Under the cover's, we'll use methods from the **OpenNLP** library (http://opennlp.apache.org/) to process the next methods from the **Weka machine learning** library (http://www.cs.waikato.ac.nz/ml/weka/) to perform the sentiment analysis. However, we'll wrap these to provide a more natural, Clojure-like interface.

Let's start in the src/sentiment/tokens.clj file, which will begin in the following way:

```
(ns sentiment.tokens
  (:require [clojure.string :as str]
            [clojure.java.io :as io])
  (:import [opennlp.tools.tokenizeSimpleTokenizer]
           [opennlp.tools.postagPOSModelPOSTaggerME]))
```

Our tokenizer will use SimpleTokenizer from the OpenNLP library and normalize all characters to lowercase:

```
(defn tokenize [s]
  (map (memfn toLowerCase)
       (seq
         (.tokenize SimpleTokenizer/INSTANCE s))))
```

I've aliased the sentiment.tokens namespace to t in the REPL. This function is used to break an input string into a sequence of token substrings:

```
user=> (t/tokenize "How would this be TOKENIZED?")
("how" "would" "this" "be" "tokenized" "?")
```

Next, we'll take the token streams and create feature vectors from them.

Creating feature vectors

A feature vector is a vector that summarizes an observation or document. Each vector contains the values associated with each variable or feature. The values may be boolean, indicating the presence or absence with 0 or 1, they may be raw counts, or they may be proportions scaled by the size of the overall document. As much of machine learning is based on linear algebra, vectors and matrices are very convenient data structures.

In order to maintain consistent indexes for each feature, we have to maintain a mapping from feature to indexes. Whenever we encounter a new feature, we need to assign it to a new index.

For example, the following table traces the steps to create a feature vector based on token frequencies from the phrase *the cat in the hat*.

Step	Feature	Index	Feature Vector
1	the	0	[1]
2	cat	1	[1, 1]
3	in	2	[1, 1, 1]
4	the	0	[2, 1, 1]
5	hat	3	[2, 1, 1, 1]

So, the final feature vector for *the cat in the hat* would be [2, 1, 1, 1]. In this case, we're counting the features. In other applications, we might use a bag-of-words approach that only tests the presence of the features. In that case, the feature vector would be [1, 1, 1, 1].

We'll include the code to do this in the sentiment.tokens namespace. First, we'll create a function that increments the value of a feature in the feature vector. It looks up the index of the feature in the vector from the feature index (f-index). If the feature hasn't been seen yet, this function also allocates an index for it:

```
(defn inc-feature [f-index f-vec feature]
  (if-let [i (f-index feature)]
    [f-index, (assoc f-veci (inc (nth f-veci)))]
    (let [i (count f-index)]
      [(assoc f-index feature i), (assoc f-veci 1)])))
```

We can use this function to convert a feature sequence into a feature vector. This function initially creates a vector of zeroes for the feature sequence, and then it reduces over the features, updating the feature index and vector as necessary:

```
(defn ->feature-vec [f-index features]
  (reduce #(inc-feature (first %1) (second %1) %2)
          [f-index (vec (repeat (count f-index) 0))]
          features))
```

Finally, for this task, we have several functions that we'll look at together. The first function, accum-features, builds the index and the list of feature vectors. Each time it's called, it takes the sequence of features passed to it and creates a feature vector. It appends this to the collection of feature vectors also passed into it. The next function, pad-to, makes sure that the feature vector has the same number of elements as the feature index. This makes it slightly easier to work with the feature vectors later on. The final function takes a list of feature vectors and returns the feature index and vectors for this data:

```
(defnaccum-features [state features]
   (let [[index accum] state
         [new-index feature] (->feature-vec index features)]
     [new-index (conj accum feature)]]))

(defn pad-to [f-index f-vec]
  (vec (take (count f-index) (concat f-vec (repeat 0)))))

(defn ->features [feature-seq]
   (let [[f-index f-vecs]
         (reduce accum-features [{} []] feature-seq)]
     [f-index (map #(pad-to f-index %) f-vecs)]))
```

We can use these functions to build up a matrix of feature vectors from a set of input sentences. Let's see how this works in the first few sentences of an *Emily Dickinson* poem:

```
user=> (def f-out
         (t/->features
           (map set
             (map t/tokenize ["I'm nobody."
                              "Who are you?"
                              "Are you nobody too?"]))))
#'user/f-out
user=> (first f-out)
{"nobody" 0, "'" 1, "i" 2, "m" 3, "." 4, "too" 9, "are" 5,
 "who" 6, "you" 7, "?" 8}
user=> (print (second f-out))
([1 1 111 0 0000] [0 0 000 1 111 0]
 [1 0 000 1 0 1 11])
```

Notice that after tokenizing each document, we created a set of the tokens. This changes the system here to use a bag-of-words approach. We're only looking at the presence or absence of a feature, not its frequency. This does put the tokens out of order, nobody was evidently the first token indexed, but this doesn't matter.

Now, by inverting the feature index, we can look up the words in a document from the features that it contains. This allows us to recreate a frequency map for each document as well as to recreate the tokens in each document. In this case, we'll look up the words from the first feature vector, I'm nobody:

```
user=> (def index (map first (sort-by second (first f-out))))
#'user/index
```

```
user=> index
("nobody" "'" "i" "m" "." "are" "who" "you" "?" "too")
user=> (->> f-out
second
first
        (map-indexed vector)
        (remove #(zero? (second %)))
        (map first)
        (map #(nth index %)))
("nobody" "'" "i" "m" ".")
```

This block of code gets the indexes for each position in the feature vector, removes the features that didn't occur, and then looks up the index in the inverted feature index. This provides us with the sequence of features that occurred in that document. Notice that they're out of order. This is to be expected because neither the input sequence of features (in this case a set) nor the feature vector itself preserves the order of the features.

Creating feature vector functions and POS tagging

We'll also include some functions to turn a list of tokens into a list of features. By wrapping these into functions, we make it easier to compose pipelines of processing functions and experiment with different feature sets.

The simplest and probably the most common type of feature is the unigram or a single token. As the `tokenize` function already outputs single functions, the `unigram` function is very simple to implement:

```
(def unigrams identity)
```

Another way to construct features is to use a number of consecutive tokens. In the abstract, these are called n-grams. Bigrams (two tokens) and trigrams (three tokens) are common instances of this type of function. We'll define all of these as functions:

```
(defn n-grams [n coll]
  (map #(str/join " " %) (partition n 1 coll)))
(defn bigrams [coll] (n-grams 2 coll))
(defn trigrams [coll] (n-grams 3 coll))
```

There are a number of different features we could create and experiment with, but we won't show them all here. However, before we move on, here's one more common type of feature: the token tagged with its **part of speech** (**POS**). POS is the category for words, which determines their range of uses in sentences. You probably remember these from elementary school. Nouns are people, places, and things. Verbs are actions.

To get this information, we'll use OpenNLP's trained POS tagger. This takes a word and associates it with a part of speech. In order to use this, we need to download the training model file. You can find it at `http://opennlp.sourceforge.net/models-1.5/`. Download **en POS tagger** (English) with a description of **Maxent model with tag dictionary**. The file itself is named `en-pos-maxent.bin`, and I put it into the `data` directory of my project.

This tagger uses the POS tags defined by the Penn Treebank (`http://www.cis.upenn.edu/~treebank/`). It uses a trained, probabilistic tagger to associate tags with each token from a sentence. For example, it might associate the token things with the NNS tag, which is the abbreviation for plural nouns. We'll create the string for this feature by putting these two together so that this feature would look like `things_NNS`.

Once we have the data file, we need to load it into a POS model. We'll write a function to do this and return the tagger object:

```
(defn read-me-tagger [filename]
  (->>filename
io/input-stream
POSModel.
POSTaggerME.))
```

Using the tagger is pretty easy. We just call its tag method as follows:

```
(defn with-pos [model coll]
  (map #(str/join "_" [%1 %2])
coll
      (.tag model (into-array coll))))
```

Now that we have these functions ready, let's take a short sentence and generate the features for it. For this set of examples, we'll use the clauses, Time flies like an arrow; fruit flies like a banana. To begin with, we'll define the input data and load the POS tagger.

```
user=> (def data
        "Time flies like an arrow; fruit flies like a banana.")
```

```
user=> (def tagger (t/read-me-tagger "data/en-pos-maxent.bin"))
user=> (def tokens (t/tokenize data))
user=> (t/unigrams tokens)
("time" "flies" "like" "an" "arrow" ";" "fruit" "flies" "like" "a"
 "banana" ".")
user=> (t/bigrams tokens)
("time flies" "flies like" "like an" "an arrow" "arrow ;"
 "; fruit" "fruit flies" "flies like" "like a" "a banana"
 "banana .")
user=> (t/trigrams tokens)
("time flies like" "flies like an" "like an arrow" "an arrow ;"
 "arrow ; fruit" "; fruit flies" "fruit flies like" "flies like a"
 "like a banana" "a banana .")
user=> (t/with-pos tagger tokens)
("time_NN" "flies_VBZ" "like_IN" "an_DT" "arrow_NN" ";_:"
 "fruit_NN" "flies_NNS" "like_IN" "a_DT" "banana_NN" "._.")
```

In the last output, the words are associated with part-of-speech tags. This output uses the tags from the Penn Treebank (http://www.cis.upenn.edu/~treebank/). You can look at it for more information, but briefly, here are the tags used in the preceding code snippet:

- NN means noun;
- VBZ means the present tense verb, third person, singular;
- IN means and, the preposition or subordinating conjunction
- DT means the determiner.

So we can see that the POS-tagged features provide the most data on the single tokens; however, the n-grams (bigrams and trigrams) provide more information about the context around each word. Later on, we'll see which one gets better results.

Now that we have the preprocessing out of way, let's turn our attention to the documents and how we want to structure the rest of the experiment.

Cross-validating the results

As I've already mentioned, the dataset for this chapter is a manually coded group of 500 hotel reviews taken from the OpinRank dataset. For this experiment, we'll break these into 10 chunks of 50 reviews each.

These chunks will allow us to use **K-fold cross validation** to test how our system is doing. Cross validation is a way of checking your algorithm and procedures by splitting your data up into equally sized chunks. You then train your data on all of the chunks but one; that is the training set. You calculate the error after running the trained system on the validation set. Then, you use the next chunk as a validation set and start over again. Finally, we can average the error for all of the trials.

For example, the validation procedure uses four folds, A, B, C, and D. For the first run, A, B, and C would be the training set, and D would be the test set. Next, A, B, and D would be the training set, and C would be the test set. This would continue until every fold is used as the test set once.

This may seem like a lot of work, but it helps us makes sure that we didn't just get lucky with our choice of training or validation data. It provides a much more robust way of estimating the error rates and accuracy of our classifier.

The main trick in implementing cross validation is that Clojure's native partitioning functions (`partition` and `partition-all`) don't handle extra items exactly the way we'd like. The `partition` function just throws the extras away, and `partition-all` sticks all of the extras to the end in a smaller group. What we'd like is to include the extras in the previous chunks. Each chunk should have one extra until all of the remainders are exhausted. To handle this, we'll define a function named `partition-spread`. It will partition the first part of the collection into larger chunks and the second part into smaller chunks.

Unfortunately, we'll need to know the size of the input collection. To do this, we must hold the entire collection in the memory at once, so this algorithm isn't good for very large sequences:

```
(defn partition-spread [k coll]
  (let [get-mod (fn [i x]
                  [(mod i k) x])
        map-second #(map second (second %))]
    (->>coll
      (map-indexed get-mod)
      (group-by first)
      (map map-second))))
```

We can now see how these partitioning functions differ:

```
user=> (partition 4 (range 10))
((0 1 2 3) (4 5 6 7))
user=> (partition-all 4 (range 10))
((0 1 2 3) (4 5 6 7) (8 9))
```

```
user=> (xv/partition-spread 4 (range 10))
((0 4 8) (1 5 9) (2 6) (3 7))
user=> (xv/partition-spread 3 (range 10))
((0 3 6 9) (1 4 7) (2 5 8))
```

We can also see that the semantics of the first parameter have changed. Instead of indicating the size of the partitions, it specifies the number of partitions. Now the partitions are all of a roughly equal size.

Next, we'll create a couple of functions that pull out each chunk to use as the validation set and concatenates all the other chunks.

```
(defn step-folds-seq [folds steps]
  (lazy-seq
    (when-let [[s &ss] (seq steps)]
      (let [[prefix [validation & suffix]] (split-at s folds)
training (flatten (concat prefix suffix))
current [validation training]]
        (cons current (step-folds-seq folds ss))))))
(defn step-folds [folds]
  (step-folds-seq folds (range (count folds))))
```

Now, by partitioning into chunks with one element each, we can clearly see just how the K-fold partitioning works. Each time, a new chunk is selected as the validation set (the first item), and the rest of the chunks are concatenated into the training set (the second item):

```
user=> (xv/step-folds (xv/partition-spread 10 (range 10)))
([(0) (1 2 3 4 5 6 7 8 9)] [(1) (0 2 3 4 5 6 7 8 9)]
 [(2) (0 1 3 4 5 6 7 8 9)] [(3) (0 1 2 4 5 6 7 8 9)]
 [(4) (0 1 2 3 5 6 7 8 9)] [(5) (0 1 2 3 4 6 7 8 9)]
 [(6) (0 1 2 3 4 5 7 8 9)] [(7) (0 1 2 3 4 5 6 8 9)]
 [(8) (0 1 2 3 4 5 6 7 9)] [(9) (0 1 2 3 4 5 6 7 8)])
```

Now we can define a function that controls the K-fold validation process. It takes the training and error steps as function parameters, and it just handles partitioning the data into groups, calling the training and error functions, and combining their output into one result:

```
(defn k-fold
  ([train error combine data]
   (k-fold train error combine 10 data))
  ([train error combine k input-data]
```

```
(->> input-data
 shuffle
     (partition-spread k)
 step-folds
     (map (fn [[v t]] [v (train t)]))
     (map (fn [[v t]] [err (error t v)]
                        (println :error err)
 err)))
     (reduce combine (combine)))))
```

Now we need to decide what constitutes an error and how we'll compute it.

Calculating error rates

To calculate the error rates on classification algorithms, we'll keep count of several things. We'll track how many positives are correctly and incorrectly identified as well as how many negatives are correctly and incorrectly identified. These values are usually called true positives, false positives, true negatives, and false negatives. The relationship of these values to the expected values and the classifier's outputs and to each other can be seen in the following diagram:

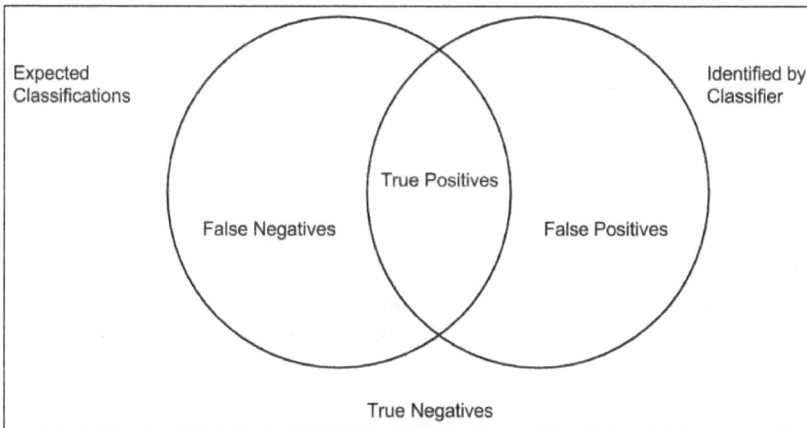

From these numbers, we'll first calculate the precision of the algorithm. This is the ratio of true positives to the number of all identified positives (both true and false positives). This tells us how many of the items that it identified as positives actually are positives.

We'll then calculate the recall. This is the ratio of true positives to all actual positives (true positives and false negatives). This gives us an idea of how many positives it's missing.

To calculate this, we'll use a standard `reduce` loop. First, we'll write the accumulator function for it. This will take a mapping of the counts that we need to tally and a pair of ratings, the expected and the actual. Depending on what they are and whether they match, we'll increment one of the counts as follows:

```
(defnaccum-error [error-counts pair]
   (let [get-key {["+" "+"] :true-pos
                  ["-" "-"] :true-neg
                  ["+" "-"] :false-neg
                  ["-" "+"] :false-pos}
  k (get-key pair)]
      (assoc error-counts k (inc (error-counts k))))))
```

Once we have the counts for a test set, we'll need to summarize these counts into the figure for precision and recall:

```
(defn summarize-error [error-counts]
   (let [{:keys [true-pos false-pos true-neg false-neg]}
error-counts]
      {:precision (float (/ true-pos (+ true-pos false-pos))),
:recall (float (/ true-pos (+ true-pos false-neg)))}))
```

With these two defined, the function to actually calculate the error is standard Clojure:

```
(defn compute-error [expecteds actuals]
   (let [start {:true-neg 0, :false-neg 0, :true-pos 0,
:false-pos 0}]
      (summarize-error
       (reduceaccum-error start (map vector expecteds actuals)))))
```

We can do something similar to determine the mean error of a collection of precision/recall mappings. We could simply figure the value for each key separately, but rather than walking over the collection multiple times, we will do something more complicated and walk over it once while calculating the sums for each key:

```
(defn mean-error [coll]
   (let [start {:precision 0, :recall 0}
accum (fn [a b]
                {:precision (+ (:precision a) (:precision b))
:recall (+ (:recall a) (:recall b))})
summarize (fn [n a]
                {:precision (/ (:precision a) n)
:recall (/ (:recall a) n)})]
      (summarize (count coll) (reduce accum start coll)))))
```

These functions will give us a good grasp of the performance of our classifiers and how well they do at identifying the sentiments expressed in the data.

Using the Weka machine learning library

We're going to test a couple of machine learning algorithms that are commonly used for sentiment analysis. Some of them are implemented in the OpenNLP library. However, they do not have anything for others algorithms. So instead, we'll use the Weka machine learning library (http://www.cs.waikato.ac.nz/ml/weka/). This doesn't have the classes to tokenize or segment the data that an application in a natural language processing requires, but it does have a more complete palette of machine learning algorithms.

All of the classes in the Weka library also have a standard, consistent interface. These classes are really designed to be used from the command line, so each takes its options as an array of strings with a command-line-like syntax. For example, the array for a naive Bayesian classifier may have a flag to indicate that it should use the kernel density estimator rather than the normal distribution. This would be indicated by the `-K` flag being included in the option array. Other options may include a parameter that would follow the option in the array. For example, the logistic regression classifier can take a parameter to indicate the maximum number of iterations it should run. This would include the items `-M` and `1000` (say) in the options array.

The Clojure interface functions for these classes are very regular. In fact, they're almost boilerplate. Unfortunately, they're also a little redundant. Option names are repeated in the functions' parameter list, the default values for those parameters, and where the parameters are fed into the options array. It would be better to have one place for a specification of each option, its name, its flag, its semantics, and its default value.

This is a perfect application of Clojure's macro system. The data to create the functions can be transformed into the function definition, which is then compiled into the interface function.

The final product of this is the `defanalysis` macro, which takes the name of the function, the class, the method it's based on, and the options it accepts. We'll see several uses of it later in this chapter.

Unfortunately, at almost 40 lines, this system is a little long and disruptive to include here, however interesting it may be. You can find this in the `src/sentiment/weka.clj` file in the code download, and I have discussed it in a bit more length in *Clojure Data Analysis Cookbook, Packt Publishing*.

We do still need to convert the `HotelReview` records that we loaded earlier into a `WekaInstances` collection. We'll need to do this several times as we train and test the classifiers, and this will provide us with a somewhat shorter example of interacting with Weka.

To store a data matrix, Weka uses an `Instances` object. This implements a number of standard Java collection interfaces, and it holds objects that implement the `Instance` interface, such as `DenseInstance` or `SparseInstance`.

Instances also keep track of which fields each item has in its collection of `Attribute` objects. To create these, we'll populate `ArrayList` with all of the features that we accumulated in the feature index. We'll also create a feature for the ratings and add it to `ArrayList`. We'll return both the full collection of the attributes and the single attribute for the review's rating:

```
(defn instances-attributes [f-index]
  (let [attrs (->> f-index
                (sort-by second)
                (map #(Attribute. (first %)))
ArrayList.)
review (Attribute. "review-rating"
                            (ArrayList. ["+" "-"]))]
    (.add attrs review)
    [attrs review]))
```

(At this point, we're hardcoding the markers for the sentiments as a plus sign and a negative sign. However, these could easily be made into parameters for a more flexible system.)

Each hotel review itself can be converted separately. As most documents will only have a fraction of the full number of features, we'll use `SparseInstance`. Sparse vectors are more memory efficient if most of the values in the instance are zero. If the feature is nonzero in the feature vector, we'll set it in `Instance`. Finally, we'll also set the rating attribute as follows:

```
(defn review->instance [attrs review]
  (let [i (SparseInstance. (.size attrs))]
    (doseq [[attr value] (map vector attrs (:feature-vec review))]
      (when-not (zero? value)
        (.setValueiattr (double value))))
    (.setValuei (last attrs) (:rating review))
i))
```

With these, we can populate `Instances` with the data from the `HotelReview` records:

```
(defn ->instances
  ([f-index review-coll]
   (->instances f-index review-coll "hotel-reviews"))
  ([f-index review-coll name]
   (let [[attrs review] (instances-attributes f-index)
```

```
instances (Instances. name attrs (count review-coll)))]
     (doseq [review review-coll]
       (let [i (review->instance attrs review)]
         (.add instances i)))
     (.setClass instances review)
instances)))
```

Now we can define some functions to sit between the cross-validation functions we defined earlier and the Weka interface functions.

Connecting Weka and cross-validation

The first of these functions will classify an instance and determine which rating symbol it is classified by (+ or -), given the distribution of probabilities for each category. This function is used to run the classifier on all data in an Instances object:

```
(defn run-instance [classifier instances instance]
  (let [dist (.distributionForInstance classifier instance)
i (first (apply max-key second
                      (map vector (range) dist)))]
    (.. instances classAttribute (value i))))
(defn run-classifier [classifier instances]
  (map #(run-instance classifier instances %) instances))
```

The next function defines the cross-validation procedure for a group of HotelReview records. This function actually takes a training function and returns a function that takes the feature index and collection of HotelReview records and actually performs the cross validation. This will allow us to create some wrapper functions for each type of classifier:

```
(defn run-k-fold [trainer]
  (fn [f-index coll]
    (let [do-train (fn [xs]
                     (let [is (w/->instances f-index xs)]
                       (trainer is)))
do-test (fn [classifier xs]
                  (->>xs
                    (w/->instances f-index)
w/filter-class-index
                    (run-classifier classifier)
                    (xv/compute-error (map :rating xs))
vector))]
      (xv/k-fold do-train do-test concat 10 coll))))
```

When executed, this function will return a list of ten of whatever the `do-test` function returns. In this case, that means a list of ten precision and recall mappings. We can average the output of this to get a summary of each classifier's performance.

Now we can start actually defining and testing classifiers.

Understanding maximum entropy classifiers

Maximum entropy (maxent) classifiers are, in a sense, very conservative classifiers. They assume nothing about hidden variables and base their classifications strictly upon the evidence they've been trained on. They are consistent with the facts that they've seen, but all other distributions are assumed to be completely uniform otherwise. What does this mean?

Let's say that we have a set of reviews and positive or negative ratings, and we wish to be able to predict the value of ratings when the ratings are unavailable, given the tokens or other features in the reviews. The probability that a rating is positive would be p(+). Initially, before we see any actual evidence, we may intuit that this probability would be uniform across all possible features. So, for a set of five features, before training, we might expect the probability function to return these values:

p(+)	½
p(-)	½

This is perfectly uniform but not very useful. We have to make observations from the data in order to train the classifier.

The process of training involves observing the features in each document and its rating and determining the probability of any given feature that is found in a document with a given rating. We'll denote this as p(x, y) or the probability as feature x and rating y.

These features impose constraints on our model. As we gather more and more constraints, figuring a consistent and uniform distribution for the non-constrained probabilities in the model becomes increasingly difficult.

Essentially, this is the maxent algorithm's job. It takes into account all of the constraints imposed by the probabilities found in the training data, but it maintains a uniform distribution on everything that's unconstrained. This provides a more consistent, stronger algorithm overall, and it still performs very well, usually. Also, cross validation can help us evaluate its performance.

Another benefit is that maxent doesn't make any assumptions about the relationships between different features. In a bit, we'll look at a naive Bayesian classifier, and it does make an assumption about the relationships between the features, an often unrealistic assumption. Because maxent does not make that assumption, it can better match the data involved.

For this chapter, we'll use the maxent classifier found in the Weka class, `weka. classifiers.functions.Logistic` (maxent is equivalent to the logistic regression, which attempts to classify data based on a binary categorical label, which is based on one or more features). We'll use the `defanalysis` macro to define a utility function that cross validates a logistic regression classifier as follows:

```
(w/defanalysis train-logistic Logistic buildClassifier
  [["-D" debugging false :flag-true]
   ["-R" ridge nil :not-nil]
   ["-M" max-iterations -1]])
(def k-fold-logistic (run-k-fold train-logistic))
```

Now let's define something similar for a naive Bayesian classifier.

Understanding naive Bayesian classifiers

A common, generally well-performing classifier is the naive Bayesian classifier. It's naive because it makes an assumption about that data and the features; it assumes that the features are independent of each other. That is, the probability of, say, *good* occurring in a document is not influenced at all by the probability of any other token or feature, such as, say, *not*. Unfortunately, language doesn't work this way, and there are dependencies all through the features of any linguistic dataset.

Fortunately, even when the data and features are not completely independent, this classifier often still performs quite well in practice. For example, in *An analysis of data characteristics that affect naive Bayes performance* by *Irina Rish, Joseph Hellerstein,* and *Jayram Thathachar*, it was found that Bayesian classifiers perform best with features that are completely independent or functionally dependent.

This classifier works by knowing several probabilities and then using Bayes' theorem to turn them around to predict the classification of the document. The following are the probabilities that it needs to know:

- It needs to know the probability for each feature in the training set. We'll call this **p(F)**. Say the word *good* occurs in 40 percent of the documents. This is the evidence of the classification.

- It needs to know the probability that a document will be part of a classification. We'll call this **p(C)**. Say that the rate of positive ratings in the corpus of reviews is 80 percent. This is the prior distribution.

- Now it needs to know the probability that the good feature is in the document if the document is rated positively. This is **p(F | C)**. For this hypothetical example, say that *good* appears in 40 percent of the positive reviews. This is the likelihood.

Bayes theorem allows us to turn this around and compute the probability that a document is positively rated, if it contains the feature *good*.

$$p\left(C \mid F\right) = \frac{p(C)p(F \mid C)}{p(F)}$$

For this example, this turns out to be `(0.8)(0.4) / 0.4`, or 0.8 (80 percent). So, if the document contains the feature *good*, it is very likely to be positively rated.

Of course, things begin to get more and more interesting as we start to track more and more features. If the document contains both *not* and *good*, for instance, the probability that the review is positive may change drastically.

The Weka implementation of a naive Bayesian classifier is found in `weka.classifiers.bayes.NaiveBayes`, and we'll wrap it in a manner that is similar to the one we used for the maxent classifier:

```
(w/defanalysis train-naive-bayesNaiveBayesbuildClassifier
  [["-K" kernel-density false :flag-true]
   ["-D" discretization false :flag-true]])
(def k-fold-naive-bayes (run-k-fold train-naive-bayes))
```

Now that we have both the classifiers in place, let's look again at the features we'll use and how we'll compare everything.

Running the experiment

Remember, earlier we defined functions to break a sequence of tokens into features of various sorts: unigrams, bigrams, trigrams, and POS-tagged unigrams. We can take these and automatically test both the classifiers against all of these types of features. Let's see how.

First, we'll define some top-level variables that associate label keywords with the functions that we want to test at that point in the process (that is, classifiers or feature-generators):

```
(def classifiers
  {:naive-bayes a/k-fold-naive-bayes
:maxent a/k-fold-logistic})
(def feature-factories
  {:unigram t/unigrams
:bigram t/bigrams
:trigram t/trigrams
:pos (let [pos-model
              (t/read-me-tagger "data/en-pos-maxent.bin")]
        (fn [ts] (t/with-pos pos-model ts)))})
```

We can now iterate over both of these hash maps and cross-validate these classifiers on these features. We'll average the error information (the precision and recall) for all of them and return the averages. Once we've executed that, we can spend some time looking at the results.

For the inner-most loop of this process, we'll take a collection of features and a classifier and cross validate them. This is pretty straightforward; it simply constructs an identifying key out of the keywords for the feature generator and the classifier, runs the cross validation, and averages the output error information as follows:

```
(defn do-class [f-key f-index features c-info]
  (let [[c-key c] c-info, k [c-key f-key]]
    (println k)
    [k (x/mean-error (c f-index features))])))
```

Now, given a set of features, we'll call do-class on each classifier one loop up. Constructing the loop this way by generating the features and then looping on the classifiers keeps us from needing to regenerate the same set of features multiple times:

```
(defn do-features [docs classifiers f-info]
  (let [[f-key f] f-info
        [f-index features] (d/add-features f docs)]
    (map #(do-class f-key f-index features %) classifiers)))
```

The controlling function for this process simply calls do-features on each set of feature-generating functions and stores all the outputs into a hash map:

```
(defn test-suite [docs]
  (into {} (mapcat #(do-features docs classifiers %)
feature-factories)))
```

This takes a while to execute:

```
user=> (def reviews (->> "data/hotels-sample" d/read-data
d/sample vals flatten))
#'user/reviews
user=> (c/test-suite reviews)
[:naive-bayes :unigram]
:error [{:precision 0.5185185, :recall 0.5}]
:error [{:precision 0.6, :recall 0.5769231}]
:error [{:precision 0.5185185, :recall 0.6666667}]
```

Now we can start looking at the data in more detail.

Examining the results

First, let's examine the precision of the classifiers. Remember that the precision is how well the classifiers do at only returning positive reviews. This indicates the percentage of reviews that each classifier has identified as being positive is actually positive in the test set:

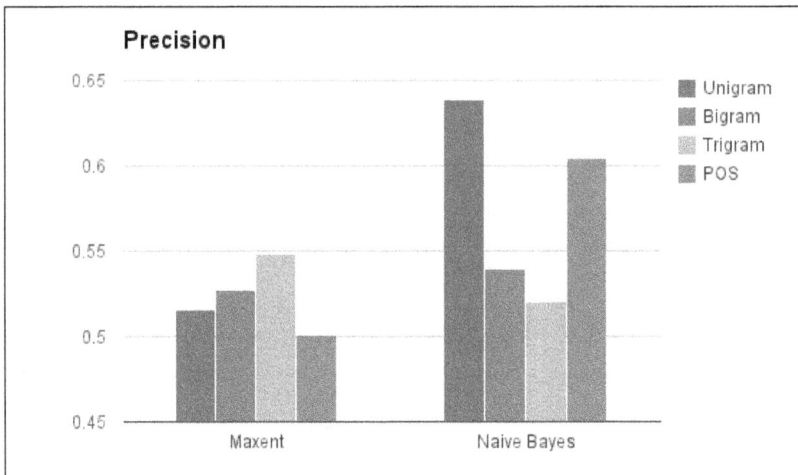

We need to remember a couple of things while looking at this graph. First, sentiment analysis is difficult, compared to other categorization tasks. Most importantly, human raters only agree about 80 percent of the time. So, the bar seen in the preceding figure that almost reaches 65 percent is actually decent, if not great. Still, we can see that the naive Bayesian classifier generally outperforms the maxent one for this dataset, especially when using unigram features. It performed less well for the bigram and trigram features, and slightly lesser for the POS-tagged unigrams.

We didn't try tagging the bigram and trigrams with POS information, but that might have been an interesting experiment. Based on what we can see here, these feature generators would not get better results than what we've already tested, but it would be good to know that more definitively.

It's interesting to see that maxent performed best with trigrams. Generally, compared to unigrams, trigrams pack more information into each feature, as they encode some implicit syntactical information into each feature. However, each feature also occurs fewer times, which makes performing some statistical processes on it more difficult. Remember that recall is the percentage of positives in the test set that were correctly identified by each classifier. Now let's look at the recall of these classifiers:

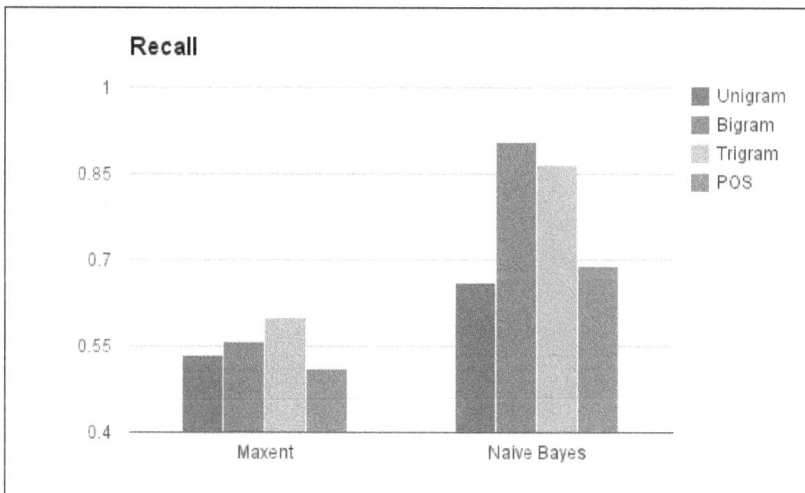

First, while the naive Bayesian classifier still outperforms the maxent classifier, this time the bigram and trigram get much better results than the unigram or POS-tagged features.

Also, the recall numbers on these two tests are better than any of the values for the precision. The best part is that the naive Bayes bigram test had a recall of just over 90 percent.

In fact, just looking at the results, there appeared to be an inverse relationship between the precision and the recall, as there typically is. Tests with high precision tended to have lower recall numbers and vice versa. This makes intuitive sense. A classifier can get a high recall number by marking more reviews as positive, but that negatively impacts its precision. Or, a classifier can have better precision by being more selective in what it marks as positive but also noting that will drag down its recall.

Combining the error rates

We can combine these two into a single metric using the harmonic mean of the precision and recall, also known as the F-measure. We'll compute this with the following function:

```
(defn f-score [error]
  (let [{:keys [precision recall]} error]
    (* 2 (/ (* precision recall) (+ precision recall)))))
```

This gives us a way to combine the precision and recall in a rational, meaningful manner. Let's see what values it gives for the F-measure:

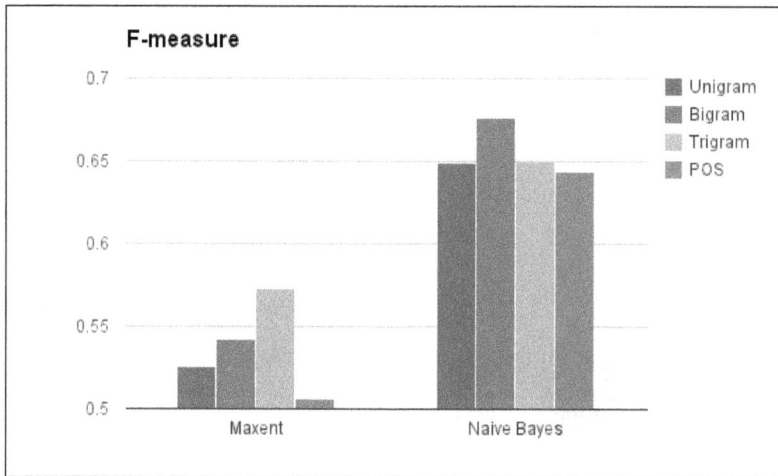

So, as we've already noticed, the naive Bayesian classifier performed better than the maxent classifier in general, and on balance, the bigram features worked best for this classifier.

While this gives us a good starting point, we'll also want to consider why we're looking for this information, how we'll use it, and what penalties are involved. If it's vitally important that we get all the positive reviews, then we will definitely want to use the naive Bayesian classifier with the bigram features. However, if the cost of missing some isn't so high but the cost of having to sort through too many false results is high, then we'll probably want to use unigram features, which would minimize the number of false results we have to manually sort through later.

Improving the results

What could we do to improve these results?

First, we should improve the test and training sets. It would be good to have multiple raters, say, have each review independently reviewed three times and use the rating that was chosen two or three times.

Most importantly, we'd like to have a larger and better test set and training set. For this type of problem, having 500 observations is really on the low end of what you can do anything useful with, and you can expect the results to improve with more observations. However, I do need to stress on the fact that more training data doesn't necessarily imply better results. It could help, but there are no guarantees.

We could also look at improving the features. We could select them more carefully, because having too many useless or unneeded features can make the classifier perform poorly. We could also select different features such as dates or information about the informants; if we had any data on them, it might be useful.

There has also been more recent work in moving beyond polarity classification, such as looking at emotional classification. Another way of being more fine grained than binary categorization is to classify the documents on a scale. For instance, instead of positive or negative, these classifiers could try to predict how the user would rate the product on a five-star scale, such as what has become popular on **Amazon** and many websites that include user ratings and reviews.

Once we have identified the positive or negative reviews, we can apply other analyses separately to those reviews, whether its topic modeling, named entity recognition, or something else.

Summary

In the end, sentiment analysis is a simple tool to analyze documents according to two complex, possibly ill-defined categories. Although language is used in complex ways, modern sentiment analysis techniques can do almost as well as humans, which, admittedly, isn't particularly efficient.

What's most powerful about these techniques is that they can provide answers to questions that cannot be answered in other ways. As such, they're an important part of the data analyst's toolbox.

In the next chapter, we'll look at null hypothesis testing, which is a standard and foundational technique of traditional statistics. This informs how we approach many experiments and how we frame the questions that we're asking. By following these guides, we can make sure that our results are more valid and generalizable.

7
Null Hypothesis Tests – Analyzing Crime Data

Getting started with data analysis can be so easy. We just plug numbers into a function or library and retrieve the results. But sometimes, it's easy to forget that we have to pay attention to how the data and experiments are constructed and how the questions are framed. Much of the reliability of statistics comes from following good practices and developed processes for framing and executing the tests and experiments.

Of course, there's a lot to setting up statistical experiments and following best practices in gathering data and applying statistical tests. We won't be able to do more than cursorily glance at this topic. Hopefully, either it will serve as a reminder of things you already know or it will outline what you need to know and point you in the right direction to learn more.

Over the course of this chapter, we'll move back and forth between looking at the problem we're tackling and seeing what null hypothesis testing is, how it can help us, and how we can apply it.

In this chapter, we will cover the following topics:

- Introducing confirmatory data analysis
- Understanding null hypothesis testing
- Understanding crime
- Getting the data
- Transforming the data
- Conducting the experiment
- Interpreting the results

So without any further delay, let's learn about the techniques and the problems we'll address with these methods in this chapter.

Introducing confirmatory data analysis

Oftentimes, data analysis seems like a menu of analyses applied to problems, but lacking an overall structure. Of course, this isn't the case, but it seems that way to programmers without a strong background in statistics.

Frameworks such as **confirmatory data analysis** and **null hypothesis testing** provide the structure that may be missing. Generally, when you begin working with data, you start by generating some summary statistics that highlight some of the basic characteristics of the data. Afterwards, you probably generate some graphs that further elucidate the essential qualities of the data. This all falls into the realm of **exploratory data analysis**.

However, as the exploration wraps up, you'll probably start to think of some theories about the data that you'd like to test. You'll generate some hypotheses, and you'll need to test whether they're true or not. And based on those tests, you'll further refine your knowledge of the data, what's in it, and what it means.

This more formal stage of data analysis represents confirmatory data analysis. At this stage, you're concerned with using reliable tests that match your data, and you're trying to determine how representative your sample is. You are minimizing error and trying to get a **pvalue** — the probability that a result so extreme could have happened by chance — that means that the results are statistically significant.

But what does all this mean, exactly? How do we go about conceptualizing, planning, and executing these tests?

Understanding null hypothesis testing

One common way of structuring and processing these tests is to use null hypothesis testing. This represents a **frequentist** approach to statistical inference. This draws inferences based upon the frequencies or proportions in the data, paying attention to confidence intervals and error rates. Another approach is Bayesian inference, which focuses on degrees of belief, but we won't go into that in this chapter.

Frequentist inference has been very successful. Its use is assumed in many fields, such as the social sciences and biology. Its techniques are widely implemented in many libraries and software packages, and it's relatively easy to start using it. It's the approach we'll use in this chapter.

Understanding the process

To use the null hypothesis process, we should understand what we'll be doing at each step of the way. The following is the basic process that we'll work through in this chapter:

1. Formulate an initial hypothesis.

2. State the null (H_0) and alternative (H_1) hypotheses.

3. Identify the statistical assumptions in the sample.

4. Determine which tests (T) are appropriate.

5. Select the significance level (a), such as $p<0.05$ or $p<0.01$.

6. Determine the critical region, that is, the region of the distribution in which the null hypothesis will be rejected.

7. Calculate the test statistic and the probability of the observation under the null hypothesis (p).

8. Either reject the null hypothesis or fail to reject it.

We'll go into these step-by-step, and we'll walk through this process twice to get a good feel for how it works. Most of this is pretty simple, really.

Formulating an initial hypothesis

Before we can start testing a theory about our data, we need to have something to test. This is generally something that might be true or false, and we want to determine which of the two it is. Some examples of initial hypotheses might be height correlating to diet, speed limit correlating to accident mortality, or a Super Bowl win for an old American Football League team (AFC division) correlating to a declining stock market (the so-called Super Bowl indicator).

Stating the null and alternative hypotheses

Now we have to reformulate the initial hypothesis into the statistical phrases that we'll use more directly the rest of the time. This is a useful point that helps to clarify the rest of the process.

In this case, the null hypothesis is the control, or what we're trying to disprove. It's the opposite of the alternative hypothesis, which is what we want to prove.

For example, in the last example from the previous section, the Super Bowl indicator, the re-cast hypotheses might be as follows:

- **Null hypothesis**: Who wins the Super Bowl has no effect upon the stock market.
- **Alternative hypothesis**: When an AFC division team wins the Super Bowl, the stock market will decline; when an NFC division team wins the Super Bowl, the stock market will be up.

For the rest of the process, we will concern ourselves with rejecting the null hypothesis. That can only happen when we've determined two things: first, that the data we have supports the alternative hypothesis, and second, that this is very unlikely to be a mistake; that is, the results we see probably are not a sample that misrepresents the underlying population.

This is going to keep coming up, so let's unpack it a little.

You're interested in making an observation about a population—all men; all women; all people; all statisticians; or past, present, and future stock market trends—but obviously you can't make an observation for every person or aspect in the population. So instead, you select a sample. It should be random. The question then becomes: does the sample accurately represent the population? Say you're interested in people's heights. How close is the sample's average height to the population's average height?

Let's assume that what we're interested in falls on a normal distribution, as height generally does. What would this look like? For the following chart, I generated some random height data. The blue bars (appearing as dark gray in physical books) represent the histogram for the population, and the red bars (appearing as light gray in physical books) are the histogram for the sample.

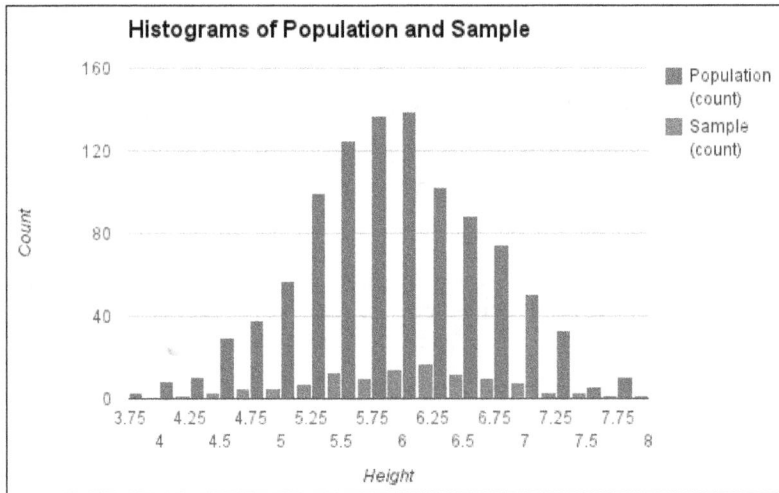

Histograms of Population and Sample

We can see from the preceding graph that the distributions are similar, but certainly not the same. And in fact, the mean for the population is 6.01, while the mean for the sample is 5.94. They're not too far apart in this case, but some samples would be much further off.

It has been proven theoretically that the difference between the population mean and the possible sample means will fall on a normal distribution. The following is the plot for the difference in the means from 500 sets of samples drawn from the same population:

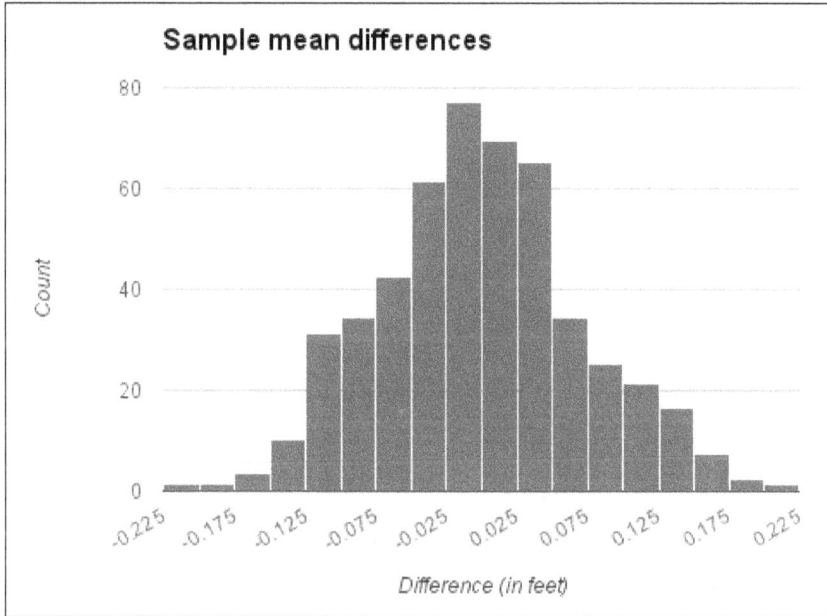

This histogram makes it clear that large differences between the population mean and the sample mean are unlikely, and the larger the difference, the more improbable it is. This is important for several reasons. First, if we know the distribution of the differences of means, it allows us to set constraints on results. If we are working with sample data, we know that the same values for the population will fall within a set bound.

Also, if we know the distribution of differences, then we know if our results are significant. This means that we can reject the null hypothesis that the averages are the same. Any two sample means should fall within the same boundaries. Large differences between any two sets of sample means are similarly improbable.

For example, one sample would be the control data, and one would be the test data. If the difference between the two samples is large enough to be improbable, then we can infer that the test behavior produced a significant difference (assuming the rest of the experiment is well designed and other things aren't complicating the experiment). If it's unlikely enough, then we say that it's significant, and we reject the null hypothesis.

Depending on what we're testing, we may be interested in results that are on the left-hand side of the graph, the right-hand side, or either. That is, the test statistic for the alternative hypothesis may be significantly less than, significantly greater than, or equal to the null hypothesis. We express this in notation using one of the following three forms. (These use the character mu, μ, using the sample mean as the test statistic.) In each of these notations, the first line states the null hypothesis, and the second states the alternative hypothesis. For instance, the first pair in the following notation says that the null hypothesis is that the test sample's mean should be greater than or equal to the control sample's mean, and the alternative hypothesis is that the test sample's mean should be less than the control sample's mean:

$$H_0 : \mu \geq \mu_0$$
$$H_a : \mu < \mu_0$$

$$H_0 : \mu \leq \mu_0$$
$$H_a : \mu > \mu_0$$

$$H_0 : \mu = \mu_0$$
$$H_a : \mu \neq \mu_0$$

We've taken our time to understand this more thoroughly because it's fundamental to the rest of the process. However, if you don't understand it at this point, throughout the rest of the chapter, we'll keep going over this. By the end, you should have a good understanding of this graph of sample mean differences and what it implies.

Determining appropriate tests

Another aspect of your data that you'll need to pay attention to is the shape of the data. This can often be easily visualized using a histogram. For example, the following screenshot shows a normal distribution and two distributions that are skewed:

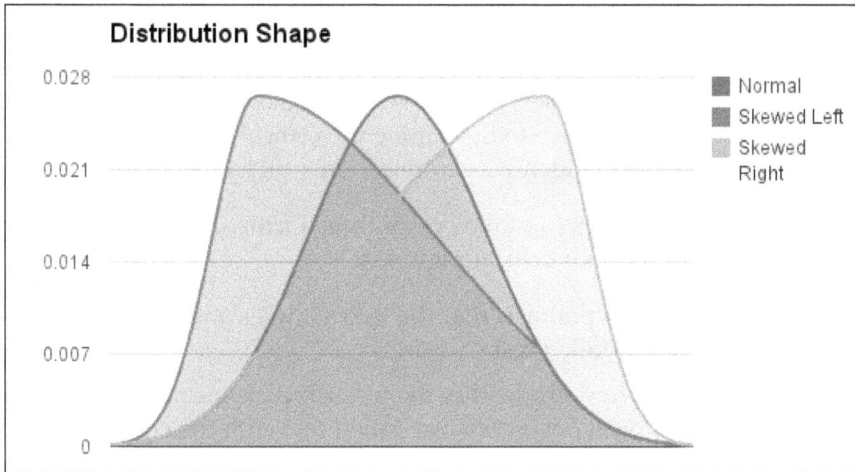

The red curve is skewed left (appearing as dark gray), and the yellow curve is skewed right (appearing as white). The blue curve (appearing as light gray) is a normal distribution with no skew.

Many statistical tests are designed for normal data, and they won't give good results for skewed data. For example, t-test and regression analysis both give good results only for normally distributed data.

Selecting the significance level

Next, we need to select the significance level that we want to achieve for our test. This is the level of certainty that we'll need to have before we can reject the null hypothesis. More to the point, this is the maximum chance that the results could be an outlying sample from the population, which would cause you to incorrectly reject the null hypothesis.

Often, the significance level, usually given as the p-value, is given as $p<0.05$ or $p<0.01$. This means that the results have a less than 5 percent or 1 percent chance of being caused by a sample with an outlying mean.

If we look at the graph of sample mean differences given earlier, we can see that we're looking at differences of about 2.4 inches to be significant. In other words, based on this population, the average difference in height would need to be more than 2 inches for it to be considered statistically significant.

Say we wanted to see if men and women were on average, of different heights. If the average height difference were only 1 inch, that could likely be the result of the samples that we picked. However, if the average height difference were 2.4 inches or more, that would be unlikely to have come from the sample.

Determining the critical region

Now we have determined two important pieces of information: we've expressed our null and alternative hypotheses, and we've decided on a needed level of significance. We can use these two to determine the critical region for the test results, that is, the region for which we can reject the null hypothesis.

Remember that our hypotheses can take one of three forms. The following conditions determine where our critical region is:

- For the alternative hypothesis that the two samples' means are not equal, we'll perform a two-tailed test.

- For the alternative hypothesis that the test sample's mean is less than the control sample's, we'll perform a one-tailed test with the critical region on the left-hand side of the graph.

- And for the alternative hypothesis that the test sample's mean is greater than the control sample's, we'll perform a one-tailed test with the critical region on the right-hand side of the graph.

The following hypothetical graph highlights the part of the curve in which the critical regions occur. The curve represents the distribution of the test statistic for the sample, and the shaded parts will be the areas that the critical region(s) might come from.

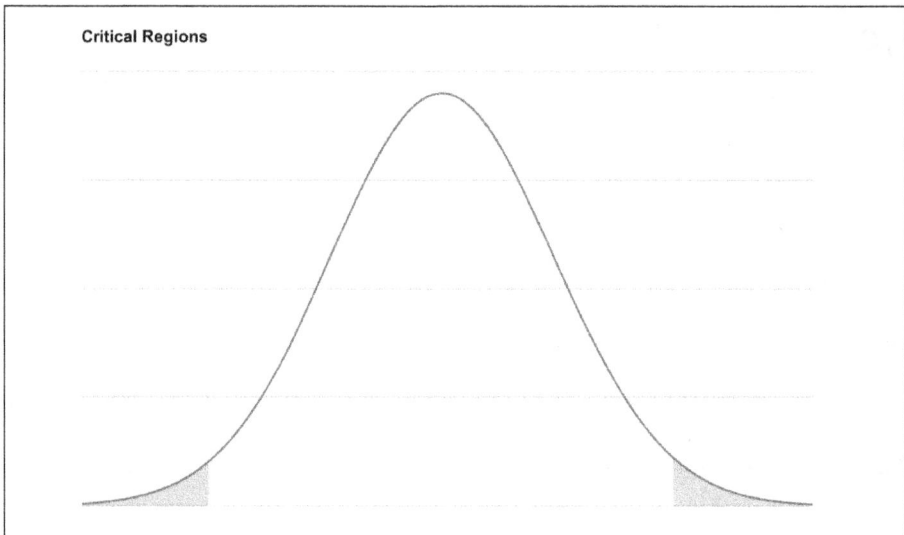

Critical Regions

The exact size of the critical regions is determined by the p value that we decided upon. In all cases, the area of the critical regions is the p percentage of the entire curve. That is, if we've decided that we're trying for $p<0.05$, and the area under the whole curve is 100, the area in the critical region will be 5.

If we are performing a two-tailed test, then that area will be divided into two, so in the example we just outlined, each side will have an area of 2.5. However, for one-tailed tests, the entire critical region will fall on one side.

Calculating the test statistics and its probability

Now we have to calculate the test statistic. Depending on the nature of the data, the sample, and on what you're trying to answer, this could involve comparing means, a student's t-test, X^2 test, or any number of other tests.

These tests will give you a number, but interpreting it directly is often not helpful. Instead, you then need to calculate the value of p for that test's distribution. If you're doing things by hand, this can involve either looking up the value in tables or if you're using a software program, this is often done for you and returned as a part of the results.

We'll use Incanter in several sections later in this chapter, starting with calculating the test statistic and its probability. Its functions generally return both the test value and the p value.

Deciding whether to reject the null hypothesis or not

Now we can find the value of p in relation to the critical regions and determine whether we can reject the null hypothesis or not.

For instance, say that we've decided that the level of significance that we want to achieve is $p<0.05$ and the actual value of p is *0.001*. This will allow us to reject the null hypothesis.

However, if the value of p is *0.055*, we would fail to reject the null hypothesis. We would have to assume that the alternative hypothesis is incorrect, at least until more information is available.

Flipping coins

Now that we've been over the process of null hypothesis testing, let's walk through the process one more time with an example. This should be simple and straightforward enough that we can focus on the process, and not on the test itself.

For that purpose, we'll test whether a dice is loaded or not. If it is balanced, then the expected probability of any given side should be 1/6, or about 16 percent. However, if the die is loaded, then the probability for rolling one side should be greater than 16 percent, and the probabilities for rolling the other sides would be less than 16 percent.

Of course, generally this isn't something that you would worry about. But before you agree to play craps with the dice that your friend 3D printed, you may want to test them.

For this test, I've rolled one die 1,000 times. The following is the table of how many times each side came up:

Side	Frequency
1	157
2	151
3	175
4	187
5	143
6	187

So we can see that the frequencies are relatively close, within a range of 44, but they aren't exactly the same. This is what we'd expect. The question is whether they're different enough that we can say with some certainty that the die is loaded.

Formulating an initial hypothesis

So we suspect that our test die is fair, but we don't know that. We'll frame our hypothesis this way: on any roll, all sides have an equal chance of appearing.

Stating the null and alternative hypotheses

Our initial hypothesis can act as our null hypothesis. And in this case, we expect to fail to reject it. Let's state both hypotheses explicitly:

- H_0: All sides have an equal chance of appearing on any roll.
- H_1: One side has a greater chance of appearing on any roll.

In this case, we let H_0 be such that the two sides are equal because we want there to be more latitude in what counts as fair, and we want to enforce a high burden of proof before we declare a die loaded.

Identifying the statistical assumptions in the sample

For our sample, we'll roll the die in question 1,000 times. We'll assume that each roll is identical: that it's being done with approximately the same arm and hand movements, and that the die is landing on a flat surface. We'll also assume that before being thrown, the die is being shaken enough to be appropriately random.

This way, no biases are introduced because of the mechanics of how the die is being thrown.

Determining appropriate tests

For this, we'll use a Pearson's X^2 goodness-of-fit test. This is used to test whether an observed frequency distribution matches a theoretical distribution. It works by calculating a normalized sum of squared deviations. We're trying to test whether some observations match an expected distribution, so this test is a great fit.

We'll see exactly how to apply this test in a minute.

Selecting the significance level

Proving that a die is loaded does require a higher burden of proof than assuming that it's fair, but we don't want the bar to be too high. Because of that, we'll use $p < 0.05$ for this.

Determining the critical region

The output of the X^2 test fits an X^2 distribution, not a normal distribution, so the graph won't look the same. Also, X^2 tests are intrinsically one sided. When the number is too far out on the right, then it indicates that the data fits the theoretical values poorly. A value to the left on the X^2 distribution just indicates that the fit is very good, which isn't really a problem.

The following is a graph comparing the normal distribution, centered on 50, with the X^2 distribution, with 3 degrees of freedom:

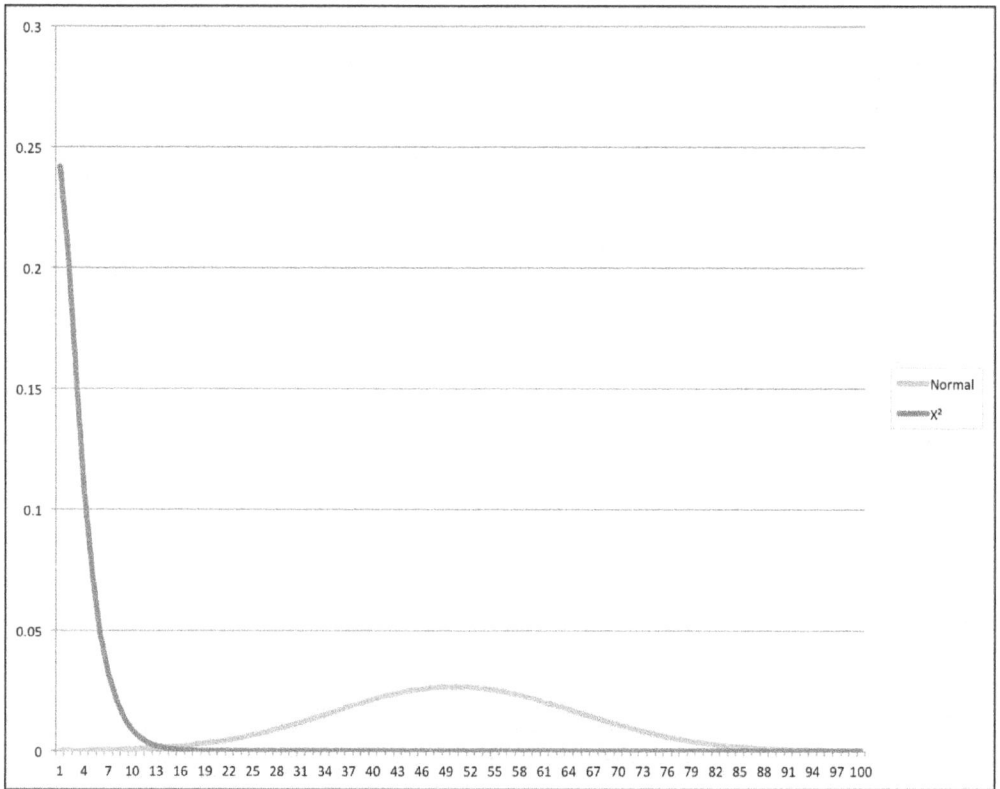

Either way, the statistics library that we're going to use (Incanter) will take care of this for us.

Calculating the test statistic and its probability

So let's fire up the Leiningen REPL and see what we can do. For this project, we're going to use the following project.clj file:

```
(defproject nullh "0.1.0-snapshot"
  :dependencies [[org.clojure/clojure "1.5.1"]
                 [enlive "1.1.4"]
                 [http.async.client "0.5.2"]
                 [org.clojure/data.csv "0.1.2"]
                 [org.clojure/data.json "0.2.3"]
                 [me.raynes/fs "1.4.5"]
```

```
                    [incanter "1.5.4"]
                    [geocoder-clj "0.2.2"]
                    [geo-clj "0.3.5"]
                    [congomongo "0.4.1"]
                    [org.apache.poi/poi-ooxml "3.9"]]
        :profiles {:dev {:dependencies
                        [[org.clojure/tools.namespace "0.2.4"]]
                        :source-paths ["dev"]}})
```

First, we'll load Incanter, then we'll create a matrix containing our data, and finally we'll run an X^2 test over it with the following code:

```
user=> (require '[incanter.core :as i] '[incanter.stats :as s])
nil
user=> (def table (i/matrix [157 151 175 187 143 187]))
#'user/table
user=> (def r (s/chisq-test :table table))
#'user/r
user=> (pprint (select-keys r [:p-value :df :X-sq]))
{:X-sq 10.771999999999998, :df 5, :p-value 0.05609271590058857}
```

Let's look at this code in more detail:

- The function `incanter.stats/chisq-test` returns a lot of information, including its own input. So, before displaying it at the end, I filtered out most of the data and only returned the three keys that we're particularly interested in. The following are those keys and the values that they returned.

    - `:X-sq`: This is the X^2 statistic. Higher values of this indicate that the data does not fit their expected values.

    - `:df`: This is the degrees of freedom. This represents the number of parameters that are free to vary. For nominal data (data without natural ordering), such as rolls of dice, this is the number of values that the data can take, minus one. In this case, since it's a six-sided die, the degree of freedom is five.

    - `:p-value`: This is the value of p that we've been talking about. This is the probability that we'd see these results from the X^2 test if the null hypothesis were true.

Now that we have these numbers, how do we apply them to our hypotheses?

Deciding whether to reject the null hypothesis or not

In this case, since $p>0.05$, we fail to reject the null hypothesis. We can't really rule it out, but we don't have enough evidence to support it either. In this case, we can assume that the die is fair.

Hopefully, this example gives you a better understanding of the null hypothesis testing process and how it works. With that under our belts, let's turn our attention to a bigger, more meaningful problem than the fairness of imaginary dice.

Understanding burglary rates

Understanding crime seems like a universal problem. Earlier, societies grappled with the problem of evil in the universe from a theological perspective; today, sociologists and criminologists construct theories and study society using a variety of tools and techniques. However the problem is cast, the aim is to better understand why some people violate social norms in ways that are often violent and harmful to those around them and even themselves. By better understanding this problem, ultimately we'd like to be able to create social programs and government policies that minimize the damage and create a safer and hopefully more just society for all involved.

Of course, as data scientists and programmers engaging in data analysis, we're inclined to approach this problem as a data problem. That's what we'll do in the rest of this chapter. We'll gather some crime and economic data and look for a tie between the two. In the course of our analysis, we'll explore the data, tentatively suggest a hypothesis, and test it against the data.

We'll look at crime data from the United Nations and see what relationships it has with data from the World Bank data site.

Getting the data

In order to get the data, perform the following steps:

1. First, we need to download the data.

2. For the crime data, we'll go to the website of the United Nations Office on Drugs and Crime (http://www.unodc.org/). It publishes crime data for countries around the world over a number of years. Their data page, http://www.unodc.org/unodc/en/data-and-analysis/statistics/data.html, has links to Excel files for a number of different categories of crime in the section of the page labeled **Statistics on crime**.

3. You should download each of these and save them to the directory `unodc
   -data`. You can extract the data from these in a minute. First, you can get
   the data that we want to correlate to the crime data.

4. We'll get this data from the World Bank's data site (`http://data.
   worldbank.org/`). Navigating the site is a little complicated, and in my
   experience it changes regularly. For the moment, at least, this seems to be
   the easiest way to get the data:

   1. Visit the **Indicators** page at `http://data.worldbank.org/
      indicator`.

   2. In the search box, enter `land area` and select **Land area (sq. km)**,
      as shown in the following screenshot:

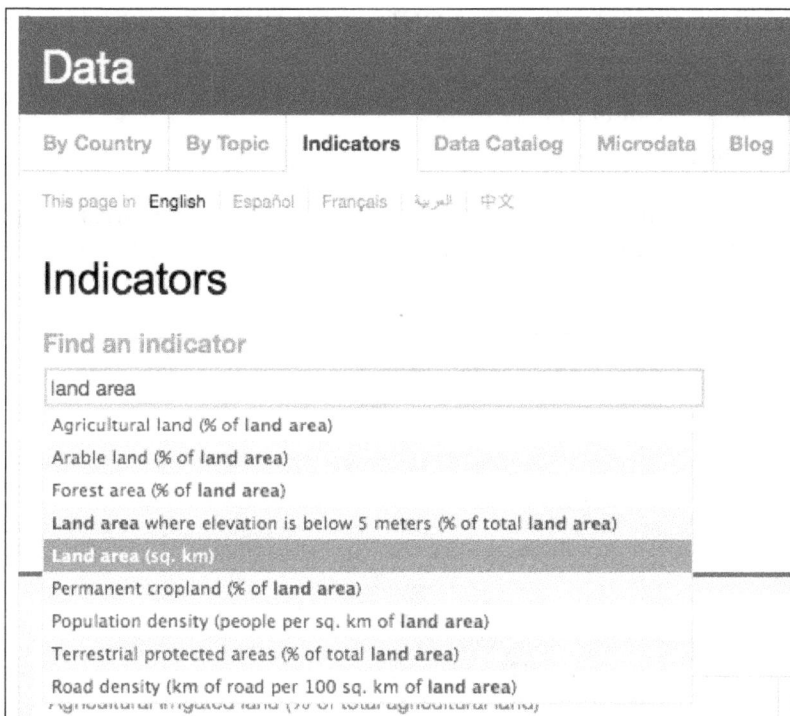

5. Then hit the **Go** button.

6. On the next page, you'll be given the option to download the dataset in
   a number of formats. Choose **CSV**.

7. Download the data and unzip it into a directory named `ag.lnd`, based on the indicator codes that the World Bank uses. (You can use a different directory name, but you'll need to modify the directions that follow.)

We'll also want some economic data. To get that, perform the following steps:

1. Go back to the **Indicators** page.

2. Search for **GNI per capita** (it's the default selection for the search box).

3. From the filtered results, select **GNI per capita, Atlas method (current US$)**.

4. Click on **Go**.

5. Download the data as CSV again.

6. Unzip the data into a directory named `ny.gnp`.

At this point, you should have a directory with several subdirectories containing data files. The structure should look something like the following screenshot:

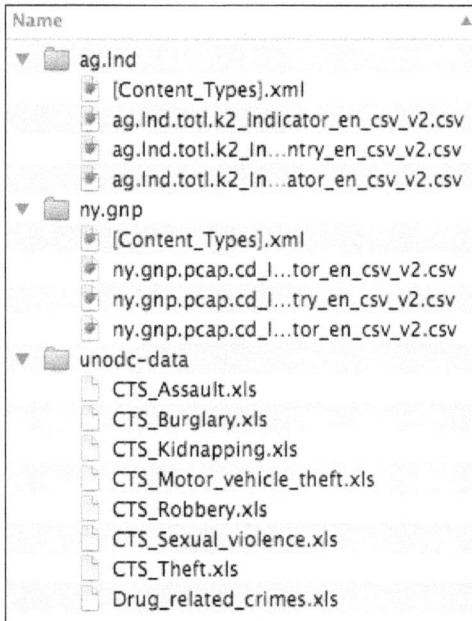

Some of the data is ready to go, but before we use it, we need to extract the data from the Excel files. Let's turn our attention there.

Parsing the Excel files

Before we can extract the data from the Excel files, we need to find out what our input for this will be. If we open up one of the Excel files, in this case CTS_Assault. xls, we'll see something similar to the following screenshot:

	A	D	E	F	G
10					
11					
12					
13					
14	**Region**	**Sub-region II**	**Country/territory**	**2003**	**200**
15	Africa	Eastern Africa	Burundi		
16	Africa		Kenya		
17	Africa		Mauritius	105	
18	Africa		Mozambique		1
19	Africa		Uganda	19,491	25,
20	Africa		Zimbabwe	78,464	95,
21	Africa	Middle Africa	Cameroon	2,998	3,
22	Africa		Sao Tome and Principe	1	
23	Africa	Northern Africa	Algeria	23,050	20,
24	Africa		Egypt		
25	Africa		Morocco	48,662	46,
26	Africa	Southern Africa	Botswana		
27	Africa		Lesotho		

Let's list out some of the features of the sheets that we'll need to take into account:

- There are about thirteen rows of headers, most of which are hidden in the preceding screenshot.
- Again, not shown in the preceding screenshot, but some of the files have more than one tab of data.
- There are some hidden columns between columns A and D.
- The subregion isn't listed on each row, so we'll need some way to carry this over.
- All the years for each crime and country combination are listed on one row. We'll probably want to pivot that so that there's a column for the crime, one for the country, one for the year, and one for the data value.
- There is a lot of missing data. We can filter that out.

To get into the Excel files, we'll use the Apache POI project (http://poi.apache. org/). This library provides access to file formats of Microsoft Office's suites.

We'll use this library to extract the data from the Excel files in several stages, as follows:

1. Pull raw data rows out of the Excel files
2. Populate a tree of data that groups the data hierarchically by region, subregion, and country

3. Flatten the hierarchically arranged data back into a sequence of maps containing all the data for each row

4. Wrap all of this in one easy-to-use function

Let's follow the preceding steps for the rest of this section, and in the end we'll add a controller function that pulls it all together.

We'll keep all of this code in a single module. The following namespace declaration for this will include all the dependencies that we'll need. For the fully specified `project.clj` file that includes all of these, refer to the code download for this chapter. I named the project `nullh`, so the file that I'm working with here is named `src/nullh/unodc.clj`.

```clojure
(ns nullh.unodc
  (:require [clojure.java.io :as io]
            [clojure.string :as str]
            [me.raynes.fs :as fs]
            [clojure.data.json :as json]
            [nullh.utils :as u])
  (:import
    [java.io FileInputStream]
    [org.apache.poi.ss.usermodel
     Cell CellStyle DataFormat Font RichTextString Row Sheet]
    [org.apache.poi.hssf.usermodel HSSFWorkbook]))
```

Now we can start populating this namespace.

Pulling out raw data

For the first stage of the process, in which we read the data into a series of raw data rows, we'll use a couple of record types, as shown in the following code. The first, `sheet-data`, associates the title of the worksheet with the data in it. The second, `xl-row`, simply stores the data in each row's cells into named fields.

```clojure
(defrecord sheet-data [sheet-name sheet-rows])
(defrecord xl-row
  [sheet region sub-region country
    count-2003 count-2004 count-2005 count-2006 count-2007
    count-2008 count-2009 count-2010 count-2011
    rate-2003 rate-2004 rate-2005 rate-2006 rate-2007
    rate-2008 rate-2009 rate-2010 rate-2011])
```

As we interact with the worksheet's data and API, we'll use a number of utilities that makes access to the worksheet objects more like working with native Clojure objects. The following are some of those utilities:

```clojure
(defn sheets [workbook]
  (->> workbook
    (.getNumberOfSheets)
    (range)
    (map #(.getSheetAt workbook %))))
(defn rows [sheet]
  (->> sheet
    (.getPhysicalNumberOfRows)
    (range)
    (map #(.getRow sheet %))
    (remove nil?)))
(defn cells [row]
  (->> row
    (.getPhysicalNumberOfRows)
    (range)
    (map #(.getCell row %))))
```

We'll spend a lot of time accessing cells' values. We'll want to make a simpler, more Clojure-like wrapper around the Java library's API for accessing them. How we do this will depend on the cell's type, and we can use *multimethods* to handle dispatching for it, as shown in the following code:

```clojure
(defn cell-type [cell]
  (if (nil? cell)
    nil
    (let [cell-types {Cell/CELL_TYPE_BLANK   :blank
                      Cell/CELL_TYPE_BOOLEAN :boolean
                      Cell/CELL_TYPE_ERROR   :error
                      Cell/CELL_TYPE_FORMULA :formula
                      Cell/CELL_TYPE_NUMERIC :numeric
                      Cell/CELL_TYPE_STRING  :string}]
      (cell-types (.getCellType cell)))))
(defmulti cell-value cell-type)
(defmethod cell-value :blank   [_] nil)
(defmethod cell-value :boolean [c] (.getBooleanCellValue c))
(defmethod cell-value :error   [c] (.getErrorCellValue   c))
(defmethod cell-value :formula [c] (.getErrorCellValue   c))
(defmethod cell-value :numeric [c] (.getNumericCellValue c))
(defmethod cell-value :string  [c] (.getStringCellValue  c))
(defmethod cell-value :default [c] nil)
```

Now, with these methods in place, we can easily read the data into a sequence of data rows. First, we'll need to open the workbook file with the following code:

```
(defn open-file [filename]
  (with-open [s (io/input-stream filename)]
    (HSSFWorkbook. s)))
```

And we can take each sheet and read it into a `sheet-data` record with the following code:

```
(defn get-sheet-data [sheet]
  (->sheet-data (.getSheetName sheet) (rows sheet)))
```

The rows themselves will need to go through a number of transformations, all without touching the sheet name field. To facilitate this, we'll define a higher order function that maps a function over the rows field, as follows:

```
(defn on-rows [sheet f]
  (assoc sheet :sheet-rows (f (:sheet-rows sheet))))
```

The first row transformation will involve skipping the header rows for each sheet, as shown in the following code:

```
(defn first-cell-empty? [cells]
  (empty? (cell-value (first cells))))
(defn skip-headers [sheet]
  (on-rows sheet (fn [r]
                   (->> r
                     (drop-while #(first-cell-empty? (cells %)))
                     (drop 1)
                     (take-while #(not (first-cell-empty? %)))))))
```

Now we can take the sequence of `sheet-data` records and flatten them by adding the sheet name onto the row data as follows:

```
(defn row-values [sheet-name row]
  (conj (mapv cell-value (cells row)) sheet-name))
(defn sheet-data->seq [sheet]
  (map #(row-values (:sheet-name sheet) %) (:sheet-rows sheet)))
```

We do need to take each row and clean it up by rearranging the field order, making sure it has exactly the right number of fields with the help of the following code:

```
(defn clean-row [row]
  (u/pad-vec 22
             (concat (list (last row) (first row))
                     (take 11 (drop 3 row))
                     (drop 15 row))))
```

Now that we've hardened our data a little, we can take the Clojure vectors and populate the `xl-row` records with them as follows:

```
(defn seq->xl-row [coll] (apply ->xl-row coll))
```

Finally, we have a fairly clean sequence of row data.

Growing a data tree

Unfortunately, we haven't yet dealt with some problems, such as the subregion not being populated in every row. Let's take care of that now.

We'll tackle that problem by changing the sequence of records into a hierarchical tree of data. The tree is represented by a number of record types as shown in the following code:

```
(defrecord region [region-name sub-regions])
(defrecord sub-region [sub-region-name countries])
(defrecord country [country-name counts rates sheet])
(defrecord yearly-data
   [year-2003 year-2004 year-2005 year-2006 year-2007 year-2008
    year-2009 year-2010 year-2011])
```

To build the tree, we'll have a number of functions. Each takes a group of data that will go into one tree or subtree. It populates that part of the tree and returns it.

The first of these functions is `xl-rows->regions`. It takes a sequence of `xl-rows`, groups them by region, and constructs a tree of `region` records for it as shown in the following code:

```
(defn xl-rows->regions [coll]
  (->> coll
    (group-by :region)
    (map #(->region
            (first %) (xl-rows->sub-regions (second %))))))
```

The most complicated part of building this tree is dealing with the missing subregions. We'll use three functions to deal with that. The first, `conj-into`, conjugates onto a value in a map, or adds a new vector containing the data if there's no data for that key. The second, `fold-sub-region`, folds each row into a map based on either the subregion referred to in the row, or the last specified subregion. Finally, `xl-rows->sub-regions` takes a sequence of rows from one region, divides them into subregions, and creates the `sub-region` records for them, as shown in the following code:

```
(defn conj into [m k v]
```

```
    (if (contains? m k)
      (assoc m k (conj (get m k) v))
      (assoc m k [v])))
(defn fold-sub-region [state row]
  (let [[current accum] state]
    (if (str/blank? (:sub-region row))
      [current
        (conj-into accum current (assoc row :sub-region current))]
      (let [new-sub-region (:sub-region row)]
        [new-sub-region
          (conj-into accum new-sub-region row)]))))
(defn xl-rows->sub-regions [coll]
  (->> coll
    (reduce fold-sub-region [nil {}])
    second
    (map #(->sub-region
            (first %) (xl-rows->countries (second %))))))
```

Now that we have the subregions identified, we can build a tree for each country. For that, we'll pull the count data and the rate data into their own structures and put it all together into a country record with the following code:

```
(defn xl-rows->countries [coll]
  (->> coll
    (group-by :country)
    (map #(let [[country-name [row & _]] %]
            (->country country-name
                        (xl-row->counts row)
                        (xl-row->rates row)
                        (:sheet row))))))
```

The counts and rates are represented by the same record type, so we'll use a shared function to pull the fields from the row that populate the fields in the type as shown in the following code:

```
(defn xl-row->yearly [coll fields]
  (apply ->yearly-data (map #(get coll %) fields)))
(defn xl-row->counts [coll]
  (xl-row->yearly
    coll
    [:count-2003 :count-2004 :count-2005 :count-2006 :count-2007
     :count-2008 :count-2009 :count-2010 :count-2011]))
(defn xl-row->rates [coll]
  (xl-row->yearly
```

```
coll
[:rate-2003 :rate-2004 :rate-2005 :rate-2006 :rate-2007
 :rate-2008 :rate-2009 :rate-2010 :rate-2011]))
```

These functions all build the hierarchy of data that's stored in the worksheets.

Cutting down the data tree

We reverse the process to flatten the data again. In the process, this implicitly populates the missing subregions into all of the rows. Let's see how this works.

To begin with, we take a sequence of regions and convert each one into a sequence of xl-row records, as shown in the following code:

```
(defn region->xl-rows [tree nil-row]
  (let [region-row (assoc nil-row :region (:region-name tree))]
    (mapcat #(sub-regions->xl-rows % region-row)
            (:sub-regions tree))))
(defn regions->xl-rows [region-coll]
  (let [nil-row (seq->xl-row (repeat 22 nil))]
    (mapcat #(region->xl-rows % nil-row) region-coll)))
```

Just as before, this work will be delegated to other functions; in this case, sub-regions->xl-rows, which again delegates to country->xl-rows. The second function in the following code is a little long (and so I've omitted some lines from it), but both are conceptually simple:

```
(defn country->xl-rows [tree sub-region-row]
  (let [counts (:counts tree), rates (:rates tree)]
    (assoc sub-region-row
           :sheet (:sheet tree)
           :country (:country-name tree)
           :count-2003 (:year-2003 counts)
           :count-2004 (:year-2004 counts)
           ;; ...
           :rate-2003 (:year-2003 rates)
           :rate-2004 (:year-2004 rates)
           ;; ...
           )))
(defn sub-regions->xl-rows [tree region-row]
  (let [sub-region-row (assoc region-row :sub-region
                              (:sub-region-name tree))]
    (map #(country->xl-rows % sub-region-row) (:countries tree))))
```

At this point, we have a sequence of data rows with the missing subregions supplied. But we're still not done.

Putting it all together

We'll provide several levels of function to make this easier. First, one that ties together everything that we've seen so far. It takes a filename and returns a sequence of `xl-row` records as follows:

```
(defn read-sheets [filename]
  (->> filename
    (open-file)
    (sheets)
    (map get-sheet-data)
    (map skip-headers)
    (map (fn [s] (on-rows s #(remove empty? %))))
    (mapcat sheet-data->seq)
    (map clean-row)
    (map seq->xl-row)
    (xl-rows->regions)
    (regions->xl-rows)))
```

That's it. We have our data read in. It's been processed a little, but it's still pretty raw. The following is an example row:

```
{:sheet "CTS 2012 Domestic Burglary",
 :region "Africa",
 :sub-region "Middle Africa",
 :country "Sao Tome and Principe",
 :count-2003 nil,
 :count-2004 nil,
 :count-2005 nil,
 :count-2006 2.0,
 :count-2007 0.0,
 :count-2008 2.0,
 :count-2009 5.0,
 :count-2010 16.0,
 :count-2011 20.0,
 :rate-2003 nil,
 :rate-2004 nil,
 :rate-2005 nil,
 :rate-2006 1.290572368845583,
 :rate-2007 0.0,
 :rate-2008 1.2511573205214825,
 :rate-2009 3.0766390794695875,
```

```
:rate-2010 9.673694202434143,
:rate-2011 11.867604998635224}
```

We still need to clean it up a little and pivot the data to put each data value into its own row. Instead of having one row with :count-2003, :count-2004, and so on, we'll have many rows, each with :count and :year.

Let's turn our attention there next.

Transforming the data

So far, we've only lightly cleaned part of our data. We haven't even looked at the data that we want to correlate the crime data with. Also, the shape of the data is awkward for the analyses that we want to conduct, so we'll need to pivot it the way we described earlier. We'll see more about this in a minute.

For this stage of processing, we want to put all of the code into a new file. We'll name this file src/nullh/data.clj, and the namespace declaration for it looks as follows:

```
(ns nullh.data
  (:require [incanter.core :as i]
            [incanter.io :as iio]
            [clojure.set :as set]
            [clojure.string :as str]
            [clojure.data.csv :as csv]
            [clojure.data.json :as json]
            [clojure.java.io :as io]
            [me.raynes.fs :as fs]
            [nullh.unodc :as unodc]
            [nullh.utils :as u]))
```

We'll now start working with Incanter datasets. We haven't used Incanter much so far in this book, and that's a little unusual, because Incanter is one of the go-to libraries for working with numbers and statistics in Clojure. It's powerful and flexible, and it makes working with data easy.

Let's take the data that we read from the Excel files and import it into an Incanter dataset. We need to read the data into one long sequence, pull out the keys for the data fields, and then create the dataset as follows:

```
(defn read-cts-data [dirname]
  (let [input (mapcat unodc/read-sheets (u/ls dirname))
        cols (keys (first input))]
    (i/dataset cols (doall (map #(map second %) input)))))
```

Now we can read the data that we downloaded from the World Bank into another dataset. Both data files have roughly the same fields, so we can use the same function for both. Unfortunately, we need to load the CSV ourselves, because Incanter's introspection doesn't quite give us the results that we want. Because of this, we'll also include a few functions for converting the data into doubles as we read it in, and we'll define those columns that the data contains, as follows:

```
(def headers [:country-name :country-code :indicator-name
              :indicator-code :1961 :1962 :1963 :1964 :1965 :1966
              :1967 :1968 :1969 :1970 :1971 :1972 :1973 :1974
              :1975 :1976 :1977 :1978 :1979 :1980 :1981 :1982
              :1983 :1984 :1985 :1986 :1987 :1988 :1989 :1990
              :1991 :1992 :1993 :1994 :1995 :1996 :1997 :1998
              :1999 :2000 :2001 :2002 :2003 :2004 :2005 :2006
              :2007 :2008 :2009 :2010 :2011 :2012 :2013])
(defn ->double [x] (if (str/blank? x) nil (Double/parseDouble x)))
(defn coerce-row [row]
  (let [[x y] (split-at 4 row)]
    (concat x (map ->double y))))
(defn read-indicator-data [filename]
  (with-open [f (io/reader filename)]
    (->> f
      csv/read-csv
      (drop 3)
      (map coerce-row)
      doall
      (i/dataset headers))))
```

We can use the `read-indicator-data` function to load data from the two World Bank indicators that we downloaded earlier.

Now we want to put all the data from UNODC together with either of the World Bank datasets. As we do that, we'll also pivot the data tables so that instead of one column for each year, there's one column containing the year and one containing the value for that year. At the same time, we'll remove rows with missing data and aggregate the counts for all of the crimes for a country for each year.

Joining the data sources

Bringing the two data sources together is relatively simple and can be done with the following code:

```
(defn join-all [indicator cts]
  (i/$join [:country-name :country] indicator cts))
```

Basically, we just let Incanter join the two data structures on the fields by matching the World Bank data's :country-name field with the UNODC data's :country field.

Pivoting the data

Now that the data has been joined, we can pivot it. In the end, we want to have the following fields on every row:

- region
- subregion
- country
- country-code
- indicator
- indicator-code
- crime
- year
- count
- rate
- indicator-value

As you can see, some of these fields are from the UNODC data and some are from the World Bank data.

We'll do this translation on a sequence of maps instead of the dataset. We'll get started with the following code:

```
(defn pivot-map [m]
  (let [years [2003 2004 2005 2006 2007 2008 2009 2010 2011]]
    (map #(pivot-year m %) years)))
(defn pivot-data [map-seq] (mapcat pivot-map map-seq))
```

First, we use ->maps to convert the dataset to a sequence of maps. Then, pass the processing off to pivot-map. This function pivots the data for each year.

We pivot the data for each year separately. We do this by repeatedly transforming the data map for a row. This is a great example of how Clojure's immutability makes things easier. We don't have to worry about copying the map or clobbering any data. We can just modify the original data multiple times, saving the result of each transformation process as a separate, new data row.

The process itself is fairly simple. First, we use the year to create keywords for the fields that we are interested in. Next, we select the rows that we want to keep from the original data map. Then we rename a few to make them clearer. And finally, we add the year to the output map as follows:

```
(defn pivot-year [m year]
  (let [count-key (keyword (str "count-" year))
        rate-key (keyword (str "rate-" year))
        year-key (keyword (str year))]
    (-> m
      (select-keys [:region :sub-region :country :country-code
                    :indicator :indicator-code
                    :sheet count-key rate-key year-key])
      (set/rename-keys {:sheet :crime,
                        count-key :count,
                        rate-key :rate,
                        year-key :indicator-value})
      (assoc :year year))))
```

That's it. This should make the data easier to work with. We can do some more transformations on the data and clean it up a bit further.

Filtering the missing data

First, there are a lot of holes in the data, and we don't want to have to worry about that. So if a row is missing any of the three data fields (`:count`, `:rate`, or `:indicator-value`), let's get rid of it with the following code:

```
(defn remove-missing [coll]
  (let [fields [:count :rate :indicator-value]
        has-missing (fn [r] (some nil? (map r fields)))]
    (remove has-missing coll)))
```

We just check whether any of these fields has a `nil` value. If any of them do, we remove that row.

Putting it all together

Let's make a wrapper function around this process. That'll help us stay consistent and make the library easier to use. This loads the data from UNODC and one of the World Bank datasets. It joins, pivots, and removes the missing rows before returning an Incanter dataset, as shown in the following code:

```
(defn ->maps [dset]
  (let [col-names (i/col-names dset)]
```

```
        (map #(zipmap col-names %) (i/to-list dset))))
  (defn load-join-pivot [cts-dir data-file]
    (let [cts (read-cts-data cts-dir)
          indicator-data (read-indicator-data data-file)]
      (->> (join-all indicator-data cts)
        ->maps
        pivot-data
        remove-missing
        i/to-dataset)))
```

Let's use these functions to load up one of the datasets as follows:

```
(def d (d/load-join-pivot
          "unodc-data"
          "ag.lnd/ag.lnd.totl.k2_Indicator_en_csv_v2.csv"))
```

At this point, the data is in decent shape—actually, as good as this data is probably going to get (more about that near the end of this chapter). So let's see what's in the data and what it has to tell us.

Exploring the data

Let's explore a little and try to get a feel for the data. First, let's try to get some summary statistics for the various datasets. Afterward, we'll generate some graphs to get a more intuitive sense for what's in the data and how they're related.

Generating summary statistics

Incanter makes generating summary statistics easy. You can pass a dataset to the `incanter.stats/summary` function. It returns a sequence of maps. Each map represents the summary data for each column in the original dataset. This includes whether the data is numeric or not. For nominal data, it returns some sample items and their counts. For numeric data, it returns the mean, median, minimum, and maximum.

Summarizing UNODC crime data

If we load the data and filter it for the crime of "burglary", we can get the summary statistics for those fields as follows:

```
(s/summary
  (i/$where {:crime {:$eq "CTS 2012 Burglary"}} by-ag-lnd))
```

And if we pick apart the data structures that it outputs, the following are the summary statistics for the primary data fields:

Column	Minimum	Maximum	Mean	Median
Rate	0.1	1939.23	376.4	292.67
Count	11	443010	60380	17184

So, from the preceding table, we see that both fields have wide variance and are skewed somewhat, based on the differences between the means and the medians. These two having similar distributions is to be expected, since the rate is derived from the count.

Charts and graphs can also help to understand our data better. Incanter makes generating charts quite simple. Let's see how to do that.

First, we'll load the data and pivot it, since that will make it easier to pull the data out of the graph. For this example, we'll load the UNODC crime data joined to the World Bank land area data as follows:

```
(def by-ag-lnd
  (d/load-join-pivot
    "unodc-data"
    "ag.lnd/ag.lnd.totl.k2_Indicator_en_csv_v2.csv"))
```

Next, we'll filter the dataset to contain only the burglary data as shown in the following code:

```
(def burglary
  (i/$where {:crime {:$eq "CTS 2012 Burglary"}} by-ag-lnd))
```

Finally, we use the `incanter.charts/histogram` function to create the graph, and the `incanter.core/view` function to display it to the screen with the following code:

```
(def h
  (c/histogram (i/sel burglary :cols :count)
               :nbins 30
               :title "Burglary Counts"
               :x-label "Burglaries"))
  (i/view h)
```

The following is the histogram of the `:count` field:

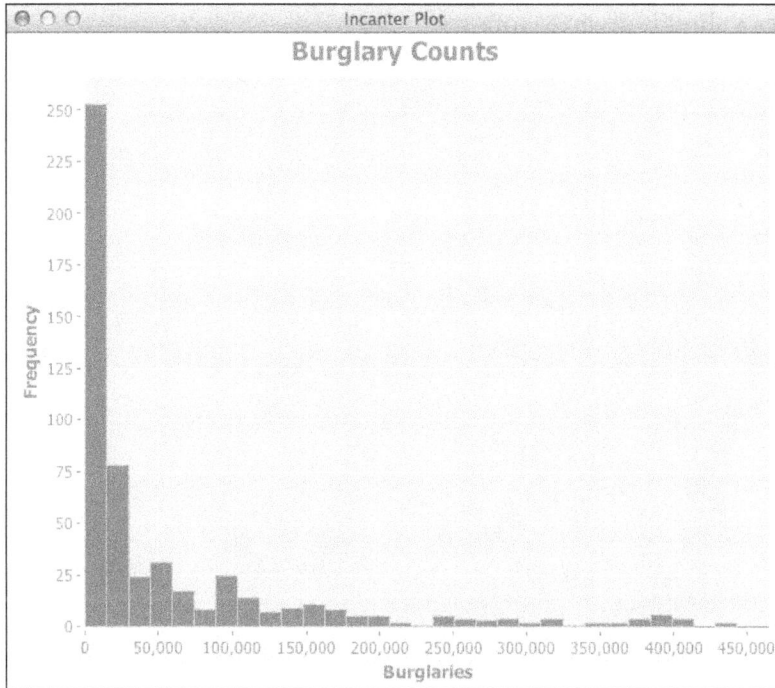

From this graph, we can see that this data does not follow a normal distribution. How does the other data correspond?

Summarizing World Bank land area and GNI data

We can use the same function, `incanter.stats/summary`, to generate the same statistics for the land area data that is given in the following table:

Column	Minimum	Maximum	Mean	Median
Land area	300	16381390	822324	100250
GNI	240	88500	17170	8140

The World Bank land area data has a distribution that is similar to the crime data. Smaller, less wealthy countries are, of course, more numerous. The distribution of the land area values is given as follows:

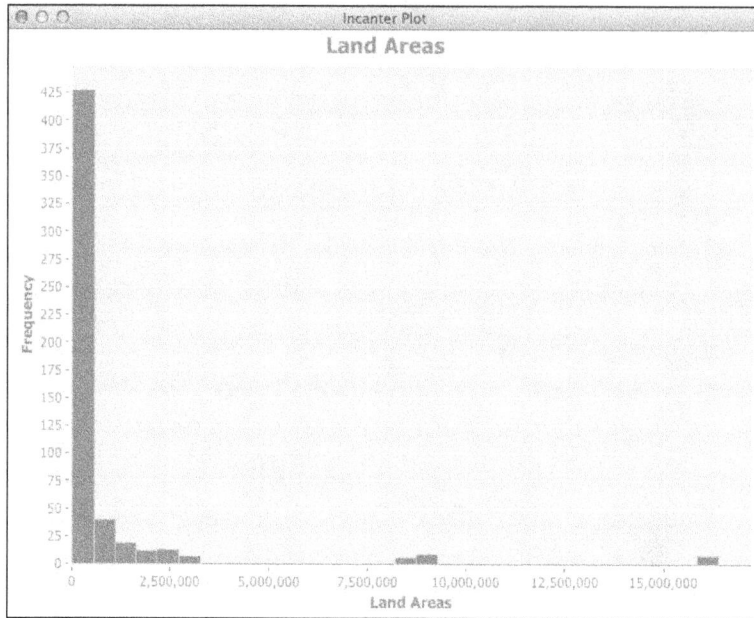

The following is the distribution of the GNI values:

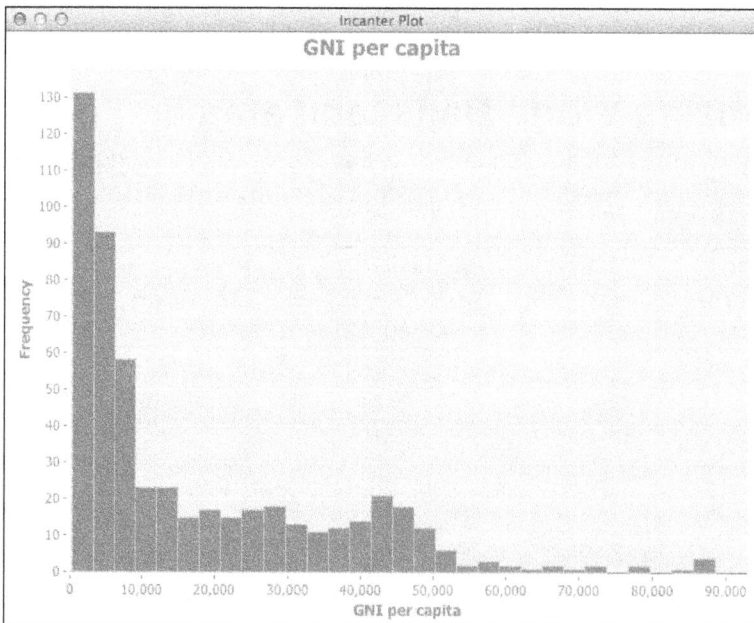

This gives us some feel for the data. All of these follow an exponential distribution, as we can see in the next graph:

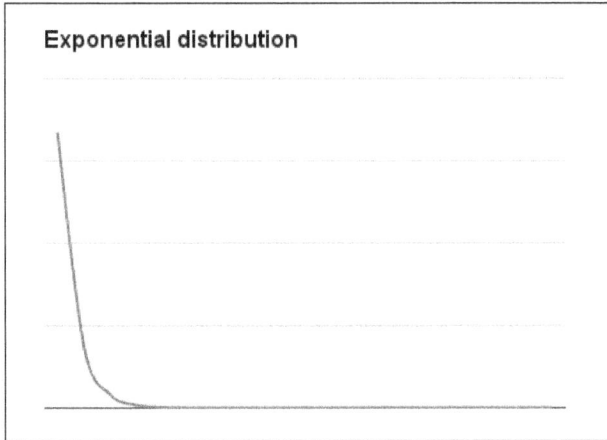

Exponential distribution

This makes it clear that all graphs with exponential distribution start with a steep drop and quickly flatten out into a near-flat line.

Generating more charts and graphs

Some more charts can help us begin to understand the relationship between some of these variables. We'll write a function to plot any crime against the World Bank indicator data joined into the current dataset.

First, however, we'll need a utility function to filter the data rows by the crime. This is a data-oriented function, so we'll store it in nullh.data, as shown in the following code:

```
(defn by-crime [dset crime-label]
  (i/$where {:crime {:$eq crime-label}} dset))
```

The next function, plot-crime, pulls out the data points and then passes everything to the incanter.charts/scatter-plot function to generate the graph:

```
(defn plot-crime [dset indicator-label crime-label]
  (let [x (i/sel dset :cols :indicator-value)
        y (i/sel dset :cols :rate)
        title (str indicator-label " and " crime-label)]
    (c/scatter-plot x y
                    :title title
                    :x-label indicator-label
                    :y-label crime-label)))
```

This makes it easy to get a quick, visual comparison of data about different types of crimes and how they relate to the World Bank indicator data.

For example, the following code shows us how the burglary ("CTS 2012 Burglary") relates to the land area data (the `plot-crime` function is in the `nullh.charts` namespace, which is aliased as `n-ch`):

```
(def by-ag-lnd
  (d/load-join-pivot
    "unodc-data"
    "ag.lnd/ag.lnd.totl.k2_Indicator_en_csv_v2.csv"))
(def ag-plot
  (n-ch/plot-crime (d/by-crime by-ag-lnd "CTS 2012 Burglary")
                   "Land Area" "Burglary"))
(i/view ag-plot)
```

The preceding code produces the following graph:

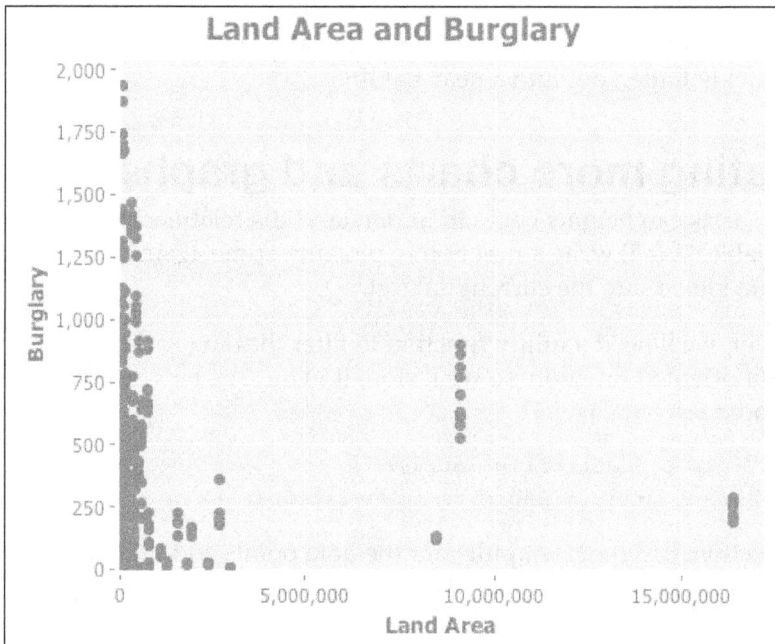

This data appears to have some strange artifacts. Look at the line of data points where the land area is around 9,000,000, stretching from about 500 burglaries per year to almost 1,000 burglaries. What is that about?

Well, when we think about it, the land area of a country rarely changes, but if a country has burglary data for several years, we'll have the land area represented those many times. We could simplify the data by getting the average of the data.

In order to do this, we aggregate all of the year data for each country. To do that, we'll use the following function:

```
(defn aggregate-years-by-country
  ([dset] (aggregate-years-by-country dset :mean))
  ([dset by]
   (let [data-cols [:count :rate :indicator-value]]
     (->> [:count :rate :indicator-value]
       (map #(i/$rollup by % :country dset))
       (reduce #(i/$join [:country :country] %1 %2))))))
```

The preceding code uses the `incanter.core/$rollup` function to get each country's average for each data column. It then uses `reduce` and `incanter.core/$join` to fold the data back into one dataset.

When we graph aggregated data, we get the following graph:

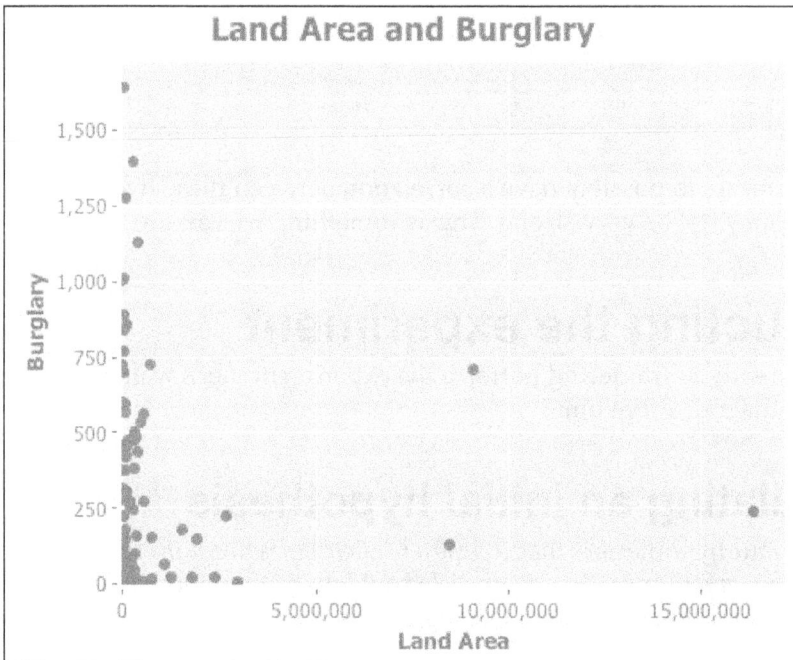

This makes it clearer that there is probably no relationship between these two variables.

The following graph compares the burglary data to the GNI per capita. Since that indicator doesn't typically vary much over the time span represented in the data (China and a few other countries not withstanding), we have again aggregated each country's data.

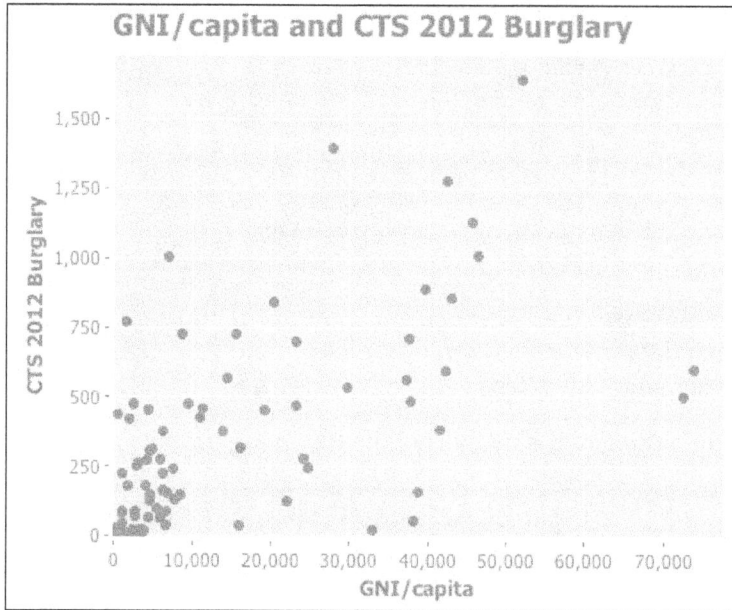

This data appears to possibly have a correlation between these two variables, although it may not be very strong. This is something we can test.

Conducting the experiment

Now we're ready to frame and perform the experiment. Let's walk through the steps to do that one more time.

Formulating an initial hypothesis

In this case, our hypothesis is that *there is a relationship between the per capita gross national income and the rate of burglaries*. We could go further and make the hypothesis stronger by specifying that higher GNI correlates to a higher burglary rate, somewhat counter-intuitively.

Stating the null and alternative hypotheses

Given that statement of our working hypothesis, we can now formulate the null and alternative hypotheses.

- H_0: There is no relationship between the per capita gross national income and a country's burglary rate.
- H_1: There is a relationship between the per capita gross national income and the country's burglary rate.

These statements will now guide us through the rest of the process.

Identifying the statistical assumptions in the sample

There are a number of assumptions in this data that we need to be aware of. First, since the crime data comes from multiple sources, there's going to be very little consistency in it.

To start with, the very definitions of these crimes may vary widely between different countries. Also, data collection procedures and practices will make the reliability of those numbers difficult.

The World Bank data is perhaps more consistent—things like land area can be measured and validated externally—but GNI can be reliant upon the own country's reporting, and that may often be inflated, as countries attempt to make themselves look more important and influential.

Moreover, there are also a lot of holes in the data. Because we haven't normalized the country names, there are no observations for the United States. It's listed as "United States" in one dataset and as "United States of America" in the other. And while this single instance would be simple to correct, we really have to do a more thorough audit of the country names.

So while there's nothing systematic that we need to take into account, there are several problems with the data that we need to keep in mind. We'll revisit these closer to the end of this chapter.

Determining which tests are appropriate

Now we have to determine which tests to run. Some tests are appropriate to different types of data and to different distributions of data. For example, nominal and numeric data require very different analyses.

If the relationship were known to be linear, we could use Pearson's correlation coefficient. Unfortunately, the relationship in our data appears to be more complicated than that.

In this case, our data is continuous numeric data. And we're interested in the relationship between two variables, but neither is truly independent, because we're not really sure exactly how the *sampling* was done, based on the description of the assumptions given earlier.

Because of all these factors, we'll use Spearman's rank correlation.

How did I pick this? It's fairly simple, but just complicated enough that we will not go into the details here.

The main point is that which statistical test you use is highly dependent on the nature of your data. Much of this knowledge comes from learning and experience, but once you've determined your data, a good statistical textbook or any of a number of online flowcharts can help you pick the right test.

But what is Spearman's rank correlation? Let's take a minute and find out.

Understanding Spearman's rank correlation coefficient

Spearman's rank correlation coefficient measures the association between two variables. It is particularly useful when only the rank of the data is known, but it can also be useful in other situations. For instance, it isn't thrown off by outliers, because it only looks at the rank.

The formula for this statistic is as follows:

$$r_x = 1 - \frac{6 \sum d_i^2}{n\left(n^2 - 1\right)}$$

The value of n is the size of the sample. The value of d is each observation's difference in rank for the two variables. For example, in the data we've been looking at, Denmark ranks first for burglary (interesting), but third for per capita GNI. So Spearman's rank correlation would look at $3 - 1 = 2$.

A coefficient of 0 means there is no relationship between the two variables, and a coefficient of -1 or $+1$ means that the two variables are perfectly related. That is, the data can be perfectly described using a **monotonic** function: a function from one variable to the other that preserves the order of the items. The function doesn't have to be linear. In fact, it could easily describe a curve. But it does capture the data.

The coefficient doesn't give us statistical significance (the p value), however. To get that, we just need to know that the Spearman's rank correlation coefficient is distributed approximately normally, when $n \geq 10$. It has a mean of 0 and a standard deviation given as follows:

$$\sqrt{\frac{1}{(n-1)}}$$

With these formulae, we can compute the z score of coefficient for our test. The z score is the distance of a data point from the mean, measured in standard deviations. The p value is closely related to the z score. So if we know the z score, we also know the p value.

Selecting the significance level

Now we need to select how high of a bar we need the significance to rise to. The target p value is known as the a value. In general, $a = 0.05$ is commonly used, although if you want to be extra careful, $a = 0.01$ is also normal.

For this test, we'll just use $a = 0.05$.

Determining the critical region

We'll accept any kind of relationship for rejecting the null hypothesis, so this will be a two-tailed test. That means that the critical region will come from both sides of the curve, with their areas being 0.05 divided equally for 0.025 on each side.

This corresponds to a z score of $z < -1.96$ or $z > 1.96$.

Calculating the test statistic and its probability

We can use Incanter's function, `incanter.stats/spearmans-rho`, to calculate the Spearman's coefficient. However, it doesn't only calculate the z score. We can easily create the following function that wraps all of these calculations. We'll put this into `src/nullh/stats.clj`. We'll name the function `spearmans`.

```
(defn spearmans
  ([col-a col-b] (spearmans col-a col-b i/$data))
  ([col-a col-b dataset]
   (let [rho (s/spearmans-rho
               (i/sel dataset :cols col-a)
               (i/sel dataset :cols col-b))
         n (i/nrow dataset)
         mu 0.0
         sigma (Math/sqrt (/ 1.0 (- n 1.0)))
         z (/ (- rho mu) sigma)]
     {:rho rho, :n n, :mu mu, :sigma sigma, :z z})))
```

Now, we can run this on the dataset. Let's start from the beginning and load the datasets from the disk with the following commands:

```
user=> (def by-ny-gnp
          (d/load-join-pivot
            "unodc-data"
            "ny.gnp/ny.gnp.pcap.cd_Indicator_en_csv_v2.csv"))
#'user/by-ny-gnp
user=> (def burglary (d/by-crime by-ny-gnp "CTS 2012 Burglary"))
#'user/burglary
user=> (pprint (n-stat/spearmans :indicator-value :rate burglary))
{:rho 0.6938241467993876,
 :n 537,
 :mu 0.0,
 :sigma 0.04319342127906801,
 :z 16.063190325134588}
```

The preceding commands allowed us to see the process from front to back, and we can take the output and consider how the test went.

Deciding whether to reject the null hypothesis or not

The final z-score was 16.03. Going by the book, a z-score this high is usually not even included on the charts. This would be a significant result, which would allow us to reject the null hypothesis. So, from this we can conclude that there is a relationship between the per capita GNI and the burglary rate.

Interpreting the results

Of course, the results don't tell us a whole lot. For one, we have to remember that just because there's a relationship, that doesn't imply causality. Moreover, because the result is so significant, we should probably be skeptical about the results and whether they're caused by some artifact in the data or the procedures.

We've already talked about the problems in the data, and some of them may be at fault. Particularly, some of the data is missing because of normalization problems, which may change the results. Another possibility is that industrialized nations keep better records, so they would appear to have more burglaries.

Summary

So, in this chapter, we learned how null hypothesis testing can help us structure our analyses. Having a well thought out and standard procedure also ensures that we are thorough in our analysis. For example, in this chapter, we were forced to confront the ugly truths about the data we were working with, and that gave us insights into the results that we achieved later.

In the next chapter, we'll actually get a chance to use these techniques again, when we look at conducting A/B testing on websites.

8

A/B Testing – Statistical Experiments for the Web

One of the most common uses of statistics on the Internet right now is **A/B testing**. This acts as an aid to design and increase interactions with users in a data-driven way. It's used all over the Web, and there have been some high-profile instances of these techniques being written about in blogs and articles online. For instance, there were several descriptions of how Baraka Obama's 2012 US Presidential campaign used A/B testing to increase both donations and how many people signed up for the e-mail updates.

Over the course of this chapter, we'll look at the following topics:

- Defining A/B testing
- Conducting an A/B test
- Analyzing the results

By the end, we'll have simulated a small A/B test to measure a click-through on two different versions of text for a button.

Defining A/B testing

At its most fundamental level, A/B testing just involves creating two different versions of a web page. Sometimes, the changes are major redesigns of the site or the user experience, but usually, the changes are as simple as changing the text on a button. Then, for a short period of time, new visitors are randomly shown one of the two versions of the page. The site tracks their behavior, and the experiment determines whether one version or the other increases the users' interaction with the site. This may mean more click-through, more purchases, or any other measurable behavior.

This is similar to other methods in other domains that use different names. The basic framework randomly tests two or more groups simultaneously and is sometimes called random-controlled experiments or online-controlled experiments. It's also sometimes referred to as split testing, as the participants are split into two groups.

These are all examples of **between-subjects experiment design**. Experiments that use these designs all split the participants into two groups. One group, the control group, gets the original environment. The other group, the test group, gets the modified environment that those conducting the experiment are interested in testing.

Experiments of this sort can be **single-blind** or **double-blind**. In single-blind experiments, the subjects don't know which group they belong to. In double-blind experiments, those conducting the experiments also don't know which group the subjects they're interacting with belong to. This safeguards the experiments against biases that can be introduced by participants being aware of which group they belong to. For example, participants could get more engaged if they believe they're in the test group because this is *newer* in some way. Or, an experimenter could treat a subject differently in a subtle way because of the group that they belong to.

As the computer is the one that directly conducts the experiment, and because those visiting your website aren't aware of which group they belong to, website A/B testing is generally an example of double-blind experiments.

Of course, this is an argument for only conducting the test on new visitors. Otherwise, the user might recognize that the design has changed and throw the experiment away. For example, the users may be more likely to click on a new button when they recognize that the button is, in fact, new. However, if they are new to the site as a whole, then the button itself may not stand out enough to warrant extra attention.

In some cases, these subjects can test more variant sites. This divides the test subjects into more groups. There needs to be more subjects available in order to compensate for this. Otherwise, the experiment's statistical validity might be in jeopardy. If each group doesn't have enough subjects, and therefore observations, then there is a larger error rate for the test, and results will need to be more extreme to be significant.

In general, though, you'll want to have as many subjects as you reasonably can. Of course, this is always a trade-off. Getting 500 or 1000 subjects may take a while, given the typical traffic of many websites, but you still need to take action within a reasonable amount of time and put the results of the experiment into effect. So we'll talk later about how to determine the number of subjects that you actually need to get a certain level of significance.

Another wrinkle that is you'll want to know as soon as possible is whether one option is clearly better or not so that you can begin to profit from it early. In the multi-armed bandit problem, this is a problem of *exploration* versus *exploitation*. This refers to the tension in the experiment design (and other domain) between exploring the problem space and exploiting the resources you've found in the experiment so far. We won't get into this further, but it is a factor to stay aware of as you perform A/B tests in the future.

Because of the power and simplicity of A/B testing, it's being widely used in a variety of domains. For example, marketing and advertising make extensive use of it. Also, it has become a powerful way to test and improve measurable interactions between your website and those who visit it online.

The primary requirement is that the interaction be somewhat limited and very measurable. Interesting would not make a good metric; the *click-through rate* or *pages visited*, however, would. Because of this, A/B tests validate changes in the placement or in the text of buttons that call for action from the users. For example, a test might compare the performance of **Click for more!** against **Learn more now!**. Another test may check whether a button placed in the upper-right section increases sales versus one in the center of the page.

These changes are all incremental, and you probably don't want to break a large site redesign into pieces and test all of them individually. In a larger redesign, several changes may work together and reinforce each other. Testing them incrementally and only applying the ones that increase some metric can result in a design that's not aesthetically pleasing, is difficult to maintain, and costs you users in the long run. In these cases, A/B testing is not recommended.

Some other things that are regularly tested in A/B tests include the following parts of a web page:

- The wording, size, and placement of a call-to-action button
- The headline and product description
- The length, layout, and fields in a form
- The overall layout and style of the website as a larger test, which is not broken down
- The pricing and promotional offers of products
- The images on the landing page
- The amount of text on a page

Now that we have an understanding of what A/B testing is and what it can do for us, let's see what it will take to set up and perform an A/B test.

Conducting an A/B test

In creating an A/B test, we need to decide several things, and then we need to put our plan into action. We'll walk through those decisions here and create a simple set of web pages that will test the aspects of design that we are interested in changing, based upon the behavior of the user.

Before we start building stuff, though, we need to think through our experiment and what we'll need to build.

Planning the experiment

For this chapter, we're going to pretend that we have a website to sell widgets (or rather, looking at the **Widgets!** website).

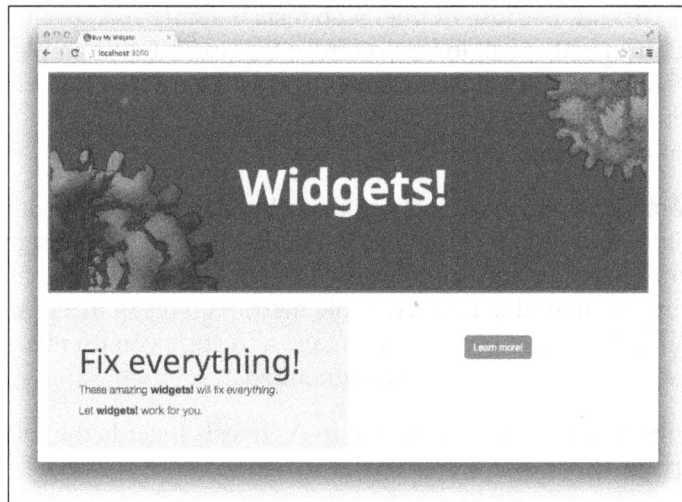

The web page in this screenshot is the **control page**. Currently, we're getting 24 percent click-through on it from the **Learn more!** button.

We're interested in the text of the button. If it read **Order now!** instead of **Learn more!**, it might generate more click-through. (Of course, actually explaining what the product is and what problems it solves might be more effective, but one can't have everything.) This will be the **test page**, and we're hoping that we can increase the click-through rate to 29 percent (a five percent absolute increase).

Now that we have two versions of the page to experiment with, we can frame the experiment statistically and figure out how many subjects we'll need for each version of the page in order to achieve a statistically meaningful increase in the click-through rate on that button.

Framing the statistics

First, we need to frame our experiment in terms of the **null-hypothesis test**. In this case, the null hypothesis would look something like this:

Changing the button copy from **Learn more!** *to* **Order now!** *Would not improve the click-through rate.*

Remember, this is the statement that we're hoping to disprove (or fail to disprove) in the course of this experiment.

Now we need to think about the sample size. This needs to be fixed in advance. To find the sample size, we'll use the standard error formula, which will be solved to get the number of observations to make for about a 95 percent confidence interval in order to get us in the ballpark of how large our sample should be:

$$n = 16 \frac{\sigma^2}{\delta^2}$$

In this, δ is the minimum effect to detect and σ^2 is the sample variance. If we are testing for something like a percent increase in the click-through, the variance is $\sigma^2 = p(1 - p)$, where p is the initial click-through rate with the control page.

So for this experiment, the variance will be *0.24(1-0.24)* or *0.1824*. This would make the sample size for each variable *16(0.1824 / 0.05²)* or almost *1170*.

The code to compute this in Clojure is fairly simple:

```
(defn get-target-sample [rate min-effect]
  (let [v (* rate (- 1.0 rate))]
    (* 16.0 (/ v (* min-effect min-effect)))))
```

Running the code from the prompt gives us the response that we expect:

```
user=> (get-target-sample 0.24 0.05)
1167.36
```

Part of the reason to calculate the number of participants needed is that monitoring the progress of the experiment and stopping it prematurely can invalidate the results of the test because it increases the risk of false positives where the experiment says it has disproved the null hypothesis when it really hasn't.

This seems counterintuitive, doesn't it? Once we have significant results, we should be able to stop the test. Let's work through it.

Let's say that in actuality, there's no difference between the control page and the test page. That is, both sets of copy for the button get approximately the same click-through rate. If we're attempting to get $p \leq 0.05$, then it means that the test will return a false positive five percent of the time. It will incorrectly say that there is a significant difference between the click-through rates of the two buttons five percent of the time.

Let's say that we're running the test and planning to get 3,000 subjects. We end up checking the results of every 1,000 participants. Let's break down what might happen:

Run	A	B	C	D	E	F	G	H
1000	No	No	No	No	Yes	Yes	Yes	Yes
2000	No	No	Yes	Yes	No	Yes	No	Yes
3000	No	Yes	No	Yes	No	No	Yes	Yes
Final	No	Yes	No	Yes	No	No	Yes	Yes
Stopped	No	Yes	Yes	Yes	Yes	Yes	Yes	Yes

Let's read this table. Each lettered column represents a scenario for how the significance of the results may change over the run of the test. The rows represent the number of observations that have been made. The row labeled *Final* represents the experiment's true finishing result, and the row labeled *Stopped* represents the result if the experiment is stopped as soon as a significant result is seen.

The final results show us that out of eight different scenarios, the final result would be significant in four cases (B, D, G, and H). However, if the experiment is stopped prematurely, then it will be significant in seven cases (all but A). The test could drastically over-generate false positives.

In fact, most statistical tests assume that the sample size is fixed before the test is run.

It's exciting to get good results, so we'll design our system so that we can't easily stop it prematurely. We'll just take that temptation away.

With this in mind, let's consider how we can implement this test.

Building the experiment

There are several options to actually implement the A/B test. We'll consider several of them and weigh their pros and cons. Ultimately, the option that works best for you really depends on your circumstances. However, we'll pick one for this chapter and use it to implement the test for it.

Looking at options to build the site

The first way to implement A/B testing is to use a server-side implementation. In this case, all of the processing and tracking is handled on the server, and visitors' actions would be tracked using GET or POST parameters on the URL for the resource that the experiment is attempting to drive traffic towards.

The steps for this process would go something like the following ones:

1. A new user visits the site and requests for the page that contains the button or copy that is being tested.

2. The server recognizes that this is a new user and assigns the user a tracking number.

3. It assigns the user to one of the test groups.

4. It adds a row in a database that contains the tracking number and the test group that the user is part of.

5. It returns the page to the user with the copy, image, or design that is reflective of the control or test group.

6. The user views the returned page and decides whether to click on the button or link or not.

7. If the server receives a request for the button's or link's target, it updates the user's row in the tracking table to show us that the interaction was a success, that is, that the user did a click-through or made a purchase.

This way of handling it keeps everything on the server, so it allows more control and configuration over exactly how you want to conduct your experiment.

A second way of implementing this would be to do everything using JavaScript (or ClojureScript, `https://github.com/clojure/clojurescript`). In this scenario, the code on the page itself would randomly decide whether the user belonged to the control or the test group, and it would notify the server that a new observation in the experiment was beginning. It would then update the page with the appropriate copy or image. Most of the rest of this interaction is the same as the one in previous scenario. However, the complete steps are as follows:

1. A new user visits the site and requests for the page that contains the button or copy being tested.

2. The server inserts some JavaScript to handle the A/B test into the page.

3. As the page is being rendered, the JavaScript library generates a new tracking number for the user.

4. It assigns the user to one of the test groups.

5. It renders that page for the group that the user belongs to, which is either the control group or the test group.

6. It notifies the server of the user's tracking number and the group.

7. The server takes this notification and adds a row for the observation in the database.

8. The JavaScript in the browser tracks the user's next move either by directly notifying the server using an AJAX call or indirectly using a GET parameter in the URL for the next page.

9. The server receives the notification whichever way it's sent and updates the row in the database.

The downside of this is that having JavaScript take care of rendering the experiment might take slightly longer and may throw off the experiment. It's also slightly more complicated, because there are more parts that have to communicate. However, the benefit is that you can create a JavaScript library, easily throw a small script tag into the page, and immediately have a new A/B experiment running.

In reality, though, you'll probably just use a service that handles this and more for you. However, it still makes sense to understand what they're providing for you, and that's what this chapter tries to do by helping you understand how to perform an A/B test so that you can be make better use of these A/B testing vendors and services.

Implementing A/B testing on the server

For the purposes of this chapter, we'll implement the A/B test on the server.

First, we'll create a new project using **Leiningen 2** (`http://leiningen.org/`) and the **Luminus web framework** (`http://www.luminusweb.net/`). We'll include some options to include the **H2 embedded database** (`http://www.h2database.com/`) and **ClojureScript support** (`https://github.com/clojure/clojurescript`). We do this with the following command line:

```
lein new luminus web-ab +h2 +cljs
```

This command creates the scaffolding for a website. We'll first get familiar with what the scaffolding provides, and then we'll fill in the parts of the site with the core site. Next, we'll add the A/B testing, and finally, we'll add a couple of pages to view the results.

Understanding the scaffolded site

Luminus is a web framework that is built by combining other libraries and tying them together. For database access and models, it uses **Korma** (http://sqlkorma.com/). For HTML templates, it uses **Selmer** (https://github.com/yogthos/Selmer), which is a port of Django-style templates. For routing, controllers, sessions, and everything else, it uses **lib-noir** (http://yogthos.github.io/lib-noir/) and **Compojure** (https://github.com/weavejester/compojure/).

Everything in the directory that contains a Luminus project will be a consistent set of subdirectories named after the project. For instance, in the project that we just created for this (web-ab), the primary directories would be as follows:

- resources is the directory of static resources. It contains the CSS, JavaScript, and image files for the site.
- src is the directory of Clojure files. Several of the subdirectories in this directory tree are important too, so I'll list them separately.
- src/web_ab/models/ is the directory that contain the Clojure files that define the model and interact with the database.
- src/web_ab/routes/ is the directory that lists the routes in a web application. Each module under this defines the routes and handlers for a particular subsection of the site.
- src/web_ab/views/templates/ is the directory that contains the Selmer templates.
- test/web_ab/test/ is the directory that contains the clojure.test tests for the site's handlers.

We'll primarily deal with the directories under src/web-ab/. We'll define the models, define the routes and handlers, and fill in the templates.

As we work, we can view the site as we're developing it by using the development server. You can start this using the following Leiningen command:

```
lein ring server
```

Once this server is executed, we can view the site by pointing our browser to http://localhost:3000/.

Building the test site

First, we need to add in the content for the main page. The file that we'll want to change will be in `src/web_ab/views/templates/home.html`. We'll add the following HTML content to that page. (There are a lot more CSS and images involved in creating the site that we saw in the screenshot earlier. All this is listed in the code download for this chapter.) Take a look at the following code:

```
{% extends "web_ab/views/templates/base.html" %}
{% block content %}
<header id="banner" class="row">
  <div class="col-md-12">
    <h1 style="width: 4.5em;" class="center-block">Widgets!</h1>
  </div>
</header>
<div id="content" class="row">
  <div id="left-panel" class="col-md-6 jumbotron">
    <h1>Fix everything!</h1>
    <p>These amazing <strong>widgets!</strong> will fix
      <em>everything</em>.</p>
    <p>Let <strong>widgets!</strong> work for you.</p>
  </div>
  <div id="right-panel" class="col-md-6 jumbotron">
    <a href="/purchase/" id="btn-more"
      class="btn btn-primary btn-lg center-block">
      Learn more!
    </a>
  </div>
</div>
{% endblock %}
```

When the time comes to add in the A/B testing features, we'll change this a little, but most of this is good as it is.

We'll also need a page to direct the users to if they want to buy a widget. We'll first define a route for this page in the `src/web_ab/routes/home.clj` file. The following is the route and the controller:

```
(defn purchase-page []
  (layout/render "purchase.html" {}))
(defroutes home-routes
  (GET "/" [] (home-page))
  (GET "/purchase/" [] (purchase-page)))
```

The view is defined in the `src/web_ab/views/templates/purchase.html` file. This file is very similar to the preceding template file, except that it's considerably simpler. It just contains a thank you message for the left panel, and there's no button or link on the right-hand side. For more details about this page, see the code download.

In fact, this is enough to define the base, control site in this project. Now let's look at what we need to do to define the A/B testing features.

Implementing A/B testing

Adding A/B testing into the site that we have so far will be pretty straightforward web development. We'll need to define a model and functions that implement the test framework's basic functionality. We can then incorporate them into the site's existing controllers and views:

1. The code that defines the data and the database settings will go into the `src/web_ab/models/schema.clj` file. It will start with the following namespace declaration:

```
(ns web-ab.models.schema
  (:require [clojure.java.jdbc :as sql]
            [noir.io :as io]))
```

2. The first facet of this section of the site that we'll define is the model. We'll add a table to the database schema that defines a table to track the A/B participants:

```
(defn create-abtracking-table []
  (sql/with-connection db-spec
    (sql/create-table :abtracking
      [:id "INTEGER IDENTITY"]
      [:testgroup "INT NOT NULL"]
      [:startat "TIMESTAMP NOT NULL DEFAULT NOW()"]
      [:succeed "TIMESTAMP DEFAULT NULL"])))
```

3. Now, in the `src/web_ab/models/db.clj` file, we'll define some low-level functions to work with the rows in this table. For this file, we'll use the following namespace declaration:

```
(ns web-ab.models.db
  (:use korma.core
        [korma.db :only (defdb)])
  (:require [web-ab.models.schema :as schema]
            [taoensso.timbre :as timbre]))
```

4. The first function in this namespace will take a group keyword (`:control` or `:test`) and insert a row into the database with a code that represents that group and the default values for the starting time (the current time) and the time in which the interaction succeeds (NULL):

```
(defn create-abtracking [group]
  (get (insert abtracking
               (values [{:testgroup (group-code group)}]))
       (keyword "scope_identity()")))
```

5. Next, we'll create a function that sets an `abtracking` object's succeed field to the current time. This will mark the interaction as a success:

```
(defn mark-succeed [id]
  (update abtracking
          (set-fields {:succeed (sqlfn :now)})
          (where {:id id})))
```

These, along with a few other functions that you can find in the code download for this chapter, will form a low-level interface with this data table. Most of the time, however, we'll deal with A/B testing using a slightly higher-level interface.

This interface will live in the `src/web_ab/ab_testing.clj` file. It will contain the following namespace declaration:

```
(ns web-ab.ab-testing
  (:require [noir.cookies :as c]
            [taoensso.timbre :as timbre]
            [web-ab.models.db :as db]
            [incanter.stats :as s]
            [clojure.set :as set]
            [web-ab.util :as util])
  (:import [java.lang Math]))
```

To understand the code in this module, we need to first talk about how the A/B testing system will work. We have the following number of requirements that we need to make sure are implemented:

- If the users have visited the site before the A/B test, they should see the control version of the site. We assume that there's a tracking cookie already being used for this. In this case, the cookie will be named *visits*, and it will simply track the number of times a user has visited the home page of the site.

- If this is the users' first visit to the site, they will be randomly assigned to the control group or the test group, and they'll be shown the appropriate page for that group. Also, they'll receive a tracking cookie for the observation that they are, and we'll insert the tracking information for them into the database.

- If the users have visited the site earlier and are participants in the A/B test, they should see the same version of the site that they saw previously.

- Finally, when a user who is a participant in the experiment visits the purchase page, that observation in the experiment will be marked as a success.

We'll write functions for most of these cases as well as a function to route the user to the right branch whenever one visits the front page. We'll write another function to handle item number four.

For the first function, we'll implement what's necessary to start a new observation in the experiment. We'll enter the functions into the database and insert the tracking cookie into the session:

```
(defn new-test [test-cases]
  (let [[group text] (rand-nth (seq test-cases))
        ab-tracking (db/get-abtracking
                      (db/create-abtracking group))]
    (c/put! :abcode (:id ab-tracking))
    text))
```

The functions in the db namespace (aliased from `web-ab.models.db`) are from the low-level model interface that we just defined. In fact, the implementation for `create-abtracking` is listed on the preceding page.

The `c/put!` function is from the `noir.cookies` namespace. It inserts the cookie value into the session. In this case, it inserts the tracking instance's database ID under the `abcode` key.

Finally, `new-test` returns the text that should be used on the page.

The next function for this level of abstraction is `get-previous-copy`. This is used whenever a user who is already a participant in the experiment visits the page again. It takes a database ID and the different versions of the site that are being used in the current test, and it retrieves the row from the database and looks up the right copy text to be used on the page, given whether the observation is in the control group or the test group:

```
(defn get-previous-copy [ab-code test-cases]
  (-> ab-code
    db/get-abtracking
    :testgroup
    db/code->group
    test-cases))
```

This function simply runs the input through a number of conversions. First, this function converts it to a full data row tuple based on the database ID. Next, it selects the `testgroup` field, and it translates it into a group keyword. This is finally translated into the appropriate text for the page, based on the group keyword.

The next function that we're going to look at ties the two previous functions together with item number one from the preceding list (where the returning visitors are shown the control page without being entered into the experiment):

```
(defn start-test [counter default test-cases]
  (let [c (Long/parseLong (c/get counter "0"))
        ab-code (get-abcode-cookie)]
    (c/put! counter (inc c))
    (cond
      (and (>= ab-code 0) (> c 0))
      (get-previous-copy ab-code test-cases)

      (and (< ab-code 0) (> c 0)) default

      :else (new-test test-cases)))))
```

First, this function expects three parameters: the cookie name for the counter, the default text for the control page, and a map from the group keywords to page text. This function looks at the value of the counter cookie and the *abtest* cookie, both of which will be -1 or 0 if they're not set, and it decides what should be displayed for the user as well as inserts whatever needs to be inserted into the database.

In the preceding code snippet, we can see that the calls to the two functions that we've just looked at are highlighted in the code listing.

Also, here we define a function that looks for the *abtest* cookie and, if it's found, we mark it as having succeeded, shown as follows:

```
(defn mark-succeed []
  (let [ab-code (get-abcode-cookie)]
    (when (> ab-code -1)
      (db/mark-succeed ab-code))))
```

Finally, once the experiment is over, we need to perform the analysis that determines whether the control page performed better or the test page:

```
(defn perform-test
  ([ab-testing] (perform-test ab-testing 0.05))
  ([ab-testing p]
   (let [groups (group-by-group ab-testing)
         t (-> (s/t-test (to-flags (:test groups))
                         :y (to-flags (:control groups))
                         :alternative :less)
               (select-keys [:p-value :t-stat
                             :x-mean :y-mean :n1 :n2])
               (set/rename-keys {:x-mean :test-p,
                                 :y-mean :control-p,
                                 :n1 :test-n,
                                 :n2 :control-n}))]
     (assoc t
            :p-target p
            :significant (<= (:p-value t) p)))))
```

To perform the actual analysis, we use the t-test function from `incanter.stats` in the **Incanter** library (`http://incanter.org/`). We'll get into this analysis in more detail later in the chapter. For now, let's just pay attention to how the data flows through this function. The `t-test` function returns a map that contains a lot of numbers. For the output, we need to select some of this information and rename the keys for some of the data that we will use. We use the core `select-keys` function to select only the information that we need, and we use `clojure.set/rename-keys` to give the rest of the names that will fit our current domain in a better manner.

To the results of the analysis, we'll also add a couple of other pieces of data. One will be the alpha value, that is, the target value for p that we're trying to improve upon. The other depends on whether the results are significant or not. This is found by testing the value of p against the significance level that we're trying for.

With the low-level and high-level interfaces to the A/B testing process in place, we can turn our attention to actually using it. First, we need to update the view template for the home page from what we listed in the preceding snippet.

Remember, the file is in `src/web_ab/views/templates/home.html`. We want to simply change the name of the link to go to the purchase page. It needs to be a parameter that we can use to insert a value into the template. For instance, the following snippet contains the updated version of the right-hand panel, including the highlighted line that we can use to insert the text into the page:

```
<div id="right-panel" class="col-md-6 jumbotron">
  <a href="/purchase/" id="btn-more"
     class="btn btn-primary btn-lg center-block">
    {{button}}
  </a>
</div>
```

The controllers will also need to change. They need to trigger the appropriate stages in the test participant's lifecycle, and they need to pass the button text into the template.

The controller for the home page does this as part of one form. It calls `start-test`, and builds the template parameters using its output directly. This addition to the controller is highlighted as follows:

```
(defn home-page []
  (layout/render
    "home.html"
    {:button (ab/start-test :visits default-button test-cases)}))
```

The controller for the purchase page just incorporates a call to `mark-succeed` in its normal flow:

```
(defn purchase-page []
  (ab/mark-succeed)
  (layout/render "purchase.html" {}))
```

At this point, everything is in place to actually conduct the test; however, we cannot tell when it's over or look at the results. We can add this section of the website in the next stage.

Viewing the results

We'll add the A/B test result's views as separate pages in a separate section of the site. It will use the same `abtracking` model as the rest of the A/B testing, but we'll define more controllers and views.

One of the primary features of this part of the site is that we don't want to display some information before the test is complete. In order to decide this, we'll first define a map that specifies how many observations from each group we need:

```
(def target-counts {:control 1200, :test 1200})
```

We can use these values to define a predicate that tests whether enough participants have been registered in order to call the experiment complete. It reads the participants from the database and categorizes them by the experiment group. It compares the counts of these groups to the target counts:

```
(defn is-over?
  ([] (is-over? (ab/get-ab-tracking)))
  ([ab-tracking]
   (let [{:keys [control test]} (ab/group-by-group ab-tracking)]
     (and (>= (count control) (:control target-counts))
          (>= (count test) (:test target-counts))))))
```

We can use this to go a step further. We'll define a function that takes the list of rows from the `abtracking` table and a function that renders a page. It tests whether the experiment has been performed. If it is complete, it passes the on processing to that function. If it's not, it displays a standard page that informs the user that the experiment has not been completed yet:

```
(defn when-is-over [ab-tracking f]
  (if (is-over? ab-tracking)
    (f ab-tracking)
    (let [{:keys [control test]} (ab/group-by-group ab-tracking)]
      (layout/render
        "ab-testing-not-done.html"
        {:counts {:control (count control)
                  :test (count test)}
         :targets target-counts
         :complete {:control (ab/pct (count control)
                                     (:control target-counts))
                    :test (ab/pct (count test)
                                  (:test target-counts))}})))
```

Now, with these utilities in place, we can define a couple of pages. The first one will list the participants from the `abtracking` table. You can find the controller function and the view template in the code download. Both are relatively straightforward.

The other is slightly more interesting for a couple of reasons. First, it uses the `when-is-over` function that we just saw, and second, it performs the statistical test to determine whether the control page performed better or the test page:

```
(defn grid []
  (when-is-over
    (ab/get-ab-tracking)
    (fn [ab-tracking]
      (let [by-group-outcome (ab/assoc-grid-totals
                                (ab/get-results-grid ab-tracking))
            stats (ab/perform-test ab-tracking 0.05)]
        (layout/render "ab-testing-grid.html"
                        {:grid by-group-outcome,
                         :stats (sort (seq stats))
                         :significant (:significant stats)})))))
```

As mentioned, this function uses the `when-is-over` function that we just defined in order to bypass this page and display a standard page that just says that the experiment has not been finished yet.

The statistical test, which is highlighted, calls the `perform-test` function that we talked about earlier.

The template for these primarily displays the results in a grid. It also has a colored alert at the top of the page, which indicates whether the control performed better or the test groups.

Looking at A/B testing as a user

Now that all the parts are together, let's walk through the user's interaction with the site. Most people who visit your site won't know that there are two different versions of the site, so they should interact with your site as they normally would.

When they first visit your site, users should see the following screen. The text on the button in the lower-right section might be different, but the rest should be the same for everyone.

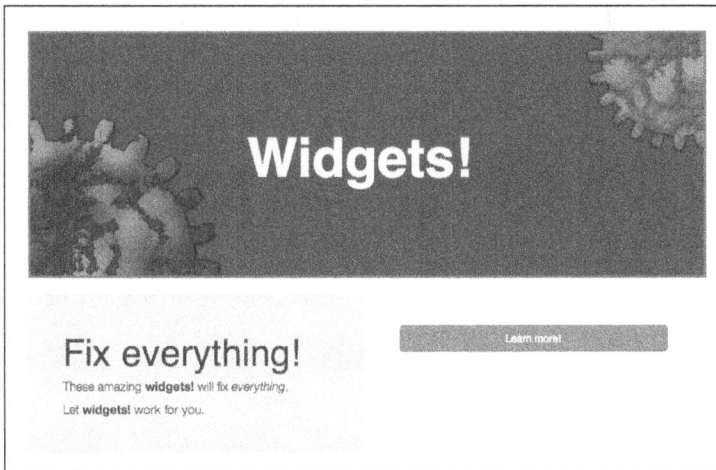

Once the user clicks on **Learn more!** (in this case), they complete the purchase, and all the users should see the following page:

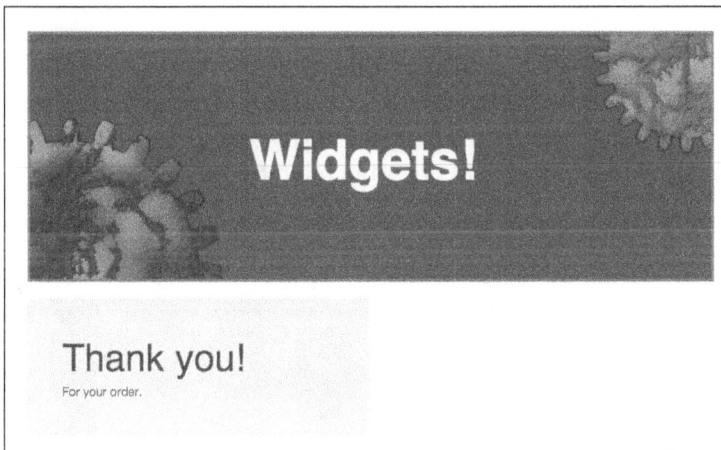

However, the more interesting part of this isn't what happens with the user but what happens afterwards when we can look at and analyze the results. We'll see some details about this in the next section.

Analyzing the results

Obviously, we're not going to be able to get a few thousand people to visit our website and purchase the widgets. In place of actual participants, I've populated the database with random data. This should allow us to see how the analysis section of the website works and what it means.

Throughout the experiment, we can get a list of the participants by visiting `http://localhost:3000/ab-testing/` on the local development server. This allows us to track the experiment's progress without really getting into the results and without having direct access to the counts.

	2426 observations.			
ID	**Group**	**Started At**		**Succeeded At**
7352	:control	2013-12-01 17:06:00.407		2013-12-01 17:11:54.208
7349	:control	2013-11-29 01:17:17.825		none
6671	:control	2013-11-29 01:16:18.302		none
5536	:control	2013-11-29 01:15:22.965		none
7012	:test	2013-11-29 01:15:16.635		2013-11-29 01:15:42.119
6839	:test	2013-11-29 01:15:11.615		none
6051	:test	2013-11-29 01:14:33.155		none

While the experiment is running, we don't really want to get more information than this page displays. This is where the `when-is-over` function, which we previously saw, comes into play. When we visited the page earlier, we had sufficient participants in the experiment, and then we got a page that explained that the experiment was not done and gave some indication as to how much longer it has to go on for.

For example, the following screenshot has about all the information we want to provide at this point in the experiment:

Not Done Yet

Group	**Current Count**
Control	306/1200 (25.5%)
Test	408/1200 (34.0%)

Back to the list of observations.

Of course, once the experiment is complete, we'd like to be able to see the final results, including whether the results allow us to reject the null hypothesis, that is, whether the test group performed better than the control group in a statistically significant way or not.

So when the experiment is complete, we get the following page:

Results Grid

The test did better than the control.

	Success	Failure	Total
Control	252	974	1226
Test	317	883	1200

There's more information included on this page. The following is a table that contains the rest of the data and a short explanation of what they are. We'll go into more detail on them in the next section, where we talk about the t-test.

Name	Value	Explanation
:control-mean	252	The average of the control group.
:control-n	1226	The number of observations in the control group.
:control-p	0.20555	The conversion rate of the control group.
:control-variance	200.20228	The variance for the control group.
:df	2401.10865	The degrees of freedom.
:p-target	0.05	The alpha value for the test: the maximum p-value for the test.
:p-value	0.00000	The actual p value for the t-test.
:se	0.59806	The standard error.
:significant	TRUE	Checking whether the results statistically significant
:t-value	108.68414	The results of the t-test.
:test-mean	317.00000	The mean of the test group.
:test-n	1200	The number of observations in the test group.
:test-p	0.26417	The conversion rate of the test group.
:test-variance	233.25917	The variance for the test group.

These values are given in another table further down the page in the preceding screenshot. To understand the statistical values in a better manner, let's dig more into exactly what test we used.

Understanding the t-test

First, we need to understand the statistical nature of the test that we're performing.

Fundamentally, the experiment is pretty simple; each observation has one of two outcomes. In many ways, this is a series of coin flips. Each flip can be heads or tails. Each site interaction can succeed or fail.

This kind of value is known as a binomial random variable. It can take one of two values, which vary according to a set probability. Binomial random variables have a number of assumptions that must be met:

- There are a fixed number of observations (n).

- Each observation will have one of the two possible outcomes.

- The n observations are independent, that is, the outcome of one observation does not in any way influence the probability of any other observation.

- The probability of the outcomes stays constant over time, that is, the probability of the outcome X ($P(X)$) will always be, say, 0.5. You can easily violate that in the design of the experiment by running the control page and the test page consecutively instead of running them simultaneously. If they're not run together, one page could be used during a busier time to get better results.

A common example of a binomial random variable is testing coin tosses. Let's use this as a first example, and then we'll apply what we've learned to our A/B test.

Testing coin tosses

Specifically, we'll have a coin that we know is fair and we'll test another coin that we suspect is biased against it. The null hypothesis is that there is no difference between the two coins and that both are true.

The following steps show us how this experiment will fulfill the assumptions of a binomial test:

1. We'll flip each coin 100 times.
2. Each coin toss (each observation) can be heads or tails.
3. Each coin toss is independent. Its probability isn't influenced by the probability of any other coin toss.
4. The probability of heads or tails won't change over time. The probability of heads (P(heads)) and the probability of tails (P(tails)) will be 0.5 during the entire test, or for the true coin, at least.

First, let's think about what will happen when we flip the true coin. We know that P(heads) = 0.5. Theoretically, every time we flip the coin for 100 times, we expect to get 50 heads and 50 tails. Of course, that isn't what happens in real life. Sometimes, we'll get 57 heads and 43 tails. Sometimes, we may get 44 heads and 56 tails. In extremely rare cases, we may get 100 heads and no tails. The distribution of coin tosses will form a binomial distribution, which is the number of successes in a series of yes/no experiments; however, as the number of coin tosses approaches infinity, the probability of all of these cases can be approximated by a normal distribution around the theoretical, expected probability of 50 heads and 50 tails.

For this experiment, let's say that we flipped a true coin 100 times, and we get heads 53 times.

Now, let's think about what will happen when we flip the other coin. It may be true, or it may be biased. If it is biased, we don't know it's biased by how much. So, when we flip it 100 times, and we get heads 58 times, we don't know if it's because P(heads) = 0.58 or because P(heads) = 0.5, P(heads) = 0.6, or something else, and we're slightly off this result on a normal distribution.

So we're interested in two things here. Primarily, we're interested in the difference between the two probabilities. Or, to express it in terms of the experiment, we're interested in the difference of means. We want to know whether the difference between 0.53 and 0.58 (0.05) is significant. The following graph illustrates the relationship that we're looking at in a continuous form. The actual data here is discrete, of course, but the continuous graph makes the relationship a little more clear.

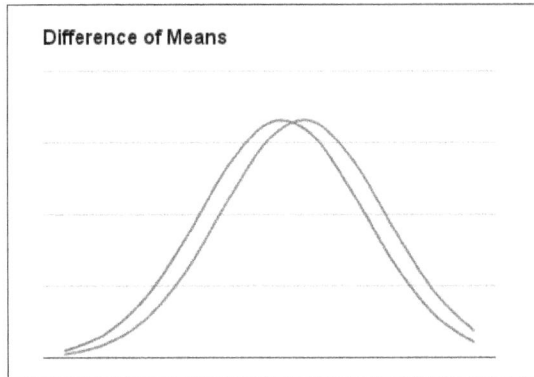

The expected number of successes of a binomial random variable is given by the following formula:

$$\mu = np$$

The Clojure code for the sample mean of a binomial variable is similarly straightforward:

```
(defn binomial-mean [coll] (reduce + 0.0 coll))
```

So, for the control group (the known true coins), the mean is 53, and for the test group (the possibly biased coins), it's 58.

In order to answer whether the difference is significant, we also have to be interested in something else: the possibility that we're wrong. We can assume that the actual means are somewhat different than the actual numbers we're dealing with, but how far off are they?

To answer this, we need to be able to calculate the standard error for our figures. Given a normal distribution, what's the probability that the figures are so far off that they'd give us the wrong result? To be able to answer this, we need to know something about how much variance the distribution has, that is, how wide the curve of the distribution's graph is.

Like the mean, the variance for a binomial random variable is pretty simple.

$$np\left(1-p\right)$$

The Clojure function for this is a little more complicated, but it's still clear:

```
(defn binomial-variance [coll]
  (let [n (count coll),
        p (/ (count (remove zero? coll)) n)]
    (* n p (- 1.0 p))))
```

This gives us variances of 24.91 and 24.36.

With the variance, we can calculate the standard error of the difference. This is an estimate of the standard deviation of all sample means, and it gives us some idea of how far off our means might be, given how variable the data is and how much data we're looking at. The following is the formula for that:

$$SE\left(\overline{X_t}-\overline{X_c}\right)=\sqrt{\frac{var_t}{n_t}+\frac{var_c}{n_c}}$$

The standard error function in Clojure is as follows:

```
(defn binomial-se [coll-t coll-c]
  (Math/sqrt (+ (/ (binomial-variance coll-t) (count coll-t))
                (/ (binomial-variance coll-c) (count coll-c)))))
```

For the coin flipping experiment, our standard error is 0.702.

We finally get to the **t-value**. This measures the difference between the means, scaled by how variable the groups are.

$$t = \frac{\overline{X_t} - \overline{X_c}}{SE}$$

Like the formula, the Clojure function for this builds upon all of the functions that we've just defined:

```
(defn binomial-t-test [coll-t coll-c]
  (/ (- (binomial-mean coll-t) (binomial-mean coll-c))
     (binomial-se coll-t coll-c)))
```

So the t-value of our coin flipping experiment is 7.123.

The output values of this formula follow a t distribution. This is very similar to a normal distribution, but the peak is smaller and the tails are heavier. However, as the degrees of freedom grow, it comes closer to a normal distribution. You can use the cumulative density function for the t-distribution or look in a table for the p value of this number.

We'll use Incanter's cumulative distribution functions to look up the probabilities of the particular t-values. In order to calculate this, we need to calculate the degrees of freedom for the test. When the variances of both the groups are equal, the formula is simple. However, for this, that will rarely be the case. For unequal variances, we'll use the Welch-Satterthwaite equation. It's a bit complicated, but it's what we have to work with.

$$v \approx \frac{\left(\frac{s_t^2}{N_t} + \frac{s_c^2}{N_c}\right)^2}{\frac{s_t^4}{N_t^2 v_t} + \frac{s_c^4}{N_c^2 v_c}}$$

In this equation, s^2 is the variation, N is the sample size, and v is $N-1$.

The Clojure code for this is only slightly less complicated:

```
(defn degrees-of-freedom [coll-t coll-c]
  (let [var-t (binomial-variance coll-t), n-t (count coll-t),
        var-c (binomial-variance coll-c), n-c (count coll-c)]
    (/ (Math/pow (+ (/ var-t n-t) (/ var-c n-c)) 2)
       (+ (/ (* var-t var-t) (* n-t n-t (dec n-t)))
          (/ (* var-c var-c) (* n-c n-c (dec n-c)))))))
```

Now, from REPL, we can test to see whether the coin toss test can reject the null hypothesis, that is, whether the second coin is biased:

```
user=> (require '[web-ab.ab-testing :as ab])
nil
user=> (require '[incanter.stats :as s])
nil
user=> (def group-c (take 100 (concat (repeat 53 1) (repeat 0))))
#'user/group-c
user=> (def group-t (take 100 (concat (repeat 58 1) (repeat 0))))
#'user/group-t
user=> (s/cdf-t (ab/binomial-t-test group-t group-c)
                :df (ab/degrees-of-freedom t c))
9.553337936305223E-12
```

So we can see that in the case of the coin flips, the coin is in fact biased and significantly so.

Testing the results

Let's take this same process and apply it again to the A/B test that we just conducted. This will help us see where the statistics in the preceding table came from:

1. First, we'll create the data sets by taking the number of observations and successes from each group:

    ```
    user=> (def c (take 1226 (concat (repeat 252 1.0)
                                     (repeat 0.0))))
    #'user/c
    user=> (def t (take 1200 (concat (repeat 317 1.0)
                                     (repeat 0.0))))
    #'user/t
    ```

2. Now, we can compute the mean and variance for each group:

```
user=> (ab/binomial-mean t)
317.0
user=> (ab/binomial-variance t)
233.25916666666666
user=> (ab/binomial-mean c)
252.0
user=> (ab/binomial-variance c)
200.20228384991844
```

3. This allows us to find the standard error:

```
user=> (ab/binomial-se t c)
0.5980633502426848
```

4. Finally, we can get the t-value, degrees of freedom, and the p-value.

```
user=> (ab/binomial-t-test t c)
108.68413851747313
user=> (ab/degrees-of-freedom t c)
2401.108650831878
user=> (s/cdf-t *2 :df *1)
1.0
```

This gives us the probability that the test results did not occur randomly. We're looking for them to be over 0.95, and they clearly are.

If this data occurred naturally, the very high p value makes us suspect that we may have a **type one error** or a false positive. However, in this case, the data wasn't generated completely randomly. In the code download, I've combined all of these into one function that gets called to perform the statistical test. This is what is used to generate the data for the table on the results page.

Summary

Over the course of this chapter, we've seen how to conceive of, create, and analyze the results of an A/B test.

The statistics themselves are really a continuation of the null-hypothesis testing that we saw in *Chapter 7, Null Hypothesis Tests – Analyzing Crime Data*. A/B testing provides a nice, complete, useful example of the workflow involved in using null-hypothesis testing and of the power and the help in the decision-making that it provides.

This allows us to use a standard and widely used way of testing exactly what variations on a website drive more interactions and allow us to identify and serve the site's users in a better manner. It allows us to decide on changes to the site in structured, testable ways.

Of course, in actuality, we'll probably want to use an existing service. There are several services out there, from bare bones but free services such as Google Analytics Content Experiments to full-featured for-pay services that cover all aspects of A/B testing, such as **Optimizely**, **Visual Website Optimizer**, or **Maxymiser**. However, knowing what's involved in A/B testing and what the best practices are means that we can evaluate and use these services and get the most from them in a better manner.

In the next chapter, we'll look at applying the data analysis to another part of the Web; we'll analyze how people participate in social sites by looking at patterns of participation in the **Stackoverflow** (`http://stackoverflow.com/`) data dumps.

9
Analyzing Social Data Participation

Social networks and websites have revolutionized the Internet. Most people online participate in some social network, either it's **Facebook**, **Twitter**, **Pinterest**, **GitHub**, **StackOverflow**, or any of the zillion other social networking websites that have sprung up. They're an important way for people to connect and stay in contact, but they're also a major source of data about people's relationships and activities.

Analyzing this data is important for a number of reasons. Of course, advertisers and marketers want to squeeze as much information out of the data as they can. But if you're running the social network, you'll want to analyze the data to figure out what's working and what's falling flat. You want to ask yourself constantly what you can do to engage users better and to make your social network a more compelling, enjoyable, or useful experience for your users.

Over the course of this chapter, we'll get an open data dump from the **StackExchange** (http://stackexchange.com) website. This includes StackOverflow (http://stackoverflow.com/) and a host of other question-and-answer sites. We'll analyze this in a number of different ways and try to learn both about how people interact and generate content on those sites and about what makes a good answer.

The following are the topics we are going to cover in this chapter:

* Understanding the analyses we can perform
* Getting the data
* Finding patterns of participation
* Comparing askers and answerers
* Finding participation patterns over time

- Finding up-voted answers
- Tagging questions automatically

Setting up the project

Before we get started, let's set up the project. I've done this using Leiningen 2 (`http://leiningen.org/`) and Stuart Sierra's reloaded project template (`https://github.com/stuartsierra/reloaded`). I named the project `social-so` by running the following code:

```
$ lein new reloaded social-so
```

Of course, we'll need more dependencies. The following is the `project.clj` file for this chapter:

```
(defproject social-so "0.1.0-SNAPSHOT"
  :dependencies [[org.clojure/clojure "1.5.1"]
                 [org.clojure/data.xml "0.0.7"]
                 [org.codehaus.jsr166-mirror/jsr166y "1.7.0"]
                 [org.clojure/data.json "0.2.4"]
                 [cc.mallet/mallet "2.0.7"]
                 [org.jsoup/jsoup "1.7.3"]]
  :profiles {:dev {:dependencies
                     [[org.clojure/tools.namespace "0.2.4"]]
                   :source-paths ["dev"]}}
  :jvm-opts ["-Xmx2048m"])
```

The highlights here are that we'll use `org.clojure/data.xml` to read XML files, `org.clojure/data.json` to read JSON, and `org.jsoup/jsoup` to clean up HTML. If you're still using Java 6, you'll need `jsr166y` to provide concurrency with the reducers library. And we'll use `cc.mallet/mallet` to handle some Naïve Bayesian classification.

Understanding the analyses

Now that we have the infrastructure out of the way, let's step back and think about what kind of data we have and what we can do with it.

Understanding social network data

Social networks come in two broad kinds:

1. There are **networking-oriented** social networks. These include the usual subjects, such as Facebook (`http://facebook.com`), LinkedIn (`http://linkedin.com`), Twitter (`http://twitter.com/`), or Sina Weibo (`http://weibo.com`). These focus on allowing people to connect with each other, build relationships, and post updates about themselves.

2. There are **knowledge-sharing-oriented** social networks. These include the StackExchange (`http://stackexchange.com`) family of social networks, including StackOverflow (`http://stackoverflow.com`) or Quora (`https://www.quora.com/`). These focus on allowing people to exchange information and knowledge. Usually, they are more structured and focused on questions and answers than web forums or wikis.

Obviously, these networks enable entirely different kinds of interactions and have different features and produce different kinds of data. Different kinds of analyses are appropriate.

Understanding knowledge-based social networks

In knowledge-based social networks, people come together to share information. Often, these are question-and-answer forums, such as the StackExchange network of sites, but also on **Quora** (`https://www.quora.com/`), **Yahoo Answers** (`http://answers.yahoo.com/`), and so on.

Generally, in this genre of social network, some users post questions. Others answer them. There's usually some kind of in-site economy, whether it's represented by badges, points, or some combination. This encourages people to keep both questions and answers on topic, to answer questions, and to set and maintain the community's tone. Sometimes, there are moderators, sometimes the communities are self-moderated, and sometimes there's a combination of the two.

Looking at the front page of StackOverflow, we can see the basic elements of the social network. Look at the following screenshot:

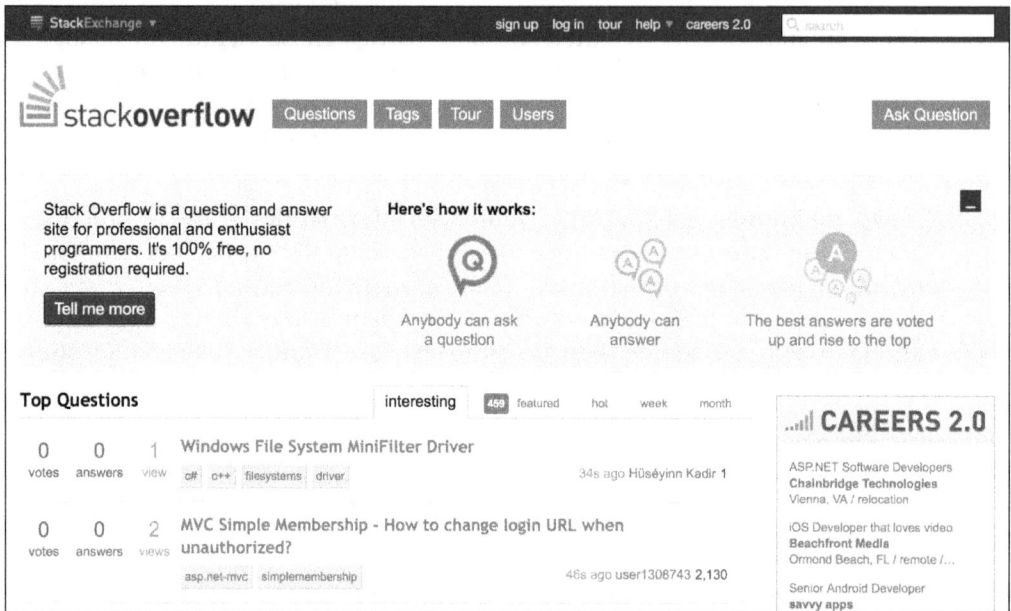

The preceding screenshot depicts a very interesting layout. You can easily notice the following two things:

- There's a button labeled **Ask Question** at the upper right-hand side for posting a question. This isn't as large as you might expect, since those asking questions are presumably motivated to find the button and are willing to click through into another page to do it. This is different than the posting boxes found on sites such as Facebook or Twitter, where they try to reduce the friction for posting new statuses in order to encourage people to do it.

- There is also a list of recently posted questions. This can be filtered to display tags that you're interested in. For example, you can use this to find either questions that you are qualified to answer or those you are interested in learning about yourself.

So we can see immediately that the primary interactions of the site are accessible from the front page. Also, the site's design makes it easier to do the more difficult interaction (answering questions).

We can already guess that most users will join to post only one or two questions and never participate on the site again. This group may potentially be quite large. Who those users are and how to motivate them to answer questions may be one critical question that StackExchange has.

There may also be a similar dynamic among the users who do answer questions. There are probably a small number of users who answer most of the questions. StackExchange may be interested in how to get contributions more evenly from all users, not just from a few *power users*.

Introducing the 80/20 rule

In fact, both of these observations are examples of the general principle of social networks. This has been called the **80/20** rule. This simply states that approximately 80 percent of the content will be created by 20 percent of the users. It's also known as the **Pareto Principle**, which states more generally that 80 percent of the effects come from 20 percent of the causes. Although in different social networks, the details may be off—for example, 15 percent of the users may create 95 percent of the content—in general this observation is surprisingly robust. One of the things that we'll look at in this chapter is exactly how the 80/20 rule applies to the StackOverflow data.

With this in mind, let's get the data so we can start looking at it.

Getting the data

In this chapter, we're going to focus on knowledge-based social networks, and in particular, we'll work with the StackExchange sites. For some time, StackExchange has made public a periodic data dump of their sites (`http://blog.stackexchange.com/category/cc-wiki-dump/`). This will provide a great test bed for working with a social network site's data.

The data dump is made available through the **Internet Archive** (https://archive.org/). The webpage for that is currently at https://archive.org/details/stackexchange. You can download the entire dump using a **BitTorrent** client (http://www.bittorrent.com/) such as **μTorrent** (http://www.utorrent.com/). However, we're only interested in the StackOverflow posts and comments, so if you'd like, you can just download those two archives. Of course, combined they're about 6 GB, so the torrent may make the most sense, anyway.

stackapps.com.7z	4.9 MB
stackexchange_archive.torrent	
stackoverflow.com-Badges.7z	61.2 MB
stackoverflow.com-Comments.7z	1.4 GB
stackoverflow.com-PostHistory.7z	7.5 GB
stackoverflow.com-PostLinks.7z	19.7 MB
stackoverflow.com-Posts.7z	4.6 GB
stackoverflow.com-Users.7z	77.3 MB
stackoverflow.com-Votes.7z	307.0 MB
stats.stackexchange.com.7z	71.9 MB
superuser.com.7z	360.3 MB
sustainability.stackexchange.com.7z	1.5 MB

The archived files are compressed using the 7z format. Windows users can get a utility for extracting this from the **7-zip** site (http://www.7-zip.org/). That site's download page also has links to some unofficial binaries for Mac OS X and Linux (http://www.7-zip.org/download.html). Both of these platforms also have command-line binaries available. For example, **Homebrew** (http://brew.sh/) has a recipe for this named **p7zip**.

Extract this data into your project directory, into a subdirectory named data, using the following lines of code:

```
cd data
7z x ~/torrents/stackexchange/stackoverflow.com-Posts.7z
```

Now we're ready to start digging into the data and see what surprises it has for us.

Looking at the amount of data

First, we need to see how much data there will be. The raw archive for this part of the data is about 6 GB. Not insignificant, but it's not petabytes, either.

So the compressed file is almost 5 GB, and the expanded file is 23 GB! We have a lot of data to look at.

Looking at the data format

All of the files are in XML format. The file labeled `Posts` contains both the questions and the answers.

The format of the data is fairly simple (but for a full description, see the `README.txt` file). The following is the first entry:

```
<row Id="4"
    PostTypeId="1"
    AcceptedAnswerId="7"
    CreationDate="2008-07-31T21:42:52.667"
    Score="251"
    ViewCount="15207"
    Body="&lt;p&gt;I want to use a track-bar to change a form's
        opacity.&lt;/p&gt;&#xA;&#xA;&lt;p&gt;This is my code
        :&lt;/p&gt;&#xA;&#xA;&lt;pre&gt;&lt;code&gt;decimal trans =
        trackBar1.Value / 5000;&#xA;this.Opacity = trans;
        &#xA;&lt;/code&gt;&lt;/pre&gt;&#xA;&#xA;&lt;p&gt;When I try
        to build it, I get this error:&lt;/p&gt;&#xA;&#xA;
        &lt;blockquote&gt;&#xA;  &lt;p&gt;Cannot implicitly convert
        type 'decimal' to 'double'.&lt;/p&gt;&#xA;&lt;
        /blockquote&gt;&#xA;&#xA;&lt;p&gt;I tried making
        &lt;strong&gt;trans&lt;/strong&gt; to &lt;strong&gt;
        double&lt;/strong&gt;, but then the control doesn't work.
        This code has worked fine for me in VB.NET in the past.
        &lt;/p&gt;&#xA;"
    OwnerUserId="8"
    LastEditorUserId="2648239"
    LastEditorDisplayName="Rich B"
    LastEditDate="2014-01-03T02:42:54.963"
    LastActivityDate="2014-01-03T02:42:54.963"
    Title="When setting a form's opacity should I use a decimal
        or double?"
    Tags="&lt;c#&gt;&lt;winforms&gt;&lt;forms&gt;&lt;type-
        conversion&gt;&lt;opacity&gt;"
    AnswerCount="13"
    CommentCount="25"
    FavoriteCount="23"
    CommunityOwnedDate="2012-10-31T16:42:47.213" />
```

As we can see from `README.txt`, this post represents a question (the `PostTypeId` field is 1). We can see its body, its tags, and its accepted answer, as well as a lot of the metadata about this post. This should give us plenty to go on.

If we look at the third entry, we'll see one of the accepted answers for this post, as follows:

```
<row Id="7"
    PostTypeId="2"
    ParentId="4"
    CreationDate="2008-07-31T22:17:57.883"
    Score="193"
    Body="&lt;p&gt;An explicit cast to double isn't
      necessary.&lt;/p&gt;&#xA;&#xA;&lt;pre&gt;&lt;code&gt;double
      trans = (double)trackBar1.Value / 5000.0;&#xA;&lt;
      /code&gt;&lt;/pre&gt;&#xA;&#xA;&lt;p&gt;Identifying the
      constant as &lt;code&gt;5000.0&lt;/code&gt; (or as
      &lt;code&gt;5000d&lt;/code&gt;) is sufficient:&lt;
      /p&gt;&#xA;&#xA;&lt;pre&gt;&lt;code&gt;double trans =
      trackBar1.Value / 5000.0;&#xA;double trans = trackBar1
      .Value / 5000d;&#xA;&lt;/code&gt;&lt;/pre&gt;&#xA;"
    OwnerUserId="9"
    LastEditorUserId="967315"
    LastEditDate="2012-10-14T11:50:16.703"
    LastActivityDate="2012-10-14T11:50:16.703"
    CommentCount="0" />
```

So, for answers (the `PostTypeId` field is 2), we can get their parents, their body texts, and their scores. Their parents indicate which child was accepted. This should be enough to help us analyze their content.

In both cases, we also have `OwnerUserId`, and this will help us understand how people interact with the site and with each other.

The text-field attributes allow rich content (`Body` and `Title`), and these are handled by encoding HTML into the fields. We'll need to escape those and probably scrub out the tags. That won't be a problem, but we'll need to keep it in mind.

Defining and loading the data

We can trace out some of the data that we'll need to use throughout this chapter. We can put these into the `src/social_so/data.clj` file.

We'll use two record types. The `CountRank` type will hold together a raw count and its rank in the list of frequencies, and the `UserInfo` type will store the user and the frequencies and ranks for the different types of posts that they've made. Look at the following code:

```
(defrecord CountRank [count rank])
(defrecord UserInfo [user post q a])
```

The post, q, and a fields will keep track of the frequencies and rank by all posts, by question posts, and by answer posts.

Together, these record structures should help us get a start in understanding this data and some of the patterns of participation.

For loading the data, let's move to a new file, named `src/social_so/xml.clj`, and let's give it the following namespace declaration:

```
(ns social-so.xml
  (:require [clojure.data.xml :as xml]
            [clojure.java.io :as io]
            [clojure.string :as str]
            [social-so.data :as d]
            [social-so.utils :as u])
  (:import [org.jsoup Jsoup]
           [org.jsoup.safety Whitelist]))
```

We'll use the functions in this namespace to read the XML file and build the records containing the data.

At the most basic level, we need to be able to read the post elements from the XML file. Look at the following code:

```
(defn read-posts [stream] (:content (xml/parse stream)))
```

We'll also need to access a little bit of data from each element. The following are some getter functions for an identifier for the user and for the post type code:

```
(defn get-user [el]
  (let [{:keys [attrs]} el]
    (or (u/->long (:OwnerUserId attrs))
        (u/to-lower (:OwnerDisplayName attrs)))))
(defn get-post-type [el]
  (u/->long (:PostTypeId (:attrs el))))
```

In this snippet, el represents the XML element being processed, and we're using a custom function to lowercase the string (`social-so.utils/to-lower`) to be a little defensive about being passed `null` values.

Loading the data from the XML files will take place in two stages. First, we'll get the raw frequencies, and then we'll sort the data several different ways and assign ranks to the data.

Counting frequencies

The way that we'll count the frequencies is to walk over the posts in the XML file. We'll maintain an index of the users with their `UserInfo` records. The first time each user is found, they will get a new `UserInfo` object. Subsequently, their `UserInfo` record will be updated with new counts.

Let's see how this works in practice.

The first function, `update-user-info`, operates on the level of a single record. It takes a `UserInfo` record and updates it based on the type of post currently being processed. If the record is nil, then a new one is created follows:

```
(defn update-user-info [user-id post-el user-info]
  (let [incrs {:question [1 0], :answer [0 1]}
        [q-inc a-inc] (incrs (get-post-type post-el))]
    (cond
      (nil? q-inc) user-info
      (nil? user-info) (d/->UserInfo user-id 1 q-inc a-inc)
      :else
      (assoc user-info
             :post (inc (:post user-info))
             :q (+ (:q user-info) q-inc)
             :a (+ (:a user-info) a-inc)))))
```

The next function operates at the level of the index from `user-id` to `UserInfo` records. It takes an XML post, and it gets the user's information from it. It tries to retrieve the `UserInfo` record for that user from the index, and it uses `update-user -info` to increment the counts in that record. Look at the following code:

```
(defn update-user-index [user-index post-el]
  (let [user (get-user post-el)]
    (->> user
      (get user-index)
      (update-user-info user post-el)
      (assoc user-index user))))
```

Finally, `load-user-infos` opens the XML file, reads in the posts, and counts the raw frequencies of the posts for each user. Finally, it forces the result with `doall`, because we're working inside of a `with-open` block, so we'll want to have the results fully realized before we close the file. Look at the following code:

```
(defn load-user-infos [filename]
  (with-open [s (io/input-stream filename)]
    (->> s
      read-posts
```

```
(reduce update-user-index {})
vals
(remove nil?)
doall)))
```

Now we're ready to walk over these, multiple times, and assign ranks based on the various counts.

Sorting and ranking

Currently, we're storing the raw frequency under the UserInfo records' fields. However, we want to move the frequencies into a CountRank record and store the rank alongside it. We will achieve this by performing the following steps:

1. We'll find the rank using the rank-on function. This sorts by one of the properties of the UserInfo records (:post, :q, or :a) and then associates each instance with a rank by containing both within a vector pair. Look at the following code:

```
(defn rank-on [user-property coll]
  (->> coll
    (sort-by user-property)
    reverse
    (map vector (range))))
```

2. The function update-rank will then take the rank-and-user pair from rank-on and associate it with the appropriate property, as follows:

```
(defn update-rank [user-property rank-info]
  (let [[rank user-info] rank-info]
    (assoc user-info user-property
           (d/->CountRank (get user-info user-property)
                          rank))))
```

3. The next function, add-rank-data, coordinates this process by calling these functions on all users. And the function controlling this process, add-all-ranks, does this on each user as follows:

```
(defn add-rank-data [user-property users]
  (map #(update-rank user-property %)
       (rank-on user-property users)))
(defn add-all-ranks [users]
  (->> users
    (add-rank-data :post)
    (add-rank-data :q)
    (add-rank-data :a)))
```

4. We can combine reading the XML file and counting the posts with sorting and ranking the users. Look at the following code:

```
(defn load-xml [filename]
  (add-all-ranks (load-user-infos filename)))
```

All of these functions make it simple to load the XML file and to assign the ranks. Look at the following code:

```
user=> (def users (x/load-xml
                    "data/stackoverflow.com-Posts"))
user=> (count users)
1594450
user=> (first users)
{:user 22656,
 :post {:count 28166, :rank 0},
 :q {:count 29, :rank 37889},
 :a {:count 28137, :rank 0}}
```

Now we have the information that we'll need to perform the first round of analyses.

Finding the patterns of participation

Now that we have some data loaded, let's roll up our sleeves and see what we can learn from it.

Before we do, however, it would be nice to have some way to generate reports of which users are the most active for each type of post. Look at the following code:

```
(defn print-top-rank [col-name key-fn n users]
  (let [fmt "%4s    %6s    %14s\n"
        sort-fn #(:rank (key-fn %))]
    (printf fmt "Rank" "User" col-name)
    (printf fmt "----" "------" "--------------")
    (doseq [user (take n (sort-by sort-fn users))]
      (let [freq (key-fn user)]
        (printf fmt (:rank freq) (:user user) (:count freq))))))
```

This allows us to create tables listing the top 10 (or so) users for each post type.

Rank	User	All Posts
0	22656	28166
1	29407	20342
2	157882	15444
3	17034	13287
4	34397	13209
5	23354	12312
6	115145	11806
7	20862	10455
8	57695	9730
9	19068	9560

Based on this table, we can see that some users are *very* active. The top user has almost 8,000 more posts than the second most active user, who is still very, very active.

The following graph, of the post counts of the top 1,000 users, shows how quickly the activity falls off and how much the top users dominate the conversation:

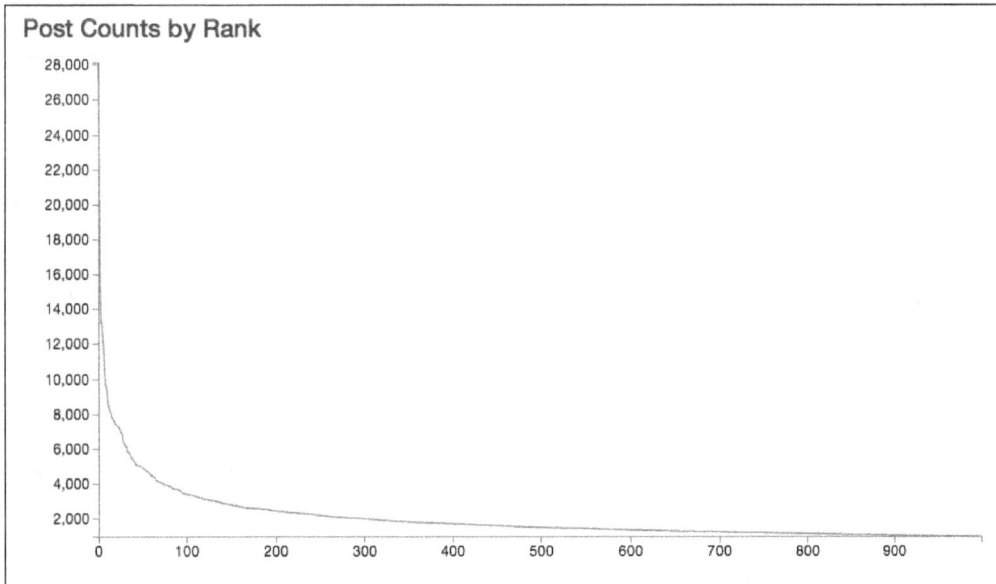

We can break this down further, however. I would expect the people who post questions to behave differently than the people who post answers.

Matching the 80/20 rule

Previously, we talked about the 80/20 rule: that 80 percent of the content is created by 20 percent of the users. That's obviously a rough estimate, but it does provide a good intuition for the dynamics of these networks.

To find the break-down, we need to perform the following steps:

1. Sort the users in descending order by the count that we're interested in.
2. Partition them into **quintiles**, that is, five equally sized buckets.
3. Sum the counts for each bucket.

To implement this, we can use a function named `quantile-on`, which sorts a collection and breaks it into the buckets. Look at the following code:

```
(defn quantile-on [n key-fn coll]
  (let [len (count coll)
        part-size (+ (quot len n)
                     (if (zero? (mod len n)) 0 1))]
    (partition-all part-size (sort-by key-fn coll)))))
```

Now we just need to pull out the appropriate fields and sum their values, as follows:

```
(defn sum-count
  ([key-fn] (partial sum-count key-fn))
  ([key-fn coll]
   (->> coll
     (map #(:count (key-fn %)))
     (remove nil?)
     (reduce + 0))))We can use these functions to find the percentage
of users in each quintile:
user=> (def p-counts
          (map (d/sum-count :post)
               (d/quantile-on 5 #(:rank (:post %)) users)))
user=> p-counts
(15587701 1282402 507654 318890 318828)
user=> (def total (reduce + 0 p-counts))
user=> (map #(float (/ % total)) p-counts)
(0.8652395 0.07118336 0.028178774 0.017700894 0.017697452)
```

So the top 20 percent of users actually produce more than 85 percent of the content. The quintiles drop off rapidly from there.

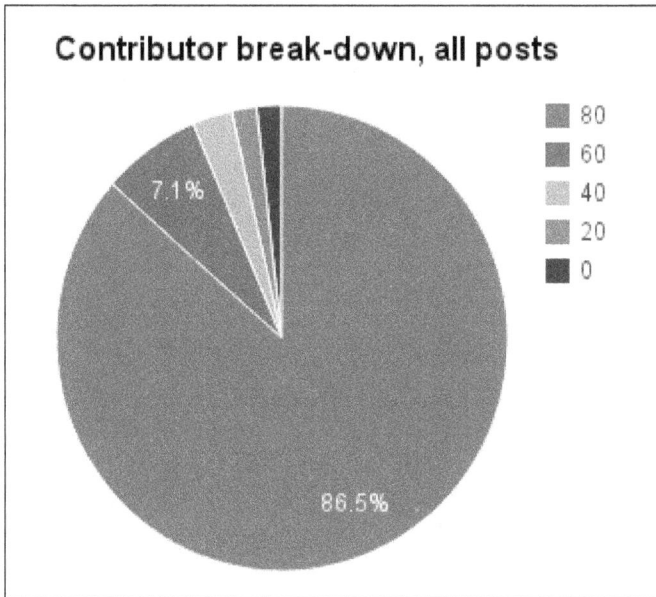

And we can pull these into a graph to be able to see the distribution of contributors more easily.

Looking for the 20 percent of questioners

While finding those who post questions, we can also see who are most active in asking questions.

Rank	User	Question Posts
0	39677	1858
1	4653	1605
2	34537	1604
3	179736	1327
4	117700	1327
5	149080	1261
6	84201	1177
7	434051	1107
8	325418	1074
9	146780	1055

When we run this, it gives us a very different set of frequencies. These are more than an order of magnitude less than the frequencies for all posts.

We can also get the numbers for the distribution of questioners.

If we use `quantile-on` and `sum-count` again, we can also see the break-down by quintile. Look at the following code:

```
user=> (def q-counts (map (d/sum-count :q)
                          (d/quantile-on 5 #(:rank (:q %)) users)))
user=> (def total (reduce + 0 q-counts))
user=> q-counts
(5182709 711037 318890 262051 0)
user=> (map #(float (/ % total)) q-counts)
(0.80045706 0.109817974 0.049251802 0.040473152 0.0)
```

And the following is the graph for this group:

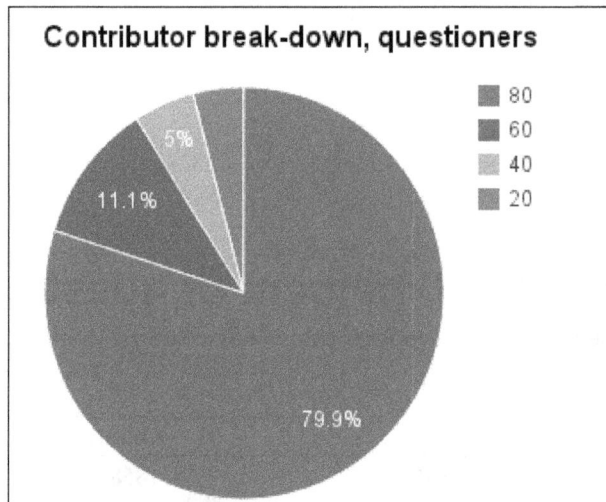

Interesting. So the lowest quintile doesn't contribute anything. Presumably, those are the users who answer questions. We'll look at this group more in a minute. But overall, the distribution of those asking questions follows what we'd expect from the 80/20 rule.

Looking for the 20 percent of respondents

Because most of the posts are answers, we can expect that these frequencies will be closer to the aggregate frequencies. We'll find this similarly to how we found the frequencies of those asking questions.

Look at the following table:

Rank	User	Answer Posts
0	22656	28137
1	29407	20310
2	157882	15431
3	17034	13285
4	34397	13157
5	23354	12270
6	115145	11784
7	20862	10447
8	57695	9711
9	19068	9557

We can see that there is a lot of similarity between this set of numbers and the first one. And in fact there is a lot of similarity between the distribution of this set of posters and the last set, as we can see in the following screenshot:

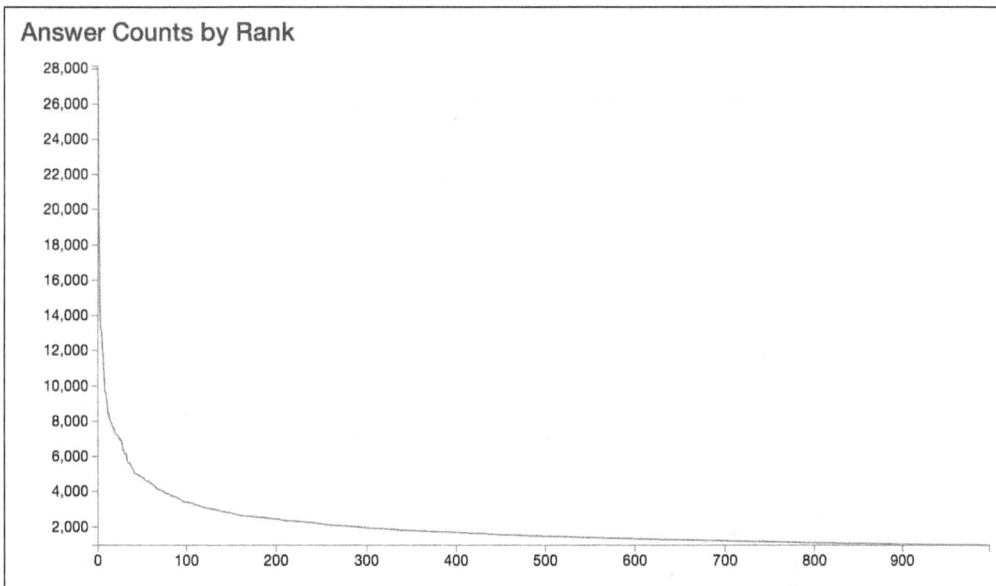

Looking at the distribution overall, however, we can see that the question answerers are even more lopsided than the question askers.

Let us try to break down the contributors who answer the questions:

```
user=> (def a-counts (map (d/sum-count :a)
                          (d/quantile-on 5 #(:rank (:a %)) users)))
user=> (def total (reduce + 0 a-counts))
user=> a-counts
(10950972 413668 176148 0 0)
user=> (map #(float (/ % total)) a-counts)
(0.9488929 0.035844 0.015263082 0.0 0.0)
```

And the following is the graph for this data:

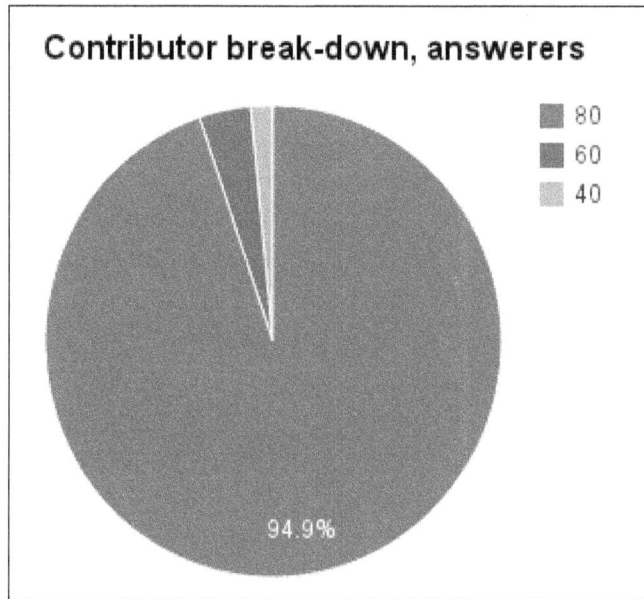

So almost half of the users never post an answer! However, the top 20 percent of users post 95 percent of the answers. So answering questions appears to be dominated by a few users, while question asking is (marginally) more widespread.

Combining ranks

We can see even more similarity if we compare the ranks. This table shows the rank for each category of post for all of the top 10 users in any category. (Note that the ranks begin at 0, not 1.)

User ID	All Post Rank	Question Post Rank	Answer Post Rank
4653	423	1	21342
17034	3	602037	3
19068	9	420772	9
20862	7	169469	7
22656	0	37889	0
23354	5	22760	5
29407	1	33177	1
34397	4	16478	4
34537	358	2	8024
39677	345	0	151684
57695	8	65071	8
84201	631	6	10521
115145	6	54339	6
117700	595	4	29654
146780	923	9	123737
149080	682	5	56862
157882	2	101282	2
179736	605	3	36463
325418	523	8	3502
434051	858	7	164416

The data in this table makes certain points clear:

- The top-ranked users asking questions are a very different set than the top-ranked users answering questions. The top questioner was ranked 141,674th as an answerer, and the top answerer was ranked 37,887th as a questioner.
- Once we're beyond the top posters, neither subgroup correlates well with the aggregate of all posts. All of these users rank within the top 1,000 for all types of posts. This just indicates that the question answerers don't completely dominate the questioners.

These observations confirm what we found looking at the quintiles and the graphs. Both of these groups look very different from each other, and from the aggregate of the two.

Let's break down the groups into those who only post questions, those who only post answers, and those who do both. That should give us more insight into the types of participation.

Looking at those who only post questions

We can get the users who only post answers fairly easily, and then running the previous analyses on that subset is also not difficult. Let's see how this will work. Look at the following code:

```
user=> (def qs (filter #(zero? (:count (:a %))) users))
user=> (def q-counts
          (map (d/sum-count :q)
             (d/quantile-on 5 #(:rank (:q %)) qs)))
user=> (def total (reduce + 0 q-counts))
user=> (count qs)
780460
user=> q-counts
(969148 272085 156092 156092 156092)
user=> (map #(float (/ % total)) q-counts)
(0.566916 0.15915973 0.09130809 0.09130809 0.09130809)
```

So first we filtered for only users who post no answers. This leaves us with 49 percent of the total number of users, so this is really an extremely large group of StackOverflow users.

However, the interesting part is that their distribution is more uniform. The most active quintile has posted less than two-thirds of the questions. The following graph makes that clear:

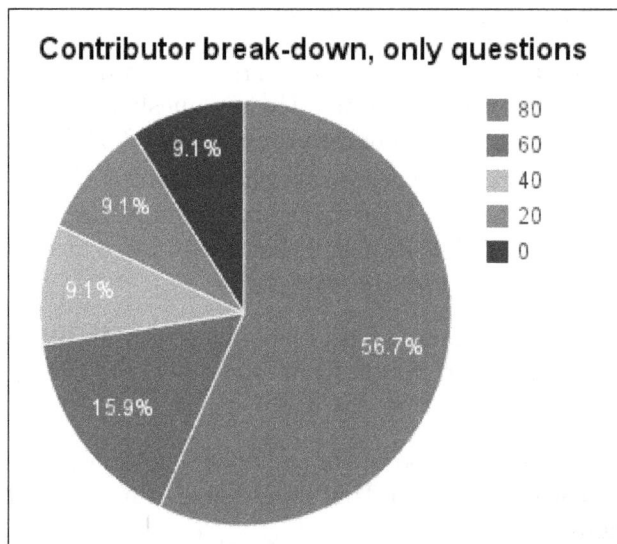

Contributor break-down, only questions

- 80
- 60
- 40
- 20
- 0

9.1%
9.1%
9.1%
56.7%
15.9%

The ratios for these are much different than we've seen so far. This group is much less driven by a few users. But when you think about it, this makes sense. Many people who come to StackOverflow only post one question, and that's the extent of their interaction. In fact, the bottom three quintiles only post one question and no answers. That's almost 33 percent of the total number of users.

Let's see how this compares to those who post only answers.

Looking at those who only post answers

Getting the users who only post answers will be almost exactly like the process we just went through. However, this time we'll switch questions and answers, of course. Look at the following code:

```
user=> (def as (filter #(zero? (:count (:q %))) users))
user=> (def a-counts (map (d/sum-count :a)
                          (d/quantile-on 5 #(:rank (:a %)) as)))
user=> (def total (reduce + 0 a-counts))
user=> (count as)
375667
user=> (float (/ (count as) (count users)))
0.23561831
user=> a-counts
(1413820 116198 75134 75134 75131)
user=> (map #(float (/ % total)) a-counts)
(0.80540407 0.06619396 0.042801227 0.042801227 0.042799518)
```

This time, we're working with a group roughly half the size of those who post only questions, roughly a quarter of the entire group of users. And the distribution of the top quintile is much closer to what we'd expect from the 80/20 rule.

Again, notice that the last few quintiles appear to have users who have only posted one answer. In fact, about 16 percent of the total number of users have posted no questions and only one answer. This seems to be one of the most curious groups, and trying to get more interaction out of them would be a priority (as I'm sure it has been for StackExchange).

The graph for this, shown following this paragraph, is somewhat between the last graph (for those who ask only questions) and the first few graphs. The first quintile is about 80 percent, but the rest don't taper off as much as they sometimes do.

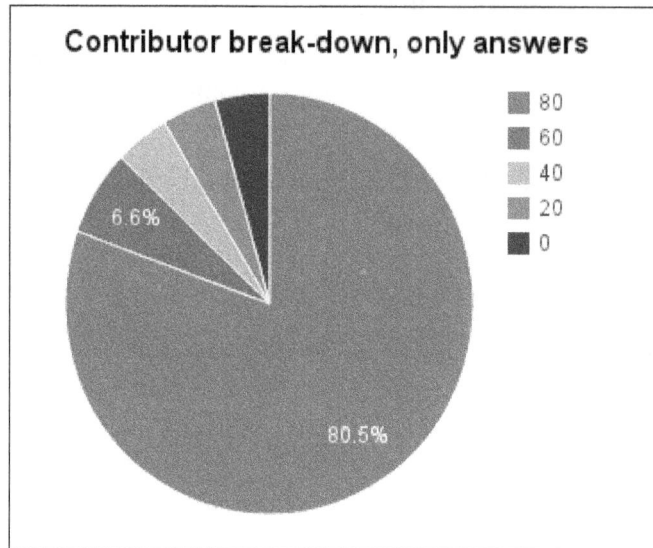

Now let's look at the breakdown for the rest of the users, those who've posted both questions and answers.

Looking at those who post both questions and answers

The predicate needed to select those users who have posted both questions and answers will be slightly different than what we've seen in the last two sections. However, once we have those users, the analysis will be the same. The only wrinkle will be that we'll get the distribution for both questions and answers.

We'll get the users who answer both using a slightly more complicated predicate, which we will page to remove. Look at the following code:

```
user=> (def both (remove #(or (zero? (:count (:q %)))
                              (zero? (:count (:a %))))
                      users))
user=> (count both)
438261
```

Now we'll also need to compute the values for both the questions and the answers. First, let's see what the questions look like:

```
user=> (def bq-counts
          (map (d/sum-count :q)
               (d/quantile-on 5 #(:rank (:q %)) both)))
user=> (def total (reduce + 0 bq-counts))
user=> bq-counts
(3450712 730467 335892 160458 87649)
user=> (map #(float (/ % total)) bq-counts)
(0.72415173 0.1532927 0.07048887 0.033673033 0.018393647)
```

The graph that follows makes clear that the ratios on this are more like the
distribution that we'd expect:

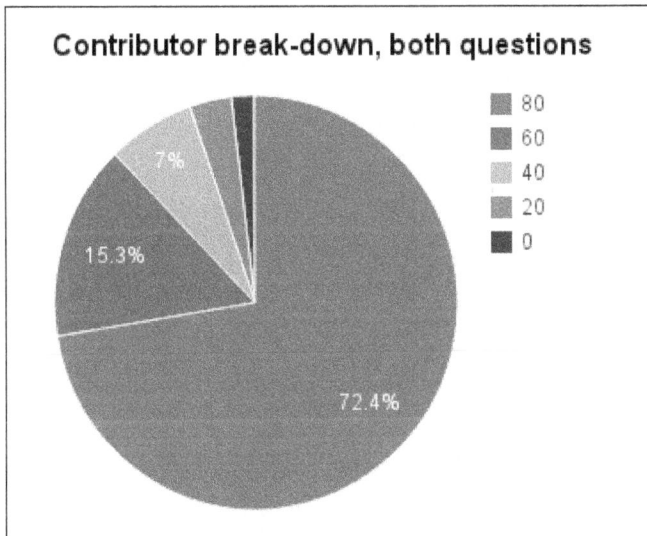

Looking at the numbers for the answers from this group, we again seem to be
following a very rough approximation of the 80/20 rule. Look at the following code:

```
user=> (def ba-counts
          (map (d/sum-count :a)
               (d/quantile-on 5 #(:rank (:a %)) both)))
user=> (def total (reduce + 0 ba-counts))
user=> ba-counts
(8564601 740590 270367 122164 87649)
user=> (map #(float (/ % total)) ba-counts)
(0.8752454 0.075683385 0.027629714 0.01248435 0.008957147)
```

And the following is the graph for this data:

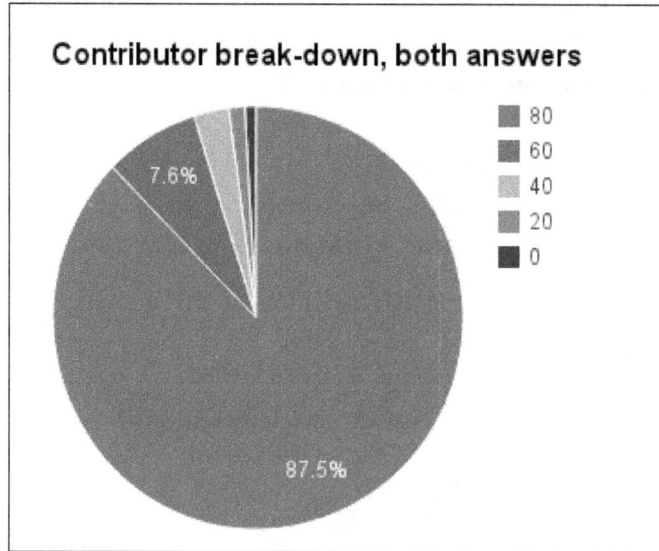

Contributor break-down, both answers

80
60
40
20
0

7.6%

87.5%

So the group who has posted both questions and answers seem to be more balanced and have a more typical interaction with the website.

Another way of looking at this data is to look at how the number of questions each user posts by the number of answers each posts. This gives us an indication of how active users are in each type of activity. Look at the following graph:

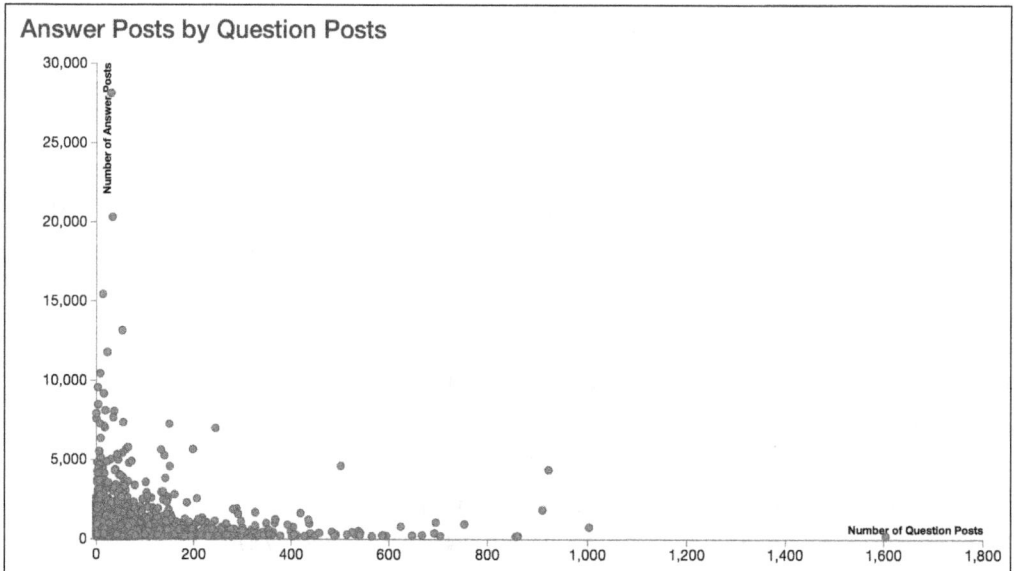

Answer Posts by Question Posts

This graph makes clear that typically users engage in one type of activity or another, and there's not as much cross-over as you might have expected. Also, the scales of the axes are a bit deceiving: the y axis is over 16 times larger than the x axis.

Now that we have a better understanding of the way that users are interacting with StackOverflow and the ways that they're generating content, let's look at that content and see if we can figure out what makes a good answer and what doesn't.

Finding the up-voted answers

Answers can be rated in a couple of different ways. The community can vote an answer up or down, and the original poster can accept an answer. For the purposes of this demonstration, we'll look at accepted answers; however, both metrics might be useful and interesting to explore.

We'll look at how we might automatically recognize answers that will be accepted.

On the one hand, this would be very useful to do. If the original poster forgets to accept an answer, the website could prompt them with a possible solution. Also, the site could send the poster an e-mail when someone posts an answer that should be considered.

But on the other hand, acceptable answers probably don't share common linguistic features that any kind of algorithm could latch on to in order to identify potential solutions. I'm doubtful that we'll be able to train an algorithm to identify acceptable answers.

Still, let's try and see how well we can actually do.

Processing the answers

There are over 18 million posts at this point. We can always work on the full data set eventually, but to get started, let's pull out a sample of the data. To make things easier, I've uploaded a random sample of 100,000 answers on `http://www.ericrochester.com/mastering-clj-data/data/post-sample-100000.json.gz`. These have been transformed into the data structure that we'll use everywhere.

You can download these with `curl` and decompress it with `gzip` as follows:

```
$ curl -O http://www.ericrochester.com/mastering-clj-data/data/
post-sample-100000.json.gz
$ gunzip post-sample-100000.json.gz
```

We'll put the code for this section into the `src/social_so/post.clj` file, and at the top we'll add the following namespace declaration:

```clojure
(ns social-so.post
  (:require [clojure.java.io :as io]
            [clojure.data.json :as json]
            [social-so.data :as d]
            [social-so.utils :as u]
            [social-so.xml :as x]))
```

To represent the data that we'll work with, we'll use the `PostInfo` record type. Look at the following code:

```clojure
(defrecord PostInfo
  [id post-type body-text score accepted-for])
```

The interesting fields here are `body-text`, which contains the answer's text, stripped of HTML, and `accepted-for`, which is nil if the post isn't accepted or contains the question's ID, if the post was accepted for its question.

This is a flat data record, so it's easy to load the JSON data into these structures. Look at the following code:

```clojure
(defn load-post-infos [filename]
  (with-open [r (io/reader filename)]
    (doall
      (->> (json/read r :key-fn keyword)
        (map map->PostInfo)
        (map #(assoc % :post-type (keyword (:post-type %))))))))
```

And now we can read the data on the REPL, assuming we've aliased this namespace to `p`. Look at the following code:

```clojure
user=> (def s (p/load-post-infos "post-sample-100000.json"))
user=> (count s)
100000
user=> (count (filter :accepted-for s))
21250
user=> (count (remove :accepted-for s))
78750
user=> (pprint (first s))
{:id 1146880,
 :post-type :a,
 :body-text
```

```
"But while processing i cancelled the transaction.  WP - Basically,
 if it was a transaction, and you canceled it before it finished,
 then whatever had started would have been undone. What your
 database looks like now should be the same as it looked before the
 UPDATE.",
:score 0,
:accepted-for nil}
```

Looking at these briefly, we can see that just over 20 percent of the posts in the sample were accepted.

Predicting the accepted answer

Now that the data is in a usable form, let's turn our attention to categorizing the posts. To do this, we'll use **MALLET** (http://mallet.cs.umass.edu/). We saw MALLET before in *Chapter 3, Topic Modeling – Changing Concerns in the State of the Union Addresses*, on topic modeling. That's usually the task that this library is used for. However, it also provides an implementation of a number of classification algorithms, and we'll use one of those now.

Over the course of this chapter, we'll categorize the posts as what MALLET calls `instances`. This will divide them into categories based on features, or clues within each instance. We'll use MALLET to take each post, create an instance from it, identify its features and categories, and finally use those to train a classifier. We can later use this classifier on new posts.

Setting up

We'll use a new namespace for this code. Open the file `src/social_so/nlp.clj` and add the following namespace declaration to the top of the file:

```
(ns social-so.nlp
  (:import [cc.mallet.types Instance InstanceList]
           [cc.mallet.pipe
            Input2CharSequence TokenSequenceLowercase
            CharSequence2TokenSequence SerialPipes
            Target2Label FeatureSequence2FeatureVector
            TokenSequenceRemoveStopwords
            TokenSequence2FeatureSequence]
           [cc.mallet.pipe.iterator ArrayDataAndTargetIterator]
           [cc.mallet.classify NaiveBayes NaiveBayesTrainer Trial]
           [cc.mallet.classify.evaluate ConfusionMatrix]))
```

That's a lot of imports. But really, that's the most complicated that this code will be. MALLET does a lot of the heavy lifting for us.

In the code to come, we'll refer to this in the REPL with the n prefix. To make this available, execute the following line (after the **user=>** prompt) in your REPL environment:

```
user=> (require '[social-so.nlp :as n])
```

Now we're ready to start filling in the blanks.

Creating the InstanceList object

MALLET represents each input as an Instance object. Instance objects contain their data, a target label, name, and other metadata.

MALLET works on collections of Instance objects as an InstanceList, which is just a collection of Instance objects. All the instances in the list are processed using the same pipe of transformations.

Each step in the pipe changes one property of each Instance object in the list. For example, one pipe (CharSequence2TokenSequence) tokenizes the input, and another (Target2Label) creates an index of the target labels.

The following figure illustrates this process:

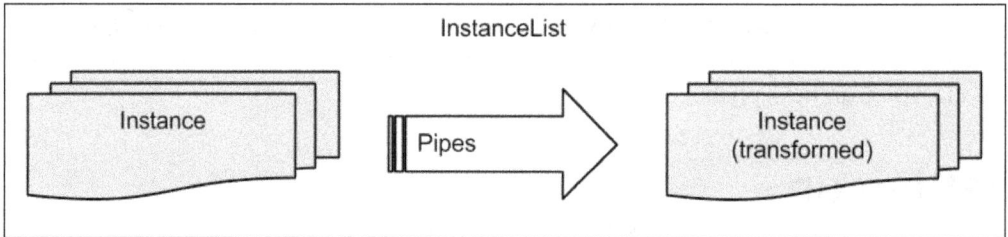

For the features in the documents and their labels, the InstanceList also maintains **alphabets**. These are indexes from the input strings to integers. The integers serve to distinguish the inputs and also act as indexes in arrays. This allows MALLET to work with frequencies as an array, which saves both space and processing time. The trick is that all of the Instance objects being processed must share the same alphabet. The InstanceList makes sure that they do.

For our processing, to make clear what transformations we'll use, we'll define them all in a function named make-pipe. The following is that function:

```
(defn make-pipe []
  (SerialPipes.
    [(Target2Label.)
     (Input2CharSequence. "UTF-8")
     (CharSequence2TokenSequence.
```

```
    #"\p{L}[\p{L}\p{P}]+\p{L}")
  (TokenSequenceLowercase.)
  (TokenSequenceRemoveStopwords. false false)
  (TokenSequence2FeatureSequence.)
  (FeatureSequence2FeatureVector.)])))
```

What's happening here? Let's take the steps apart.

1. `Target2Label` builds the alphabet for the `Instance` objects' target property.

2. `Input2CharSequence` reads the input from a string, file, or URL named in the data property and replaces it with the resource's content.

3. `CharSequence2TokenSequence` tokenizes the string in the data property.

4. `TokenSequenceLowercase` lowercases the tokens in the data property.

5. `TokenSequenceRemoveStopwords` filters out stop words (common words) from the tokens in the data.

6. `TokenSequence2FeatureSequence` creates the alphabet of tokens and convert the sequence of tokens to a sequence of feature indexes.

7. `FeatureSequence2FeatureVector` converts the sequence of feature indexes to a vector for a bag-of-words approach.

So, at the end of this pipeline, each document will be represented by a vector indicating how many times each feature appears in that document. Features can be almost anything, but usually they are words that appear in the document or metadata (author, date, tags) associated with that document. This is the format that the classifiers—as well as many other machine learning and natural language algorithms—expect.

This handles the processing of the `Instance` objects, but before we can do that, we'll need to convert the `PostInfo` objects into `Instance` objects.

MALLET has a number of classes that do this from more primitive data types. They take some kind of collection of primitive inputs and iterate over the `Instance` objects they represent. In our case, we'll use `ArrayDataAndTargetIterator`. This iterates over two string arrays. One contains each input's data, and the other contains each input's target.

We'll wrap creating this with the function `post-info-iterator`. This uses the `accepted-tag` function to decide whether the post was accepted or not and tag it appropriately. Look at the following code:

```
(defn accepted-tag [post-info]
  (if (:accepted-for post-info) "accepted" "not"))
(defn post-info-iterator [post-infos]
```

```
(ArrayDataAndTargetIterator.
  (into-array (map :body-text post-infos))
  (into-array (map accepted-tag post-infos)))))
```

Once we have these functions, we can use them to populate an `InstanceList` that will run all the documents through the transformation pipeline that we defined earlier. Look at the following code:

```
(defn post-info-instances [post-infos]
  (doto (InstanceList. (make-pipe))
    (.addThruPipe (post-info-iterator post-infos))))
```

Now we're ready. Let's pick up with the `PostInfo` sample that we extracted earlier and bound to s in the *Processing the answers* section. This contains a sequence of `PostInfo` instances. In the REPL, we can create an `InstanceList` using the functions that we just defined as follows:

user=> (def ilist (n/post-info-instances s))

Now we can think about how we're going to use these documents to train and test a classifier.

Training sets and Test sets

Now that we've processed our data into a format that MALLET can use, we'll divide the input corpus into a test set and a training set. We can use different relative sizes for each, but often we'll train on more documents than we'll test on.

MALLET's `InstanceList` class has a `split` method, but we'll define a thin wrapper over it to make it easier to use. MALLET's `split` method takes an array listing the proportions of the total for each group. Since we only want two groups that completely divide the input, we can pass in the proportion for one group and compute the value of the other group's proportion. We'll also return a hash-map indicating which of the output lists is for testing and which is for training.

The following is the `split-sets` function that acts as the wrapper:

```
(defn split-sets [test-ratio ilist]
  (let [split-on (double-array [test-ratio (- 1.0 test-ratio)])
        [test-set training-set] (.split ilist split-on)]
    {:test test-set, :training training-set}))
```

And we can use the following on the command line to divide the input:

user=> (def tt-sets (n/split-sets 0.2 ilist))

Now we're ready to use these for training and testing.

Training

Before we can use a classifier, we have to train it on the training set that we just created.

For this example, we'll create a Naive Bayesian classifier. Again, we'll just create a thin wrapper function. In this case, it's not that significantly simpler than creating the Bayesian trainer and calling it on the data. However, it will allow us to use the trainer without having to tease out which MALLET packages we have to import. This allows us to require our `social-so.nlp` namespace into the REPL and execute the entire process.

The following is the wrapper:

```
(defn bayes-train [ilist] (.train (NaiveBayesTrainer.) ilist))
```

And we can use the following in the REPL to get a trained Bayesian classifier:

```
user=> (def bayes (n/bayes-train (:training tt-sets)))
```

That's it. We've trained our classifier. Now let's see how to use it.

Testing

To test the classifier, MALLET provides a `Trial` class that encapsulates running a classifier over some inputs that are already tagged. It provides counts over how accurate the classifier is and calculates statistics to show how well it does.

To make it easier to load the development environment and to use this class, we'll create a factory function for it as follows:

```
(defn trial [classifier ilist] (Trial. classifier ilist))
```

And now let's use this function at the REPL as follows:

```
user=> (def trial (n/trial bayes (:test tt-sets)))
```

Well, great. Now what can we do with this?

Evaluating the outcome

There are several factors to consider when evaluating a classifier's ability to identify inputs as belonging to category X. Let's consider what they are and see how we can get them from the `Trial` object.

First, we need to think about the classifier's **precision or positive predictive value (PPV)**. This takes into account how many items the classifier incorrectly included in category X, and it's given by the ratio of the true positives with all labeled positive. In our case, that means the number of items that were correctly identified as `accepted` divided by all of those identified as `accepted`. You can get this using the `getPrecision` method, as follows:

```
user=> (.getPrecision trial "accepted")
0.2837067983289024
```

So we can see that it correctly identified the accepted rows rather poorly.

The next number that we need to consider is the classifier's **recall**. This is sometimes referred to as its **sensitivity** or **true positive rate (TPR)**. This is the percentage of all positives that it found, and it's found by dividing the true positives by the true positives and the false negatives. MALLET exposes this with the `getRecall` method as follows:

```
user=> (.getRecall trial "accepted")
0.1808716707021792
```

In this case, the recall is actually worse than the precision, which is *saying* something.

Next, we'll consider the **accuracy (ACC)** of the classifier. This is the ratio of true classifications, both positive and negative, to the total number of items. This is rendered from the `getAccuracy` method. Look at the following code:

```
user=> (.getAccuracy trial)
0.73655
```

Presumably, this classifier's precision and recall are better when identifying not-accepted answers. Let's test that as follows:

```
user=> (.getPrecision trial "not")
0.8052052743709334
user=> (.getRecall trial "not")
0.881159420289855
```

These results aren't great. A simple baseline that classifies everything as *not accepted* would actually score slightly better than this (80 percent). The criteria involved in accepting an answer don't appear to be captured by the simple token features that we've used here.

The performance here is likely because `not accepted` is the default state for an answer, and the status of most answers.

There's one final number that we want to pay attention to. The F1 score is a measure of the classifier's accuracy. This combines the precision and recall into a single number ranging from 0 (poor) to 1 (perfect). Look at the following code:

```
user=> (.getF1 trial "accepted")

0.22090788111784712
```

Again, we can see that the classifier doesn't do a good job.

We can get more detailed information about how well the classifier did by looking at its **confusion** matrix. This is a matrix that breaks down how many items are predicated to be in both categories, and how many actually are.

MALLET has a `ConfusionMatrix` class for displaying these charts. We'll again wrap that class in a function to make it easier to call. Look at the following code:

```
(defn confusion-matrix [trial] (str (ConfusionMatrix. trial)))
```

This generates the confusion matrix and returns it as a string. Let's call this and print the matrix out as follows:

```
user=> (println (n/confusion-matrix trial))
Confusion Matrix, row=true, column=predicted  accuracy=0.73655
       label   0   1  |total
  0      not 13984 1886  |15870
  1 accepted 3383 747   |4130
```

Now we can see where the numbers came from. Rows are the actual classes, and columns are how the classifier predicted the classes. The true positives in the lower right-hand side are much smaller than the total number of positives in the bottom row. On the other hand, the true negatives in the upper left-hand side are the majority of the total number of negatives in the top row.

Naive Bayesian classifiers don't perform well here, but it's possible (although unlikely) that other classifiers might. It's also possible that adding more metadata as features might help. For example, the length of time between when the question was posted and when the answer was posted might be fruitful. Other features that might help are the length of the answer or the answerer's reputation. Reputation is the points awarded for accepted answers, though, so including them introduces circularity – we'd be training directly on what we're attempting to classify.

Summary

However the results of the last experiment, we can see that there's a lot of information embedded in social networks. Depending on the nature of the network, we can have different kinds of interactions and different kinds of data in the network.

In the final chapter, which is next, we'll look at whether analyzing financial data and using machine learning to examine news documents help predict the future of stock prices.

10
Modeling Stock Data

Automated stock analysis has gotten a lot of press recently. High-frequency trading firms are a flashpoint. People either believe that they're great for the markets and increasing liquidity, or that they're precursors to the apocalypse. Smaller traders have also gotten into the mix in a slower fashion. Some sites, such as Quantopian (https://www.quantopian.com/) and AlgoTrader (http://www.algotrader.ch/) provide services that allow you to create models for automated trading. Many others allow you to use automated analysis to inform your trading decisions.

Whatever your view of this phenomena, it's an area with a lot of data begging to be analyzed. It's also a nice domain in which to experiment with some analysis and machine learning techniques.

For this chapter, we're going to look for relationships between news articles and stock prices in the future.

In the course of this chapter, we will cover the following topics:

- Learn about financial data analysis
- Set up our project and acquire our data
- Prepare the data
- Analyze the text
- Analyze the stock prices
- Learn patterns in both text and stock prices with neural networks
- Use this system to predict the future
- Talk about the limitations of these systems

Learning about financial data analysis

Finance has always relied heavily on data. Earnings statements, forecasting, and portfolio management are just some of the areas that make use of data to quantify their decisions. Because of this, financial data analysis and its related field, financial engineering, are extremely broad fields that are difficult to summarize in a short amount of space.

However, lately, quantitative finance, high-frequency trading, and similar fields have gotten a lot of press and really come into their own. As I mentioned, some people hate them and the added volatility that the markets seem to have. Others maintain that they bring the necessary liquidity that helps the market function better.

All of these fields apply statistical or machine learning methods to financial data. Some of these techniques can be quite simple. Others are more sophisticated. Some of these analyses are used to inform a human analyst or manager to make better financial decisions. Others are used as inputs to automated algorithmic processes that operate with varying degrees of human oversight, but perhaps with little to no intervention.

For this chapter, we'll focus on adding information to the human analyst's repertoire. We'll develop a simple machine learning system to look at past, current, and future stock prices, alongside the text of news articles, in order to identify potentially interesting articles that may indicate future fluctuations in stock price. These articles, with the possible future price vector, could provide important information to an investor or analyst attempting to decide how to shuffle his/her money around. We'll talk more about the purpose and limitations of this system toward the end of the chapter.

Setting up the basics

Before we really dig into the project and the data, we need to prepare. We'll set up the code and the library, and then we'll download the data.

Setting up the library

First, we'll need to initialize the library. We can do this using Leiningen 2 (http://leiningen.org/) and Stuart Sierra's reloaded plugin for it (https://github.com/stuartsierra/reloaded). This will initialize the development environment and project.

To do this, just execute the following command at the prompt (I've named the project `financial` in this case):

```
lein new reloaded financial
```

Now, we can specify the libraries that we'll need to use. We can do this in the `project.clj` file. Open it and replace its current contents with the following lines:

```
(defproject financial "0.1.0-SNAPSHOT"
  :dependencies [[org.clojure/clojure "1.5.1"]
                 [org.clojure/data.xml "0.0.7"]
                 [org.clojure/data.csv "0.1.2"]
                 [clj-time "0.6.0"]
                 [me.raynes/fs "1.4.4"]
                 [org.encog/encog-core "3.1.0"]
                 [enclog "0.6.3"]]
  :profiles
  {:dev {:dependencies [[org.clojure/tools.namespace "0.2.4"]]
         :source-paths ["dev"]}})
```

The primary library that we'll use is Enclog (`https://github.com/jimpil/enclog`). This is a Clojure wrapper around the Java library Encog (`http://www.heatonresearch.com/encog`), which is a machine learning library, including classes for artificial neural networks.

We now have the basics in place. We can get the data at this point.

Getting the data

We'll need data from two different sources. To begin with, we'll focus on getting the stock data.

In this case, we're going to use the historical stock data for Dominion Resources, Inc. They're a power company that operates in the eastern United States. Their New York Stock Exchange symbol is D. Focusing on one stock like this will reduce possible noise and allow us to focus on the simple system that we'll be working on in this chapter.

To download the stock data, I went to Google Finance (`https://finance.google.com/`). In the search box, I entered NYSE:D. On the left-hand side menu bar, there is an option to download **Historical prices**. Click on it.

In the table header, set the date range to be from `Sept 1, 1995` to `Jan 1, 2001`. Refer to the following screenshot as an example:

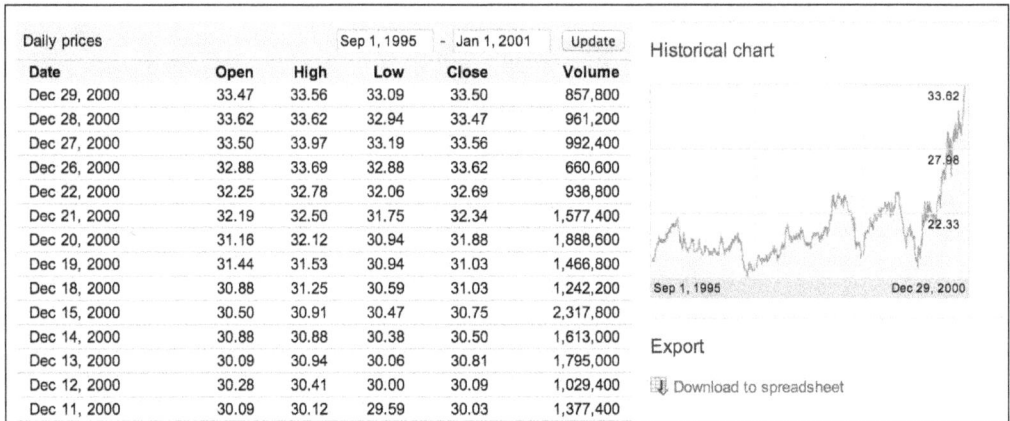

Daily prices			Sep 1, 1995	- Jan 1, 2001	Update
Date	**Open**	**High**	**Low**	**Close**	**Volume**
Dec 29, 2000	33.47	33.56	33.09	33.50	857,800
Dec 28, 2000	33.62	33.62	32.94	33.47	961,200
Dec 27, 2000	33.50	33.97	33.19	33.56	992,400
Dec 26, 2000	32.88	33.69	32.88	33.62	660,600
Dec 22, 2000	32.25	32.78	32.06	32.69	938,800
Dec 21, 2000	32.19	32.50	31.75	32.34	1,577,400
Dec 20, 2000	31.16	32.12	30.94	31.88	1,888,600
Dec 19, 2000	31.44	31.53	30.94	31.03	1,466,800
Dec 18, 2000	30.88	31.25	30.59	31.03	1,242,200
Dec 15, 2000	30.50	30.91	30.47	30.75	2,317,800
Dec 14, 2000	30.88	30.88	30.38	30.50	1,613,000
Dec 13, 2000	30.09	30.94	30.06	30.81	1,795,000
Dec 12, 2000	30.28	30.41	30.00	30.09	1,029,400
Dec 11, 2000	30.09	30.12	29.59	30.03	1,377,400

If you look at the lower-right corner of the screenshot, there's a link that reads **Download to spreadsheet**. Click on this link to download the data. By default, the filename is `d.csv`. I moved it into a directory named `d` inside my project folder and renamed it to `d-1995-2001.csv`.

We'll also need some news article data to correlate with the stock data. Freely available news articles are difficult to come by. There are good corpora available for modest fees (several hundred dollars). However, in order to make this exercise as accessible as possible, I've limited the data to what's freely available.

At the moment, the best collection appears to be the journalism segment of the Open American National Corpus (`http://www.anc.org/data/oanc/`). The **American National Corpus (ANC)** is a collection of texts from a variety of registers and genres that are assembled for linguistic research. The **Open ANC (OANC)** is the subset of the ANC that is available for open access downloading. The journalism genre is represented by articles from Slate (`http://www.slate.com/`). This has some benefits and introduces some problems. The primary benefit is that the data will be quite manageable. It means that we won't have a lot of documents to use for training and testing, and we'll need to be pickier about what features we pull from the documents. We'll see how we need to handle this later.

To download the dataset, visit the download page at `http://www.anc.org/data/oanc/download/` and get the data in your preferred format, either a TAR ball or a ZIP file. I decompressed that data into the `d` directory. It created a directory named `OANC-GrAF` that contained the data.

Your d directory should now look something as follows:

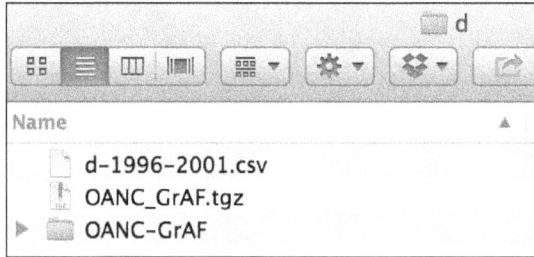

Getting prepared with data

As usual, now we need to clean up the data and put it into a shape that we can work with. The news article dataset particularly will require some attention, so let's turn our attention to it first.

Working with news articles

The OANC is published in an XML format that includes a lot of information and annotations about the data. Specifically, this marks off:

- Sections and chapters
- Sentences
- Words with part-of-speech lemma
- Noun chunks
- Verb chunks
- Named entities

However, we want the option to use raw text later when the system is actually being used. Because of that, we will ignore the annotations and just extract the raw tokens. In fact, all we're really interested in is each document's text—either as a raw string or a feature vector—and the date it was published. Let's create a record type for this.

We'll put this into the `types.clj` file in `src/financial/`. Put this simple namespace header into the file:

```
(ns financial.types)
```

This data record will be similarly simple. It can be defined as follows:

```
(dcfrecord NewsArticle [title pub-date text])
```

So let's see what the XML looks like and what we need to do to get it to work with the data structures we just defined.

The Slate data is in the `OANC-GrAF/data/written_1/journal/slate/` directory. The data files are spread through 55 subdirectories as follows:

```
$ ls d/OANC-GrAF/data/written_1/journal/slate/
.  ..  1 10 11 12 13 14 15 16 17 18 19 2 20 21 22 23 24 25 26 27 28 29 3 30
31 32
33 34 35 36 37 38 39 4 40 41 42 43 44 45 46 47 48 49 5 50 51 52 53 54 55
6 7 8
9
```

Digging in deeper, each document is represented by a number of files. From the `slate` directory, we can see the following details:

```
$ ls 1/Article247_99*
1/Article247_99-hepple.xml   1/Article247_99-s.xml
1/Article247_99.txt
1/Article247_99-logical.xml  1/Article247_99-vp.xml
1/Article247_99-np.xml       1/Article247_99.anc
```

So we can see the different annotations files are the files with the `xml` extension. The ANC file contains metadata about the file. We'll need to access that file for the date and other information. But most importantly, there's also a `.txt` file containing the raw text of the document. That will make working with this dataset much easier!

But let's take a minute to write some functions that will help us work with each document's text and its metadata as an entity. These will represent the knowledge we've just gained about the directory and file structure of the OANC corpus.

We'll call this file `src/financial/oanc.clj`, and its namespace header should look as follows:

```clojure
(ns financial.oanc
  (:require [clojure.data.xml :as xml]
            [clojure.java.io :as io]
            [clojure.string :as str]
            [me.raynes.fs :as fs]
            [clj-time.core :as clj-time]
            [clj-time.format :as time-format])
  (:use [financial types utils]))
```

If we examine the directory structure that the OANC uses, we can see that it's divided into a clear hierarchy. Let's trace that structure in the `slate` directory that we discussed earlier, `OANC-GrAF/data/written_1/journal/slate/`. In this example, `written_1` represents a category, `journal` is a genre, and `slate` is a source. We can leverage this information as we walk the directory structure to get to the data files.

Our first bit of code contains four functions. Let's list them first, and then we can talk about them:

```
(defn list-category-genres [category-dir]
  (map #(hash-map :genre % :dirname (io/file category-dir %))
       (fs/list-dir category-dir)))
(defn list-genres [oanc-dir]
  (mapcat list-category-genres (ls (io/file oanc-dir "data"))))
(defn find-genre-dir [genre oanc-dir]
  (->> oanc-dir
    list-genres
    (filter #(= (:genre %) genre))
    first
    :dirname))
(defn find-source-data [genre source oanc-dir]
  (-> (find-genre-dir genre oanc-dir)
    (io/file source)
    (fs/find-files #".*\.anc")))
```

The functions used in the preceding code are described as follows:

- The first of these functions, `list-category-genre`, takes a category directory (`OANC-GrAF/data/written_1/`) and returns the genres that it contains. This could be `journal`, as in our example here, or fiction, letters, or a number of other options. Each item returned is a hash map of the full directory and the name of the genre.

- The second function is `list-genres`. It lists all of the genres within the OANC data directory.

- The third function is `find-genre-dir`. It looks for one particular genre and returns the full directory for it.

- Finally, we have `find-source-data`. This takes a genre and source and lists all of the files with an anc extension.

Using these functions, we can iterate over the documents for a source. We can see how to do that in the next function, `find-slate-files`, which returns a sequence of maps pointing to each document's metadata ANC file and to its raw text file, as shown in the following code:

```
(defn find-slate-files [oanc-dir]
  (map #(hash-map :anc % :txt (chext % ".txt"))
       (find-source-data "journal" "slate" oanc-dir)))
```

Now we can get at the metadata in the ANC file. We'll use the `clojure.data.xml` library to parse the file, and we'll define a couple of utility functions to make descending into the file easier. Look at the following code:

```
(defn find-all [xml tag-name]
  (lazy-seq
    (if (= (:tag xml) tag-name)
        (cons xml (mapcat #(find-all % tag-name) (:content xml)))
        (mapcat #(find-all % tag-name) (:content xml)))))
(defn content-str [xml]
  (apply str (filter string? (:content xml))))
```

The first utility function, `find-all`, lazily walks the XML document and returns all elements with a given tag name. The second function, `content-str`, returns all the text children of a tag.

Also, we'll need to parse the date from the `pubDate` elements. Some of these have a `value` attribute, but this isn't consistent. Instead, we'll parse the elements' content directly using the `clj-time` library (https://github.com/clj-time/clj-time), which is a wrapper over the Joda time library for Java (http://joda-time.sourceforge.net/). From our end, we'll use a few functions.

Before we do, though, we'll need to define a date format string. The dates inside the `pubDate` functions look like *2/13/97 4:30:00 PM*. The formatting string, then, should look as follows:

```
(def date-time-format
    (time-format/formatter "M/d/yyyy h:mm:ss a"))
```

We can use this formatter to pull data out of a `pubDate` element and parse it into an `org.joda.time.DateTime` object as follows:

```
(defn parse-pub-date [pub-date-el]
  (time-format/parse date-time-format (content-str pub-date-el)))
```

Unfortunately, some of these dates are about 2000 years off. We can normalize the dates and correct these errors fairly quickly, as shown in the following code:

```
(defn norm-date [date]
  (cond
    (= (clj-time/year date) 0)
      (clj-time/plus date (clj-time/years 2000))
    (< (clj-time/year date) 100)
      (clj-time/plus date (clj-time/years 1900))
    :else date))
```

With all of these parts in place, we can write a function that takes the XML from an ANC file and returns date and time for the publication date as follows:

```
(defn find-pub-date [anc-xml]
  (-> anc-xml
    (find-all :pubDate)
    first
    parse-pub-date
    norm-date))
```

The other piece of data that we'll load from the ANC metadata XML is the title. We get that from the title element, of course, as follows:

```
(defn find-title [anc-xml]
  (content-str (first (find-all anc-xml :title))))
```

Now, loading a NewsArticle object is straightforward. In fact, it's so simple that we'll also include a version of this that reads in the text from a plain file. Look at the following code:

```
(defn load-article [data-info]
  (let [{:keys [anc txt]} data-info
        anc-xml (xml/parse (io/reader anc))]
    (->NewsArticle (find-title anc-xml)
                   (find-pub-date anc-xml)
                   (slurp txt))))
(defn load-text-file [data filename]
  (->NewsArticle filename date (slurp filename)))
```

And using these functions to load all of the Slate articles just involves repeating the earlier steps, as shown in the following commands:

```
user=> (def articles (doall (map oanc/load-article
                         (oanc/find-slate-files
                           (io/file "d/OANC-GrAF")))))
user=> (count articles)
4531
```

```
user=> (let [a (first articles)]
        [(:title a) (:pub-date a) (count (:text a))]])
["Article247_4" #<DateTime 1999-03-09T07:47:21.000Z> 3662]
```

The last command in the preceding code just prints the title, publication date, and the length of the text in the document.

With these functions in place, we now have access to the article dataset.

Working with stock data

Loading the news articles was complicated. Fortunately, the stock price data is in **comma-separated values** (CSV) format. Although not the richest data format, it is very popular, and `clojure.data.csv` (https://github.com/clojure/data.csv/) is an excellent library for loading it.

As I just mentioned, though, CSV isn't the richest data format. We will want to convert this data into a richer format, so we'll still create a record type and some wrapper functions to make it easier to work with the data as we read it in.

The data in this will closely follow the columns in the CSV file that we downloaded from Google Finance earlier. Open `src/financial/types.clj` again and add the following line to represent the data type for the stock data:

```
(defrecord StockData [date open high low close volume])
```

For the rest of the code in this section, we'll use a new namespace. Open the `src/financial/cvs_data.clj` file and add the following namespace declaration:

```
(ns financial.csv-data
  (:require [clojure.data.csv :as csv]
            [clojure.java.io :as io]
            [clj-time.core :as clj-time]
            [clj-time.format :as time-format])
  (:use [financial types utils]))
```

Just like the Slate news article data, this data also has a field with a date, which we'll need to parse. Unlike the Slate data, this value is formatted differently. Glancing at the first few lines of the file gives us all the information that we need, as follows:

```
Date,Open,High,Low,Close,Volume
29-Dec-00,33.47,33.56,33.09,33.50,857800
28-Dec-00,33.62,33.62,32.94,33.47,961200
27-Dec-00,33.50,33.97,33.19,33.56,992400
26-Dec-00,32.88,33.69,32.88,33.62,660600
```

To parse dates in this format (29-Dec-00), we can use the following format specification:

```
(def date-format (time-format/formatter "d-MMM-YY"))
```

Now, we build on this and a few other function—which you can find in the code download in the file `src/financial/utils.clj`—to create a `StockData` instance from a row of data, as shown in the following code:

```
(defn row->StockData [row]
  (let [[date open high low close vol] row]
    (->StockData (time-format/parse date-format date)
                 (->double open)
                 (->double high)
                 (->double low)
                 (->double close)
                 (->long vol)))))
```

This is all straightforward. Basically, every value in the row must be converted to a native Clojure/Java type, and then all of those values are used to create the `StockData` instance.

To read in an entire file, we just do this for every row returned by the CSV library as follows:

```
(defn read-stock-prices [filename]
  (with-open [f (io/reader filename)]
    (doall (map row->StockData (drop 1 (csv/read-csv f))))))
```

The only wrinkle is that we have to drop the first row, since it's the header.

And now, to load the data, we just call the following function (we've aliased the `financial.csv-data` namespace to `csvd`):

```
user=> (def sp (csvd/read-stock-prices "d/d-1995-2001.csv"))
user=> (first sp)
#financial.types.StockData{:date #<DateTime 2000-12-29T00:00:00.000Z>,
   :open 33.47, :high 33.56, :low 33.09, :close 33.5, :volume 857800}
user=> (count sp)
1263
```

Everything appears to be working correctly. Let's turn our attention back to the news article dataset and begin analyzing it.

Analyzing the text

Our goal for analyzing the news articles is to generate a vector space model of the collection of documents. This attempts to pull the salient features for the documents into a vector of floating-point numbers. Features can be words or information from the documents' metadata encoded for the vector. The feature values can be 0 or 1 for presence, an integer for raw frequency, or the frequency scaled in some form.

In our case, we'll use the feature vector to represent a selection of the tokens in a document. Often, we can use all the tokens, or all the tokens that occur more than once or twice. However, in this case, we don't have a lot of data, so we'll need to be more selective in the features that we include. We'll consider how we select these in a few sections.

For the feature values, we'll use a scaled version of the token frequency called **term frequency-inverse document frequency (tf-idf)**. There are good libraries for this, but this is a basic metric in working with free text data, so we'll take this algorithm apart and implement it ourselves for this chapter. That way, we'll understand it better.

For the rest of this section, we'll put the code into `src/financial/nlp.clj`. Open this file and add the following for the namespace header:

```
(ns financial.nlp
  (:require [clojure.string :as str]
            [clojure.set :as set])
  (:use [financial types utils]))
```

With this in place, we can now start to pick the documents apart.

Analyzing vocabulary

The first step for analyzing a document, of course, is tokenizing. We'll use a simple tokenize function that just pulls out sequences of letters or numbers, including any single punctuation marks.

Now, we can use this function to see what words are present in the text and how frequent they are. The core Clojure function, `frequencies`, makes this especially easy, but we do still need to pull out the data that we'll use.

For each step, we'll first work on raw input, and then we'll write an additional utility function that modifies the `:text` property of the input `NewsArticle`.

To tokenize the text, we'll search for the matches for a regular expression and convert the output to lowercase. This won't work well for a lot of cases — contractions, abbreviations, and hyphenations in English, for example — but it will take care of simple needs. Look at the following code:

```
(defn tokenize [string]
  (map str/lower-case (re-seq #"[\p{L}\p{M}]+" string)))
(defn tokenize-text [m] (update-in m [:text] tokenize))
```

The actual tokenization is handled by the `tokenize` function. The `tokenize-text` function takes a `NewsArticle` instance and replaces its raw text property with the sequence of tokens generated from the text.

The function `token-freqs` replaces the sequence of tokens with a mapping of their frequencies. It uses the Clojure core function frequencies as shown in the following code:

```
(defn token-freqs [m] (update-in m [:text] frequencies))
```

We can then take a sequence of `NewsArticle` instances that contain the token frequencies and generate the frequencies for the entire corpus. The function `corpus-freqs` takes care of that. Look at the following code:

```
(defn corpus-freqs [coll]
  (reduce #(merge-with + %1 %2) {} (map :text coll)))
```

Let's use the following functions to get the frequencies:

- We'll get the tokens for each article. Then we'll print out the first ten tokens from the first article, as follows:

  ```
  user=> (def tokens (map nlp/tokenize-text articles))
  user=> (take 10 (:text (first tokens)))
  ("harmonic" "convergences" "you" "re" "right" "maxim" "s" "strong"
  "point" "is")
  ```

- Now, we'll get the frequencies of the tokens in each document and print out ten of the token-frequency pairs from the first document, as follows:

  ```
  user=> (def freqs (map nlp/token-freqs tokens))
  user=> (take 10 (:text (first freqs)))
  (["sillier" 1] ["partly" 2] ["mags" 4] ["new" 1] ["advisor" 1]
  ["a" 13] ["worry" 1] ["unsentimental" 1] ["method" 1] ["pampering"
  1])
  ```

- Finally, we can reduce those down into one set of frequencies over the entire collection. I've pretty-printed out the top ten most frequent tokens. Look at the following code:

```
user=> (def c-freqs (nlp/corpus-freqs freqs))
user=> (take 10 (reverse (sort-by second c-freqs)))
(["the" 266011]
 ["of" 115973]
 ["to" 107951]
 ["a" 101017]
 ["and" 96375]
 ["in" 74558]
 ["s" 66349]
 ["that" 64447]
 ["is" 49311]
 ["it" 38175])
```

We can see that the most frequent words are common words with little semantic value. In the next section, we'll see what we need to do with them.

Stop lists

The words identified as the most common words in the code in the previous section are often referred to as **function** words, because they're performing functions in the sentence, but not really carrying meaning. For some kinds of analyses, such as grammatical and stylistic analyses, these are vitally important. However, for this particular chapter, we're more interested in the documents' content words, or the words that carry semantic meaning.

To filter these out, the typical technique is to use a stop word list. This is a list of common words to remove from the list of tokens.

If you type english stop list into Google, you'll get a lot of workable stop lists. I've downloaded one from http://jmlr.org/papers/volume5/lewis04a/all-smart-stop-list/english.stop. Download this file too, and place it into the d directory along with the data files.

To load the stop words, we'll use the following function. It simply takes the filename and returns a set of the tokens in it.

```
(defn load-stop-words [filename]
  (set (tokenize (slurp filename))))
```

Using this set directly is easy enough on raw strings. However, we'll want a function to make calling it on NewsArticle instances easier. Look at the following code:

```
(defn remove-stop-words [stop-words m]
  (update-in m [:text] #(remove stop-words %)))
```

Now, we can load those words and remove them from the lists of tokens. We'll start with the definition of tokens that we just created. Look at the following code:

```
user=> (def stop-words (nlp/load-stop-words "d/english.stop"))
user=> (def filtered
         (map #(nlp/remove-stop-words stop-words %) tokens))
user=> (take 10 (:text (first filtered)))
("harmonic" "convergences" "maxim" "strong" "point" "totally"
"unsentimental" "ungenteel" "sendup" "model")
```

First, we can tell that we've removed a number of tokens that weren't really adding much. You, re, and s were all taken out, along with others.

Now let's regenerate the corpus frequencies with the following code:

```
user=> (def freqs (map nlp/token-freqs filtered))
user=> (def c-freqs (nlp/corpus-freqs freqs))
user=> (pprint (take 10 (reverse (sort-by second c-freqs))))
(["clinton" 8567]
 ["times" 6528]
 ["people" 6351]
 ["time" 6091]
 ["story" 5645]
 ["president" 5223]
 ["year" 4539]
 ["york" 4516]
 ["world" 4256]
 ["years" 4144])
```

This list seems much more reasonable. It focuses on Bill Clinton, who was the US President during this period.

Another way of dealing with this is to use a white list. This would be a set of words or features that represent the entire collection of those that we want to deal with. We could implement this as a simple function, `keep-white-list`, as shown in the following code:

```
(defn keep-white-list [white-list-set m]
  (over :text #(filter white-list-set %) m))
```

This function seems academic now, but we'll need it before we're done.

Hapax and Dis Legomena

Now, let's look at a graph of the frequencies:

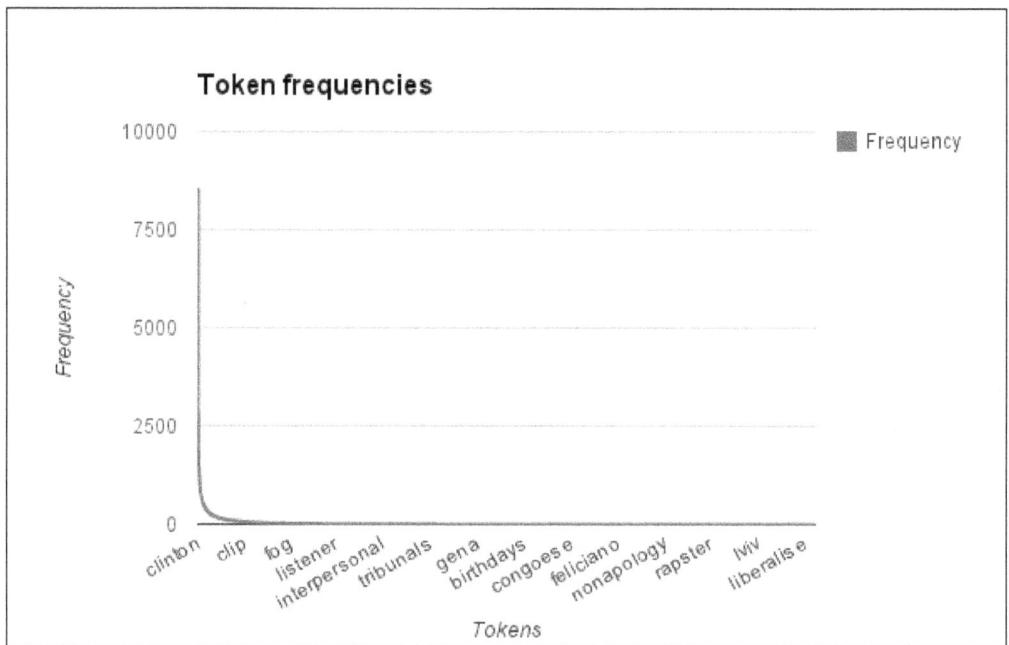

That's a lot of words that don't occur very much. This is actually expected. A few words occur a lot, but most just don't.

We can get another view of the data by looking at the log-log plot of the frequencies and ranks. Functions that represent a value raised to a power should be linear in these line charts. We can see that the relationship isn't quite on a line in this plot, but it's very close. Look at the following graph:

Token Frequency by Rank

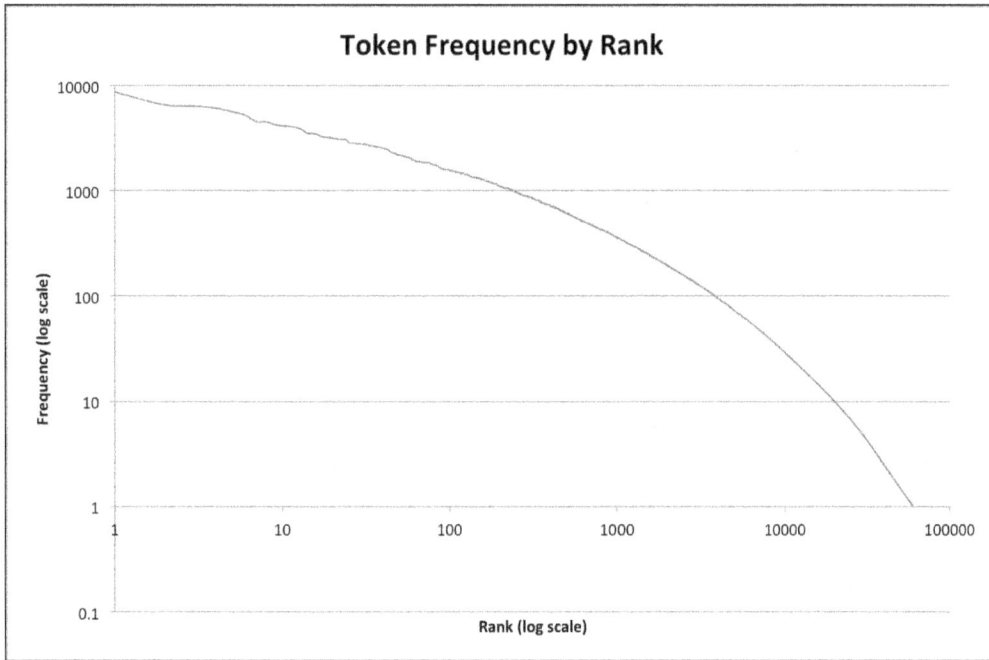

In fact, let's turn the frequency mapping around in the following code to look at how often different frequencies occur:

```
user=> (def ffreqs (frequencies (vals c-freqs)))
user=> (pprint (take 10 (reverse (sort-by second ffreqs))))
([1 23342]
 [2 8814]
 [3 5310]
 [4 3749]
 [5 2809]
 [6 2320]
 [7 1870]
 [8 1593]
 [9 1352]
 [10 1183])
```

So there are more than 23,000 words that only occur once and more than 8,000 words that only occur twice. Words like these are very interesting for authorship studies. The words that are found only once are referred to as **hapax legomena**, from Greek for "said once", and words that occur only twice are **dis legomena**.

Looking at a random 10 hapax legomena gives us a good indication of the types of words these are. The 10 words are: shanties, merrifield, cyberguru, alighting, roomfor, sciaretto, borisyeltsin, vermes, fugs, and gandhian. Some of these appear to be unusual or rare words. Others are mistakes or two words that were joined together for some reason, possibly by a dash.

Unfortunately, they do not contribute much to our study, since they don't occur often enough to contribute to the results statistically. In fact, we'll just get rid of any words that occur less than 10 times. This will form a second stop list, this time of rare words. Let's generate this list. Another, probably better performing, option is to create a whitelist of the words that aren't rare, but we can easily integrate this with our existing stop-list infrastructure, so we'll do it by just creating another list here.

To create it from the frequencies, we'll define a `make-rare-word-list` function. It takes a frequency mapping and returns the items with fewer than *n* occurrences, as follows:

```
(defn make-rare-word-list [freqs n]
  (map first (filter #(< (second %) n) freqs)))
```

We can now use this function to generate the `d/english.rare` file. We can use this file just like we used the stop list to remove items that aren't common and to further clean up the tokens that we'll have to deal with (you can also find this file in the code download for this chapter):

```
(with-open [f (io/writer "d/english.rare")]
  (binding [*out* f]
    (doseq [t (sort (nlp/make-rare-word-list c-freqs 8))]
      (println t))))
```

Now, we have a list of more than 48,000 tokens that will get removed. For perspective, after removing the common stop words, there were more than 71,000 token types.

We can now use that just like we did for the previous stop word list. Starting from `filtered`, which we defined in the earlier code after removing the common stop words, we'll now define `filtered2` and recalculate the frequencies as follows:

```
user=> (def rare (nlp/load-stop-words "d/english.rare"))
user=> (def filtered2
        (map #(nlp/remove-stop-words rare %) filtered))
user=> (take 10 (:text (first filtered2)))
("maxim" "strong" "point" "totally" "unsentimental" "sendup" "model"
"hustler" "difference" "surprise")
```

So we can see that the process has removed some uncommon words, such as `harmonic` and `convergences`.

This process is pretty piecemeal so far, but it's one that we would need to do multiple times, probably. Many natural language processing and text analysis tasks begin by taking a text, converting it to a sequence of features (tokenization, normalization, and filtering), and then counting them. Let's package that into one function as follows:

```
(defn process-articles
  ([articles]
   (process-articles
     articles ["d/english.stop" "d/english.rare"]))
  ([articles stop-files]
   (let [stop-words (reduce set/union #{}
                             (map load-stop-words stop-files))
         process (fn [text]
                   (frequencies
                     (remove stop-words (tokenize text))))]
     (map #(over :text process %) articles))))
```

The preceding function allows us to call it with just a list of articles. We can also specify a list of stop word files. The entries in all the lists are added together to create a master list of stop words. Then the articles' text is tokenized, filtered by the stop words, and counted. Doing it this way should save on creating and possibly hanging on to multiple lists of intermediate processing stages that we won't ever use later.

Now we can skip to the document-level frequencies with the following command:

```
user=> (def freqs (nlp/process-articles articles))
```

Now that we've filtered these out, let's look at the graph of token frequencies again:

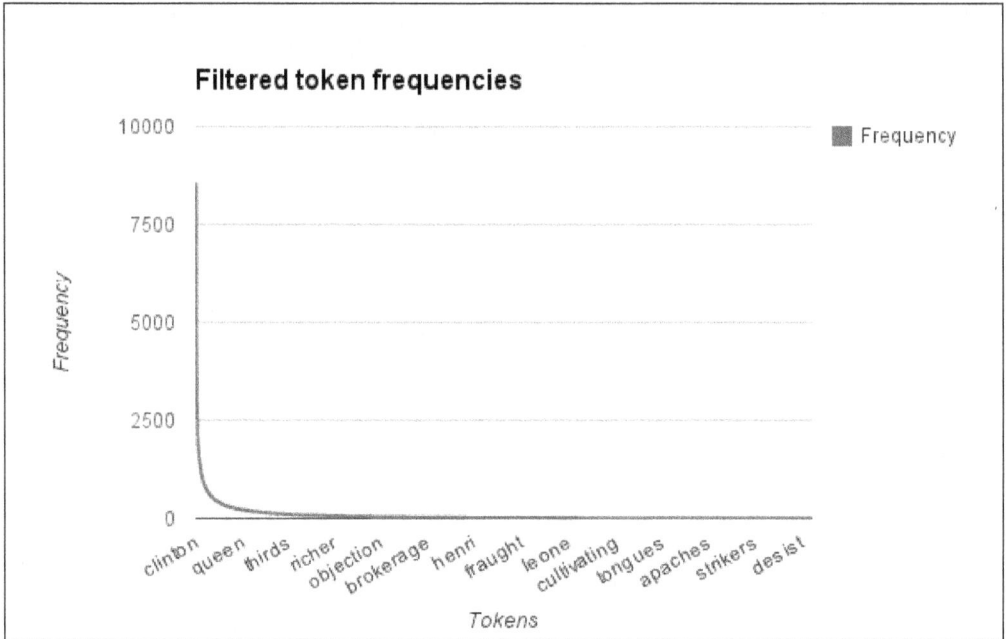

The distribution stayed the same, as we would expect, but the number of words should be more manageable.

Again, we can see from the following log-log plot that the previous power relationship—almost, but not quite, linear—holds for this frequency distribution as well:

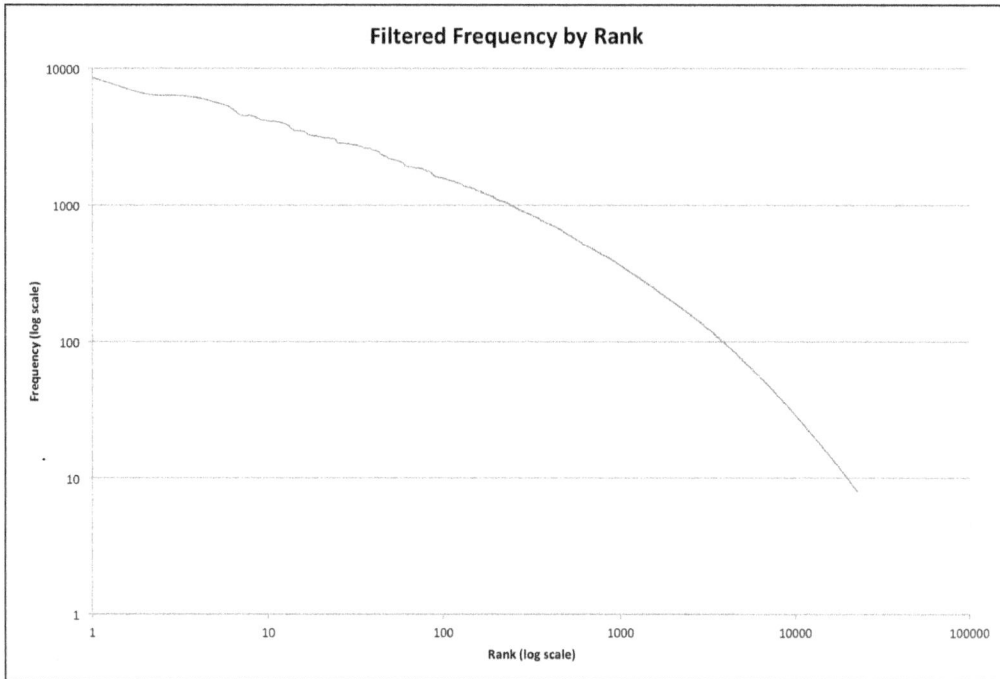

Filtered Frequency by Rank

Another way to approach this would be to use a whitelist, as we mentioned earlier. We could load files and keep only the tokens that we've seen before by using the following function:

```
(defn load-articles [white-list-set articles]
  (let [process (fn [text]
                  (frequencies
                    (filter white-list-set (tokenize text))))]
    (map #(over :text process %) articles)))
```

Again, this will come up later. We'll find this necessary when we need to load unseen documents to analyze.

TF-IDF

The frequencies as we currently have them will present a couple of difficulties. For one thing, if we have a document with 100 words and one with 500 words, we can't really compare the frequencies. For another thing, if a word occurs three times in every document, say in a header, it's not as interesting as one that occurs in only a few documents three times and nowhere else.

In order to work around both of these, we'll use a metric called **term frequency -inverse document frequency (TF-IDF)**. This combines some kind of document -term frequency with the log of the percentage of documents that contain that term.

For the first part, term frequency, we could use a number of metrics. We could use a boolean 0 or 1 to show absence or presence. We could use the raw frequency or the raw frequency scaled. In this case, we're going to use an augmented frequency that scales the raw frequency by the maximum frequency of any word in the document. Look at the following code:

```
(defn tf [term-freq max-freq]
  (+ 0.5 (/ (* 0.5 term-freq) max-freq)))
(defn tf-article [article term]
  (let [freqs (:text article)]
    (tf (freqs term 0) (reduce max 0 (vals freqs)))))
```

The first function in the preceding code, `tf`, is a basic augmented frequency equation and takes the raw values as parameters. The second function, `tf-article`, wraps `tf` but takes a `NewsArticle` instance and a word and generates the TF value for that pair.

For the second part of this equation, the inverse document frequency, we'll use the log of the total number of documents divided by the number of documents containing that term. We'll also add one to the last number to protect against division-by-zero errors.

The `idf` function calculates the inverse document frequency for a term over the given corpus, as shown in the following code:

```
(defn has-term?
  ([term] (fn [a] (has-term? term a)))
  ([term a] (not (nil? (get (:text a) term)))))
(defn idf [corpus term]
  (Math/log
    (/ (count corpus)
       (inc (count (filter (has-term? term) corpus)))))))
```

The IDF for a word won't change between different documents. Because of this, we can calculate all of the IDF values for all the words represented in the corpus once and cache them. The following two functions take care of this scenario:

```
(defn get-vocabulary [corpus]
  (reduce set/union #{} (map #(set (keys (:text %))) corpus)))
(defn get-idf-cache [corpus]
  (reduce #(assoc %1 %2 (idf corpus %2)) {}
          (get-vocabulary corpus)))
```

The first function in the preceding code, get-vocabulary, returns a set of all the words used in the corpus. The next function, get-idf-cache, iterates over the vocabulary set to construct a mapping of the cached IDF values. We'll use this cache to generate the TF-IDF values for each document.

The tf-idf function combines the output of tf and idf (via get-idf-cache) to calculate the TF-IDF value. In this case, we simply take the raw frequencies and the IDF value and multiply them together as shown in the following code:

```
(defn tf-idf [idf-value freq max-freq]
  (* (tf freq max-freq) idf-value))
```

This works at the most basic level; however, we'll want some adapters to work with NewsArticle instances and higher-level Clojure data structures.

The first level up will take the IDF cache and a map of frequencies and return a new map of TF-IDF values based off of those frequencies. To do this, we have to find the maximum frequency represented in the mapping. Then we can calculate the TF-IDF for each token type in the frequency map as follows:

```
(defn tf-idf-freqs [idf-cache freqs]
  (let [max-freq (reduce max 0 (vals freqs))]
    (into {}
          (map #(vector (first %)
                        (tf-idf
                          (idf-cache (first %))
                          (second %)
                          max-freq))
               freqs)))))
```

The `tf-idf-freqs` function does most of the work for us. Now we can build on it further. First, we'll write `tf-idf-over` to calculate the TF-IDF values for all the tokens in a `NewsArticle` instance. Then we'll write `tf-idf-cached`, which takes a cache of IDF values for each word in a corpus. It returns those documents with their frequencies converted if TF-IDF. Finally, `tf-idf-all` will call this function on a collection of `NewsArticle` instances as shown in the following code:

```
(defn tf-idf-over [idf-cache article]
  (over :text (fn [f] (tf-idf-freqs idf-cache f)) article))
(defn tf-idf-cached [idf-cache corpus]
  (map #(tf-idf-over idf-cache %) corpus))
(defn tf-idf-all [corpus]
  (tf-idf-cached (get-idf-cache corpus) corpus))
```

We've implemented TF-IDF, but now we should play with it some more to get a feel for how it works in practice.

We'll start with the definition of `filtered2` that we implemented in the *Hapax and Dis Legomena* section. This section contained the corpus of `NewsArticles` instances, and the `:text` property is the frequency of tokens without the tokens from the stop word lists of both rare and common words.

Now we can generate the scaled TF-IDF frequencies for these articles by calling `tf-idf-all` on them. Once we have that, we can compare the frequencies for one article. Look at the following code:

```
(def tf-idfs (nlp/tf-idf-all filtered2))
(doseq [[t f] (sort-by second (:text (first filtered2)))]
  (println t \tab f \tab (get (:text (first tf-idfs)) t)))
```

The table's too long to reproduce here (176 tokens). Instead, I'll just pick 10 interesting terms to look at more closely. The following table includes not only each term's raw frequencies and TF-IDF scores, but also the number of documents that they are found in:

Token	Raw frequency	Document frequency	TF-IDF
sillier	1	8	3.35002
politics	1	749	0.96849
british	1	594	1.09315
reason	2	851	0.96410
make	2	2,350	0.37852
military	3	700	1.14842
time	3	2,810	0.29378

Token	Raw frequency	Document frequency	TF-IDF
mags	4	18	3.57932
women	11	930	1.46071
men	13	856	1.66526

The tokens in the preceding table are ordered by their raw frequencies. However, notice how badly that correlates with the TF-IDF.

- First, notice the numbers for "sillier" and "politics". Both are found once in this document. But "sillier" probably doesn't occur much in the entire collection, and it has a TF-IDF score of more than 3. However, "politics" is common, so it scores slightly less than 1.

- Next, notice the numbers for "time" (raw frequency of 3) and "mags" (4). "Time" is a very common word that kind of straddles the categories of function words and content words. On the one hand, you can be using expressions like "time after time", but you can also talk about "time" as an abstract concept. "Mags" is a slangy version of "magazines", and it occurs roughly the same number of times as "time". However, since "mags" is rarely found in the entire corpus (only 18 times), it has the highest TF-IDF score of any word in this document.

- Finally, look at "women" and "men". These are the two most common words in this article. However, because they're found in so many documents, both are given TF-IDF scores of around 1.5.

What we wind up with is a measure of how important a term is in that document. Words that are more common have to appear more to be considered significant. Words that are found in only a few documents can be important with just one mention.

As a final step before we move on, we can also write a utility function that loads a set of articles, given a token whitelist and an IDF cache. This will be important } after we've trained the neural network when we're actually using it. That's because we will need to keep the same features, in the same order, and to scale between the two runs. Thus, it's important to scale by the same IDF values. Look at the following code:

```
(defn load-text-files [token-white-list idf-cache articles]
  (tf-idf-cached idf-cache
               (load-articles token-white-list articles)))
```

The preceding code will allow us to analyze documents and actually use our neural network after we've trained it.

Inspecting the stock prices

Now that we have some hold on the textual data, let's turn our attention to the stock prices. Previously, we loaded it from the CSV file using the `financial.csv-data/read-stock-prices` function. Let's reload that data with the following commands:

```
user=> (def stock (csvd/read-stock-prices "d/d-1995-2001.csv"))
user=> (count stock)
1263
```

Let's start with a graph that shows how the closing price has changed over the years:

So the price started in the low 30s, fluctuated a bit, and finished in the low 20s. During that time, there were some periods where it climbed rapidly. Hopefully, we'll be able to capture and predict those changes.

Merging text and stock features

Before we can start to train the neural network, however, we'll need to figure out how we need to represent the data and what information the neural network needs to have.

The code for this section will be present in the `src/financial/nn.clj` file. Open it up and add the following namespace header:

```
(ns financial.nn
  (:require [clj-time.core :as time]
            [clj-time.coerce :as time-coerce]
            [clojure.java.io :as io]
            [enclog.nnets :as nnets]
            [enclog.training :as training]
            [financial.utils :as u]
            [financial.validate :as v])
  (:import [org.encog.neural.networks PersistBasicNetwork]))
```

However, we first need to be clear about what we're trying to do. That will allow us to properly format and present the data.

Let's break it down like this: for each document, based on the previous stock prices and the tokens in a document, can we predict the direction of future stock prices.

So one set of features will be the tokens in the document. We already have those identified earlier. Other features can represent the stock prices. Since we're actually interested in the direction of the future prices, we can actually use the difference between the stock prices of a point in the past and of the day the article was published. Offhand, we're not sure what time frames will be helpful, so we can select several and include them all.

The output is another difference in stock prices. Again, we don't know at what difference in time we'll be able to get good results (if any!), so we'll try to look out into the future at various distances.

For the ranges of time, we'll use some standard time periods, gradually getting further and further out: a day, two days, three days, four days, five days, two weeks, three weeks, one month, two months, six months, and one year. Days that fall on a weekend have the value of the previous business day. Months will be 30 days, and a year is 365 days. This way, the time periods will be more or less regular.

We can represent those periods in Clojure using the `clj-time` library (https://github.com/clj-time/clj-time) as follows:

```
(def periods [(time/days 1)
              (time/days 2)
              (time/days 3)
              (time/days 4)
              (time/days 5)
              (time/days (* 7 2))
```

```
      (time/days (* 7 3))
      (time/days 30)
      (time/days (* 30 2))
      (time/days (* 30 6))
      (time/days 365)])
```

For the features, we'll use the difference in price over those periods. The easiest way to get at that information would be to index the stock prices by date and then access the prices from there using some utility functions. Let's see what that would look like:

```
(defn index-by [key-fn coll]
  (into {} (map #(vector (key-fn %) %) coll)))
(defn get-stock-date [stock-index date]
  (if-let [price (stock-index date)]
    price
    (if (<= (time/year date) 1990)
      nil
      (get-stock-date
        stock-index (time/minus date (time/days 1))))))
```

We can use `index-by` to index a collection of anything into a map. The other function, `get-stock-date`, then attempts to get the `StockData` instance from the index. If it doesn't find one, it tries the previous day. If it ever works its way before 1990, it just returns nil.

Now let's get the input feature vector from a `NewsArticle` instance and the stock index.

The easy part of this will be getting the token vector. Getting the price vector will be more complicated, and we'll be doing almost the same thing twice: once looking backward from the article for the input vector, and once looking forward from the article for the output vector. Since generating these two vectors will be mostly the same, we'll write a function that does it and accepts function parameters for the differences, as shown in the following code:

```
(defn make-price-vector [stock-index article date-op]
  (let [pub-date (:pub-date article)
        base-price (:close (get-stock-date stock-index pub-date))
        price-feature
        (fn [period]
          (let [date-key (date-op pub-date period)]
            (if-let [stock (get-stock-date stock-index date-key)]
              (/ (price-diff base-price (:close stock))
                 base-price)
              0.0)))]
    (vec (remove nil? (map price-feature periods)))))
```

The `make-price-vector` function gets the base price from the day the article was published. It then gets the day offsets that we outlined previously and finds the closing stock price for each of those days. It finds the difference between the two prices.

The parameter for this function is `date-op`, which gets the second day to find the stock price for. It will either add the period to the article's publish date or subtract it, depending on whether we're looking in the future or the past.

We can build on this to make the input vector, which will contain the token vector and the price vector, as shown in the following code:

```
(defn make-feature-vector [stock-index vocab article]
  (let [freqs (:text article)
        token-features (map #(freqs % 0.0) (sort vocab))
        price-features (make-price-vector
                         stock-index article time/minus)]
    (vec (concat token-features price-features))))
```

For the token vector, we get the frequencies from the `NewsArticle` instance in the order given by the vocab collection. This should be the same across all `NewsArticle` instances. We call `make-price-vector` to get the prices for the offset days. Then we concatenate all of them into one (Clojure) vector.

The following code gives us the input vector. However, we'll also want to have future prices as the output vector.

```
(defn make-training-vector [stock-index article]
  (vec (make-price-vector stock-index article time/plus)))
```

The preceding code is just a thin wrapper over `make-price-vector`. It calls this function with the appropriate arguments to get the future stock price.

Finally, we'll write a function that takes a stock index, a vocabulary, and a collection of articles. It will generate both the input vector and the expected output vector, and it will return both stored in a hash map. The code for this function is given as follows:

```
(defn make-training-set [stock-index vocab articles]
  (let [make-pair
        (fn [article]
          {:input (make-feature-vector stock-index vocab article)
           :outputs (zipmap periods
                            (make-training-vector
                              stock-index article))})]
    (map make-pair articles)))
```

This code will make it easy to generate a training set from the data that we've been working with.

Analyzing both text and stock features together with neural nets

We now have everything ready to perform the analysis, except for the engine that will actually attempt to learn the training data.

In this instance, we're going to try to train an artificial neural network to learn the direction of change of the future prices of the input data. In other words, we'll try to train it to tell whether the price will go up or down in the near future. We want to create a simple binary classifier from the past price changes and the text of an article.

Understanding neural nets

As the name implies, artificial neural networks are machine learning structures modeled on the architecture and behavior of neurons, such as the ones found in the human brain. Artificial neural networks come in many forms, but today we're going to use one of the oldest and most common forms: the three-layer feed-forward network.

We can see the structure of a unit outlined in the following figure:

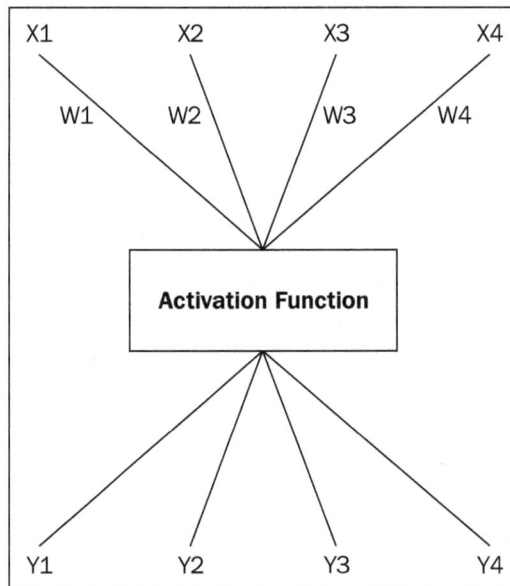

Each unit is able to realize linearly separable functions. That is, functions that divide their n-dimensional output space along a hyperplane. To emulate more complex functions, however, we have to go beyond a single unit and create a network of them.

These networks have three layers: an input layer, a hidden layer, and an output layer. Each layer is made up of one or more neurons. Each neuron takes one or more inputs and produces an output, which is broadcast to one or more outputs. The inputs are weighted, and each input is weighted individually. All of the inputs are added together, and the sum is passed through an activation function that normalizes and scales the input. The inputs are x, the weights are w, and the outputs are y.

A simple schematic of this structure is shown as follows:

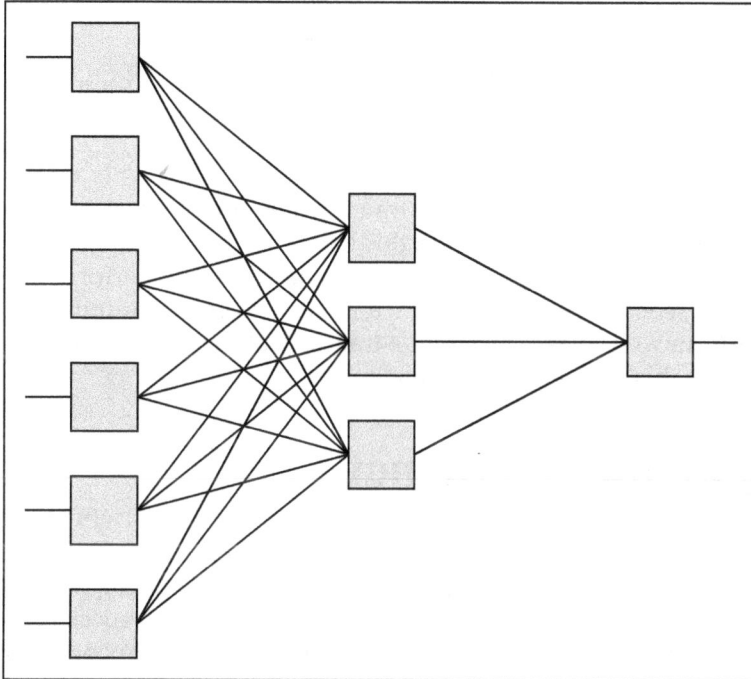

The network operates in a fairly simple manner, following the process called feed forward activation. It is described as follows:

1. The input vector is fed to the input layer of the network. Depending on how the network is set up, these may be passed through the activation function for each neuron. This determines the activation of each neuron, or the amount of signal coming into it from that channel and how excited it is.

2. The weighted connections between the input and hidden layers are then activated and used to excite the nodes in the hidden layer. This is done by getting the dot product of the input neurons with the weights going into each hidden node. These values are then passed through the activation function for the hidden neurons.

3. The forward propagation process is repeated again between the hidden layer and the output layer.

4. The activation of the neurons in the output layer is the output of the network.

Initially, the weights are usually randomly selected. Then the weights are trained using a variety of techniques. A common one is called backward propagation. This involves computing the error between the output neurons and the desired outputs. This error is then fed backward into the network. This is used to dampen some weights and increase others. The net effect is to nudge the output of the network slightly closer to the target.

Other training methods work differently, but attempt to do the same thing: each tries to modify the weights so that the outputs are close to the targets for each input in the training set.

Note that I said *close to the targets*. When training a neural network, you don't want the outputs to align exactly. When this happens, the network is said to have memorized the training set. This means that the network will perform great for inputs that it has seen previously. But when it encounters new inputs, it is brittle and won't perform well. It has learned the training set too well, but it won't be able to generalize that information to new inputs.

Setting up the neural net

Implementing neural networks isn't difficult—and doing so is a useful exercise —but there are good libraries for neural networks available for Java and Clojure, and we'll choose one of those here. For our case, we'll use the Encog Machine Learning Framework (http://www.heatonresearch.com/encog), which specializes in neural networks. But we'll primarily be using it through the Clojure wrapper library Enclog (https://github.com/jimpil/enclog/). We'll build on these to write some facade functions over Enclog to customize this library for our processes.

The first step is to create the neural network. The make-network function takes the vocabulary size and the number of hidden nodes (the variables for our purposes), but it defines the rest of the parameters internally, as follows:

```
(defn make-network [vocab-size hidden-nodes]
  (nnets/network (nnets/neural-pattern :feed-forward)
                 :activation :sigmoid
                 :input (+ vocab-size (count periods))
                 :hidden [hidden-nodes]
                 :output 1))
```

The number of input nodes is a function of the size of the vocabulary in addition to the number of periods. (Periods is a non-dynamic, namespace-level binding. We may want to rethink that and make it dynamic to provide a little more flexibility, but for our needs right now this is sufficient.) And since from the output node, we just want a single value indicating whether the stock went up or down, we hardcoded the number of output nodes to one. However, the number of hidden nodes that will perform best is an open question. We'll include that as a parameter so we can experiment with it.

For the output, we'll need a way to take our expected output and run it through the same activation function as that output. That way, we can directly compare the two as follows:

```
(defn activated [act-fn output]
  (let [a (double-array 1 [output])]
    (.activationFunction act-fn a 0 1)
    a)
```

The activated function takes an object that implements org.encog.engine.network.activation.ActivationFunction. We can get these from the neural network. It then puts the output for a period into a double array. The activation function scales this and then returns the array.

We will also need to prepare the data and insert it into a data structure that Encog can work with. The primary transformation in the following code is pulling out the output prices for the period that we're training for:

```
(defn build-data [nnet period training-set]
  (let [act (.getActivation nnet (dec (.getLayerCount nnet)))
        output (mapv #(activated act (get (:outputs %) period))
                     training-set)]
    (training/data :basic-dataset
                   (mapv :input training-set)
                   output)))
```

There's nothing particularly exciting here. We pull the inputs and the outputs for one time period out into two separate vectors and create a dataset with them.

Training the neural net

Now we have a neural network, but it's been initialized to random weights, so it will perform very, very poorly. We'll need to train it immediately.

To do this, we will put the training set together with the network in the following code. Like the previous functions, `train-for` accepts the parameters that we're interested in being able to change, uses reasonable defaults for ones that we'll probably leave alone, but hardcodes parameters that we won't touch. The function creates a trainer object and calls its `train` method. Finally, we return the neural network, which was modified in place.

```
(defn train-for
  ([nnet period training-set]
    (train-for nnet period training-set 0.01 500 []))
  ([nnet period training-set error-tolerance
    iterations strategies]
    (let [data (build-data nnet period training-set)
          trainer (training/trainer :back-prop
                                    :network nnet
                                    :training-set data)]
      (training/train
        trainer error-tolerance iterations strategies)
      nnet)))
```

When it is time to validate a network, it will be a little easier to combine creating a network with training it into one function. We'll do that with `make-train` as follows:

```
(defn make-train [vocab-size hidden-count period coll]
  (let [nn (make-network vocab-size hidden-count)]
    (train-for nn period coll 0.01 100 [])
    nn))
```

This allows us to train a new neural network in one call.

Running the neural net

Once we've trained the network, we'll want to run it on new inputs, ones for which we don't know the expected output. We can do that with the `run-network` function. This takes a trained network and an input collection and returns an array of the network's output as follows:

```
(defn run-network [nnet input]
  (let [input (double-array (count input) input)
        output (double-array (.getOutputCount nnet))]
    (.compute nnet input output)
    output))
```

We can use this function in one of two ways:

- We can pass it data that we don't know the output for to see how the network classifies it.
- We can pass it input data that we do know the output for in order to evaluate how well this network performs against data it hasn't previously encountered.

We'll see an example of the latter in the next section.

Validating the neural net

We can build on all of these functions to validate the neural network, train it, test it against new data, and evaluate how it does.

The `test-on` utility gets the **sum of squared errors** (**SSE**) for running the network on a test set for a given period. This trains and runs a neural network on the training set for a given period. It then returns the SSE for that run as follows:

```
(defn test-on [nnet period test-set]
  "Runs the net on the test set and calculates the SSE."
  (let [act (.getActivation nnet (dec (.getLayerCount nnet)))
        sqr (fn [x] (* x x))
        error (fn [{:keys [input outputs]}]
                (- (first (activated act (get outputs period)))
                   (first (run-network nnet input))))]
    (reduce + 0.0 (map sqr (map error test-set)))))
```

Running this train-test combination once gives us a very rough idea of how the network will perform with those parameters. However, if we want a better idea, we can use K-fold cross-validation. This divides the data into *K* equally sized groups. It then runs the train-test combination *K* times. Each time, it holds out a different partition as a test group. It trains the network on the rest of the partitions and evaluates it on the test group. The errors returned by `test-on` can be averaged to get a better idea of how the network will perform with those parameters.

For example, say we use K=4. We'll divide the training input into four groups: A, B, C, and D. This means that we'll train the following four different classifiers:

- We'll use A as the test set and train on B, C, and D combined
- We'll use B as the test set and train on A, C, and D
- We'll use C as the test set and train on A, B, and D
- We'll use D as the test set and train on A, B, and C

For each classifier, we'll compute the SSE, and we'll take the mean of these to see how well the classification should perform with those parameters, on average.

> I've defined the K-fold function in the `validate.clj` file at `src/financial/`. You can see how it's implemented in the source code download. I've also aliased that namespace to v in the current namespace.

The `x-validate` function will perform the cross validation on the inputs. The other function, `accum`, is simply a small utility that accumulates the error values into a vector. The `v/k-fold` function expects the accumulator to return the base case (an empty vector) when called with no arguments, as shown in the following code:

```
(defn accum
  ([] [])
  ([v x] (conj v x)))
(defn x-validate [vocab-size hidden-count period coll]
  (v/k-fold #(make-train vocab-size hidden-count period %)
            #(test-on %1 period %2)
            accum
            10
            coll))
```

The `x-validate` function uses `make-train` to create a new network and train it. It tests that network using `test-on`, and it gathers the resulting error rates together with `accum`.

Finding the best parameters

We've defined this system to let us play with a couple of parameters. First, we can set the number of neurons in the hidden layer. Also, we can set the time period that we are to predict for into the future (one day, two days, three days, a month, a year, and so on).

These parameters create a large space of possible solutions, some of which may perform better than others. We can make some educated guesses about some of the parameters—that it will predict the movement of the stock prices one day in the future better than it will the movement a year in the future—but we don't know that, and we should perhaps try it out.

These parameters present a search space. It would take too much time to try all the combinations, but we can try a number of them, just to see how they perform. This lets us tune the neural network to get the best results.

To explore this search space, let's first define what happens when we test one point, one combination of time period in the future, and a number of hidden nodes. The `explore-point` function will take care of this in the following code:

```
(defn explore-point [vocab-count period hidden-count training]
  (println period hidden-count)
  (let [error (x-validate
                vocab-count hidden-count period training)]
    (println period hidden-count
             '=> \tab (u/mean error) \tab error)
    (println)
    error))
```

The preceding code basically just takes the information and passes it to `x-validate`. It returns that function's return value (`error`) too. Along the way, it prints out a number of status messages. Then we need something that walks over the search space, calls `explore-point`, and collects the error rates returned for the output.

We'll define a dynamic global called `*hidden-counts*` that defines the range of hidden neuron counts that we're interested in exploring. The `periods` value that we bound earlier will define the search space for how far to look into the future.

To make sure that we don't train the networks too specifically on the data that we're using to find the best parameters, we'll first break the data into a development set and a test set. We'll use the development set to try out the different parameters, further breaking it up into a training set and a development-test set. At the end, we'll take the best set of parameters and test those against the test set that we originally held out. This will give us a better idea of how the neural network performs. The `final-eval` function will perform this last set and return the information that it creates.

The following function walks over these values and is named `explore-params`:

```
(def ^:dynamic *hidden-counts* [5 10 25 50 75])
(defn final-eval [vocab-size period hidden-count
                  training-set test-set]
  (let [nnet (make-train
                vocab-size hidden-count period training-set)
        error (test-on nnet period test-set)]
    {:period period
     :hidden-count hidden-count
     :nnet nnet
     :error error}))

(defn explore-params
  ([error-ref vocab-count training]
```

```
(explore-params
  error-ref vocab-count training *hidden-counts* 0.2))
([error-ref vocab-count training hidden-counts test-ratio]
(let [[test-set dev-set] (u/rand-split training test-ratio)
      search-space (for [p periods, h hidden-counts] [p h])]
  (doseq [pair search-space]
    (let [[p h] pair,
          error (explore-point vocab-count p h dev-set)]
      (dosync
        (commute error-ref assoc pair error))))
  (println "Final evaluation against the test set.")
  (let [[period hidden-count]
        (first (min-key #(u/mean (second %)) @error-ref))
        final (final-eval
                vocab-count period hidden-count
                dev-set test-set)]
    (dosync
      (commute error-ref assoc :final final))))
  @error-ref))
```

I've made a slightly unusual design decision in writing `explore-params`. Instead of initializing a hash map to contain the period-hidden count pairs and their associated error rates, I need the caller to pass in a reference containing a hash map. During the course of the processing, `explore-params` fills the hash map and finally returns it.

I've done this for one reason: exploring this search space still takes a long time. Over the course of writing this chapter, I needed to stop the validation, tweak the possible parameter values, and start it again. Setting up the function this way allowed me to be able to stop the processing, but still have access to what's happened thus far. I can look at the values, play around with them, and allow a more thorough examination of them to influence my decisions about what direction to take.

Predicting the future

Now is the time to bring together everything that we've assembled over the course of this chapter, so it seems appropriate to start over from scratch, just using the Clojure source code that we've written over the course of the chapter.

We'll take this one block at a time, loading and processing the data, creating training and test sets, training and validating the neural network, and finally viewing and analyzing its results.

Before we do any of this, we'll need to load the proper namespaces into the REPL. We can do that with the following `require` statement:

```
user=> (require
        [me.raynes.fs :as fs]
        [financial]
        [financial.types :as t]
        [financial.nlp :as nlp]
        [financial.nn :as nn]
        [financial.oanc :as oanc]
        [financial.csv-data :as csvd]
        [financial.utils :as u])
```

This will give us access to everything that we've implemented so far.

Loading stock prices

First, we'll load the stock prices with the following commands:

```
user=> (def stocks (csvd/read-stock-prices "d/d-1996-2001.csv"))
user=> (def stock-index (nn/index-by :date stocks))
```

The preceding code loads the stock prices from the CSV file and indexes them by date. This will make it easy to integrate them with the new article data in a few steps.

Loading news articles

Now we can load the news articles. We'll need two pieces of data from them: the TF-IDF scaled frequencies and the vocabulary list. Look at the following commands:

```
user=> (def slate (doall
                (map oanc/load-article
                    (oanc/find-slate-files
                        (io/file "d/OANC-GrAF")))))
user=> (def corpus (nlp/process-articles slate))
user=> (def freqs (nlp/tf-idf-all corpus))
user=> (def vocab (nlp/get-vocabulary corpus))
```

This code binds the frequencies as `freqs` and the vocabulary as `vocab`.

Creating training and test sets

Since we bundled the entire process into one function, merging our two data sources together into one training set is simple, as shown in the following command:

```
user=> (def training
          (nn/make-training-set stock-index vocab freqs))
```

Now, for each article, we have an input vector and a series of output for different stock prices related to the data.

Finding the best parameters for the neural network

The training data and the parameters' value ranges are the input for exploring the network parameter space. Look at the following commands:

```
user=> (def error-rates (ref {}))
user=> (nn/explore-params error-rates (count vocab) training)
```

This takes a very long time to run. Actually, I looked at the output it was producing and realized that it wouldn't be able to predict well beyond a day or two, so I stopped it after that. Thanks to my decision to pass in a reference, I was able to stop it and still have access to the results generated by that point.

The output is a mapping from the period and number of hidden nodes to a list of SSE values generated from each partition in the K-fold cross-validation. A more meaningful metric would be the average of the errors. We can generate that here and print out the results as follows:

```
user=> (def error-means
          (into {}
                (map #(vector (first %) (u/mean (second %)))
                     @error-rates)))
user=> (pprint (sort-by second error-means))
([[#<Days P1D> 10] 1.0435393]
 [[#<Days P1D> 5] 1.5253379]
 [[#<Days P1D> 25] 5.0099998]
 [[#<Days P1D> 50] 32.00977]
 [[#<Days P1D> 100] 34.264244]
 [[#<Days P1D> 200] 60.73007]
 [[#<Days P1D> 300] 100.29568])
```

So the squared sum of errors for predicting one day ahead go from about 1 for 10 hidden units to 100 for 300 hidden units. So, based on that, we'll only train a network to predict one day into the future and to use 10 hidden nodes.

Training and validating the neural network

Actually, training the neural network is pretty easy from our end, but it does take a while. The following commands should somewhat produce better results than we saw before, but at the cost of some time. Remember that the training process may not take this long, but we should probably be prepared.

```
user=> (def nn (nn/make-network (count vocab) 10))
user=> (def day1 (first nn/periods))
user=> (nn/train-for nn day1 training)
Iteration # 1 Error: 22.025400% Target-Error: 1.000000%
Iteration # 2 Error: 19.332094% Target-Error: 1.000000%
Iteration # 3 Error: 14.241920% Target-Error: 1.000000%
Iteration # 4 Error: 6.283643% Target-Error: 1.000000%
Iteration # 5 Error: 0.766110% Target-Error: 1.000000%
```

Well, that was quick.

This gives us a trained, ready-to-use neural network bound to the name nn.

Running the network on new data

We can now run our trained network on some new data. Just to have something to look at, I downloaded 10 articles off the Slate website and saved them to files in the directory d/slate/. I also downloaded the stock prices for Dominion, Inc.

Now, how would I analyze this data?

Before we really start, we'll need to pull some data from the processes we've been using, and we'll need to set up some reference values, such as the date of the documents. Look at the following code:

```
(def idf-cache (nlp/get-idf-cache corpus))
(def sample-day (time/date-time 2014 3 20 0 0 0))
(def used-vocab (set (map first idf-cache)))
```

So we get the IDF cache, the date the articles were downloaded on, and the vocabulary that we used in training. That vocabulary set will serve as the token whitelist for loading the news articles.

Let's see how to get the documents ready to analyze. Look at the following code:

```
(def articles (doall
               (->> "d/slate/"
                 fs/list-dir
                 (map #(str "d/slate/" %))
                 (map #(oanc/load-text-file sample-day %))
                 (nlp/load-text-files used-vocab idf-cache))))
```

This is a little more complicated than it was when we loaded them earlier. Basically, we just read the directory list and load the text from each one. Then we tokenize and filter it before determining the TF-IDF value for each token.

On the other hand, reading the stocks is very similar to what we just did. Look at the following code:

```
(def recent-stocks (csvd/read-stock-prices "d/d-2013-2014.csv"))
(def recent-index (nn/index-by :date recent-stocks))
```

With these in hand, we can put both together to make the input vectors as shown in the following code:

```
(def inputs
  (map #(nn/make-feature-vector recent-index used-vocab %)
       articles))
```

Now let's see how to run the network and see what happens. Look at the following:

```
user=> (pprint
         (flatten
           (map vec
             (map #(nn/run-network nn %) inputs))))
(0.5046613110846201
 0.5046613110846201
 0.5046613135395166
 0.5046613110846201
 0.5046613110846201
 0.5046613110846201
 0.5046613110846201
 0.5046613110846201
 0.5046613112651592
 0.5046613110846201)
```

These items are very consistent. To quite a few decimal places, they're all clustered right around 0.5. From the sigmoid function, this means that it doesn't really anticipate a stock change over the next day.

In fact, this tracks what actually happened fairly well. On March 20, the stock closed at $69.77, and on March 21, it closed at $70.06. This was a gain of $0.29.

Taking it with a grain of salt

Any analysis like the one presented in this chapter has a number of things that we need to question. This chapter is no exception.

Related to this project

The main weakness of this project was that it was carried out on far too little data. This cuts in several ways:

- We need articles from a number of data sources
- We need articles from a wider range of time
- We need more density of articles in the time period

For all of these, there are reasons we didn't address the issues in this chapter. However, if you plan to take this further, you'd need to figure out some way around these.

There are several ways to look at the results too. The day we looked at, the results all clustered close to zero. In fact, this stock if relatively stable, so if it always indicated little change, then it would always have a fairly low SSE. Large changes seem to happen occasionally, and the error from not predicting them has a low impact on the SSE.

Related to machine learning and market modeling in general

Second, and more importantly, simply putting some stock data into a jar with some machine learning and shaking it is a risky endeavor. This isn't a get-rich-quick scheme, and by approaching it so naively, you're asking for trouble. In this case, that means losing money.

For one thing, there's not much noise in news articles, and the relationship between their content and stock prices is tenuous enough that in general, stock prices may not be predictable from news reports in the first place, whatever results we achieve is this study, particularly given how small it is.

Really, to do this well, you need to understand at least two things:

- **Financial modeling**: You need to understand how to model financial transactions and dynamics mathematically
- **Machine learning**: You need to understand how machine learning works and how it models things

With this knowledge, you should be able to formulate a better model of how the stock prices change and which prices you should pay attention to.

But keep in mind, André Christoffer Andersen and Stian Mikelsen have published a master's thesis in 2012 showing that it's very, very difficult to do better than buying and holding index funds (`http://blog.andersen.im/wp-content/uploads/2012/12/ANovelAlgorithmicTradingFramework.pdf`). So, if you do try this route, you have a hard, hard task in front of you.

Summary

Over the course of this chapter, we've gotten a hold of some news articles and some stock prices, and we've managed to train a neural network that projects just a little into the future. This is a risky thing to put into production, but we've also outlined what we'd need to learn to do this correctly.

And this is also the end of this book. Thank you for staying with me this far. You've been a great reader. I hope that you've learned something as we've looked at the 10 data analysis projects that we've covered. If programming and data are both eating this world, hopefully you've seen how to have fun with both.

Index

neural nets
about 298-300
best parameters, finding 304-306
running 302
setting up 300, 301
stock features, analyzing 298
text, analyzing 298
training 301, 302
validating 303, 304
news articles
loading 307
working with 273-277
noir
about 215
URL 215
NUFORC
URL 93, 114
NUFORC comments
splitting out 114, 115
null hypothesis
stating 167-170
null hypothesis process
critical region, determining 172, 173
initial hypothesis, formulating 167
probability, calculating 173
rejection, deciding 173
significance level, selecting 171
tests appropriateness, determining 170, 171
test statistic, calculating 173
using 167
null-hypothesis test 211
null hypothesis testing
about 166
flipping coins 173, 174

O

online-controlled experiments 208
Open ANC (OANC)
about 272
URL 272
OpenNLP library
URL 143
OpinRank Review dataset
URL 141

P

Pareto Principle 239
partition-all function 149
partition function 149
partition-spread function 149
part of speech. *See* **POS**
POS annotated unigrams 142
paths metric, social network graphs 18
perform-test function 224
pie chart 34-36
Pinterest 235
POS 147
POS tagging 146-148
prior or assumed probability 118
process-speech-page function 69
project
setting up, for topic modeling 67
p-value 166

Q

Quantopian
URL 269
Quantum GIS
about 40
URL 40
quintiles 248
Quora
URL 237

R

random-controlled experiments 208
ranks, combining
about 252, 253
looking at those who only post answers 255, 256
looking at those who only post questions 254, 255
looking at those who post both questions and answers 256-259
raw data, burglary rates
about 182-185
data, pivoting 191, 192
data sources, joining 190

text, analyzing 280
text, analyzing with neutral nets 298
text, and stock features merging 294-297
weakness 311
working, with news articles 273-277
stock features
analyzing, with neural nets 298
stock prices
inspecting 294
loading 307
stop lists 282, 283
subdirectories, Luminus project
resources 215
src 215
src/web_ab/models/ 215
src/web_ab/routes/ 215
src/web_ab/views/templates/ 215
test/web_ab/test/ 215
sum of squared errors (SSE) 303

T

tab separated values file. *See* TSV file
term frequency-inverse document
frequency. *See* TF-IDF
test-on utility 303
test page 210
tests appropriateness, flipping coins
critical region, determining 175, 176
probability, calculating 176, 177
rejection, deciding for null hypothesis 178
significance level, selecting 175
test statistic, calculating 176, 177
test site, A/B test
building 216, 217
text
analyzing, with neural nets 298
text analysis, stock data modeling project
about 280
dis legomena 286
graph, viewing of frequencies 284-289
hapax legomena 286
stop lists 282, 283
TF-IDF 290-293
vocabulary, analyzing 280, 281

text, and stock features
merging 294-297
text, stock data modeling project
graph, viewing of frequencies 286
TF-IDF 280, 290-293
tf-idf-freqs function 292
tokenizing 142, 143, 280
TokenSequence2FeatureSequence 73
TokenSequenceLowercase 73
TokenSequenceRemoveStopwords 73
tools, for GIS specialists
ArcGIS 40
GDAL 40
GeoServer 40
GeoTools 40
Quantum GIS 40
topic 26
exploring 86-88
topic 42
exploring 89-91
topic 43
exploring 83-86
topic model 65
topic modeling
about 63
overview 65, 66
project, setting up for 67
URLs, for articles 65
topic modeling descriptions 107-110
topics
about 63
exploring 82, 83
topological modeling 40
trigrams 142
TripAdvisor
URL 141
TSV file 94, 142
t-test
coin tosses, testing 228-232
overview 228
t-test function 221
Twitter
about 7, 235
URL 237
type one error 233

[PACKT] open source

PUBLISHING

community experience distilled

Thank you for buying
Mastering Clojure Data Analysis

About Packt Publishing

Packt, pronounced 'packed', published its first book "*Mastering phpMyAdmin for Effective MySQL Management*" in April 2004 and subsequently continued to specialize in publishing highly focused books on specific technologies and solutions.

Our books and publications share the experiences of your fellow IT professionals in adapting and customizing today's systems, applications, and frameworks. Our solution based books give you the knowledge and power to customize the software and technologies you're using to get the job done. Packt books are more specific and less general than the IT books you have seen in the past. Our unique business model allows us to bring you more focused information, giving you more of what you need to know, and less of what you don't.

Packt is a modern, yet unique publishing company, which focuses on producing quality, cutting-edge books for communities of developers, administrators, and newbies alike. For more information, please visit our website: www.packtpub.com.

About Packt Open Source

In 2010, Packt launched two new brands, Packt Open Source and Packt Enterprise, in order to continue its focus on specialization. This book is part of the Packt Open Source brand, home to books published on software built around Open Source licenses, and offering information to anybody from advanced developers to budding web designers. The Open Source brand also runs Packt's Open Source Royalty Scheme, by which Packt gives a royalty to each Open Source project about whose software a book is sold.

Writing for Packt

We welcome all inquiries from people who are interested in authoring. Book proposals should be sent to author@packtpub.com. If your book idea is still at an early stage and you would like to discuss it first before writing a formal book proposal, contact us; one of our commissioning editors will get in touch with you.

We're not just looking for published authors; if you have strong technical skills but no writing experience, our experienced editors can help you develop a writing career, or simply get some additional reward for your expertise.

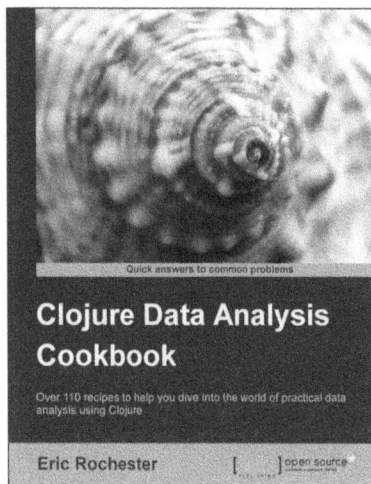

Clojure Data Analysis Cookbook

ISBN: 978-1-78216-264-3   Paperback: 342 pages

Over 110 recipes to help you dive into the world of practical data analysis using Clojure

1. Get a handle on the torrent of data the modern Internet has created.

2. Recipes for every stage from collection to analysis.

3. A practical approach to analyzing data to help you make informed decisions.

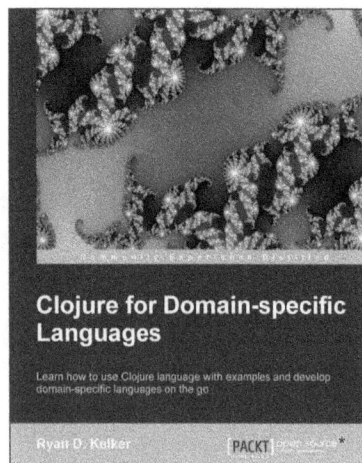

Clojure for Domain-specific Languages

ISBN: 978-1-78216-650-4   Paperback: 268 pages

Learn how to use Clojure language with examples and develop domain-specific languages on the go

1. Explore DSL concepts from existing Clojure DSLs and libraries.

2. Bring Clojure into your Java applications as Clojure can be hosted on a Java platform.

3. A tutorial-based guide to develop custom domain-specific languages.

Please check **www.PacktPub.com** for information on our titles

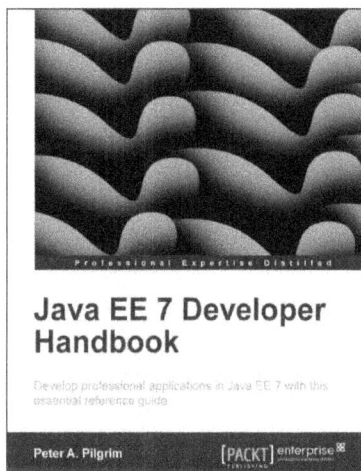

Java EE 7 Developer Handbook

ISBN: 978-1-84968-794-2   Paperback: 634 pages

Develop professional applications in Java EE 7 with this essential reference guide

1. Learn about local and remote service endpoints, containers, architecture, synchronous and asynchronous invocations, and remote communications in a concise reference.

2. Understand the architecture of the Java EE platform and then apply the new Java EE 7 enhancements to benefit your own business-critical applications.

3. Learn about integration test development on Java EE with Arquillian Framework and the Gradle build system.

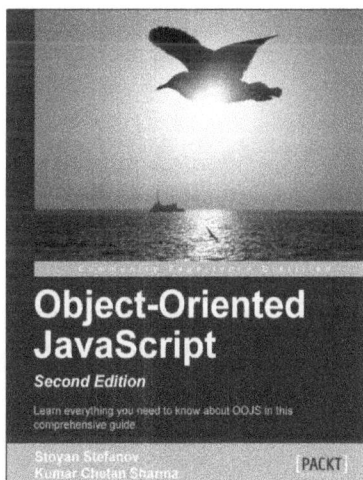

Object-Oriented JavaScript
Second Edition

ISBN: 978-1-84969-312-7   Paperback: 382 pages

Learn everything you need to know about OOJS in this comprehensive guide

1. Think in JavaScript.

2. Make object-oriented programming accessible and understandable to web developers.

3. Apply design patterns to solve JavaScript coding problems.

4. Learn coding patterns that unleash the unique power of the language.

Please check **www.PacktPub.com** for information on our titles